# Sectarian Religion in Contemporary Britain

## Nigel Scotland

paternoster
press

Copyright © 2000 Nigel Scotland
First published in 2000 by Paternoster Press

06 05 04 03 02 01 00   7 6 5 4 3 2 1

Paternoster Press is an imprint of
Paternoster Publishing,
P.O. Box 300, Carlisle, Cumbria, CA3 0QS, UK
and
Paternoster Publishing USA
P.O. Box 1047, Waynesboro, GA 30830-2047, USA

Website - www.paternoster-publishing.com

**British Library Cataloguing in Publication Data**
A catalogue record for this book is available from the British Library

ISBN 0-85364-917-0

Cover Design by Mainstream, Lancaster
Typeset by WestKey Ltd, Falmouth, Cornwall
Printed in Great Britain by
Biddles Ltd, Guildford, Surrey

# Contents

# Preface

We are living at a time when, generally speaking, the mainstream historic and denominational churches are in decline. This drift away from the practice of institutional religion has been a persistent feature of religious life in the UK since the time of the Great War. Indeed it accelerated during the 1960s and 1970s and since then has continued much as before into the present new millennium. In this same period of time some, although not all, of the newer, smaller and more intensive religious groups which are generally categorised as 'sects' have demonstrated a capacity to retain a greater hold over their membership. In fact a few of them have even expanded numerically. This volume examines in some detail the early history, life, worship and teaching of nine of the most significant sectarian movements current in the English religious landscape.

Many books have been written about 'sectarian' movements. However, the majority are either hostile productions on the part of escapees or anti-cultist organisations or they are brief factual accounts which offer only minimal information and little in the way of assessment. The intention of this book has been to adopt a rather different approach and to let each movement speak for itself and where possible in its own words. For this reason extensive use of primary sources has been made. Additionally I have visited most of the groups concerned and where possible taken part in worship and personal discussion with members of the congregations concerned. The aim has been to provide both accuracy and a high degree of objectivity. Where, however, the faith or practice of any of these movements runs contrary to that of the historic denominational churches these differences have been indicated. Thus I trust that this study will provide a fair-minded understanding of what is an important and growing sector of British religion. The concluding chapter seeks to assess reasons for the appeal and popularity of sectarian movements in the hope that this may prove of use to those whose interests lie in the growth and decline of religious institutions.

Those who are familiar with modern religious movements will doubtless be aware that all the groups considered in the subsequent pages of this book have emerged from the denominational Christian churches. All still make use of the Bible as their primary or base text and claim that their views represent an authentic development of the New Testament. I hope that what is written here will serve to promote greater dialogue and understanding among all those who see Bible-based religion as a significant aspect of life.

Finally, thanks are particularly due to Susan Napper, Glenville Sherif, David Vaughan, David Shorto, Ben Lowater, John Campbell, Nigel Antrobus, Rupert McKenzie, Clive Lloyd and Paul Northup who read the individual chapters and gave constructive, helpful advice and correction. Christine Preston very kindly word-processed my untidy manuscript.

# Chapter 1

# The Nature of Sectarian Religion

When we hear the word 'sect' or 'sectarian' it most likely conjures up in our mind something sinister and possibly occult. At the very least, sects are regarded by those who have not encountered them personally as groups which are likely to be patronised by extremists and fanatics. Such however, in most instances, is not the case. To define a group as a 'sect' does not necessarily mean that they are weird or are indulging in deviant behaviour. Sects, like churches, have both their good and their bad moments. In fact many sects have a better track record than the historical denominational churches when it comes to maintaining orthodox Christian doctrine. As Andrew Walker observed 'sects have resisted rationalism and modernism far better than most denominations and in particular the Church of England and Methodism'.[1] In addition their moral standards are often more rigorous and definite than those of the historic churches. Most members of what are called 'sects' are solid, upright, well-meaning people. They work hard, pay their taxes and many of them put as much into their family lives and children's upbringing as their counterparts in the Christian churches.

So what do we mean by 'sects'? The term was first used by a German sociologist of religion, Ernst Troeltsch (1864–1920). He studied religion in sixteenth-century Europe just after the Reformation when Martin Luther and other religious leaders broke away from the Roman Catholic Church and formed national Protestant churches which took the Bible as their supreme source of belief and practice, rather than the Pope and the teachings and

---

[1] A. Walker, *Restoring the Kingdom,* 220.

pronouncements of the Roman Church. Such churches included the Church of England, the Scottish Presbyterian Church, the German Lutheran Church and the Dutch Reformed Church. In addition to these large Church organisations, Troeltsch also observed that springing up all over Europe were clusters of much smaller breakaway groups. Often they were based in one town or in a small geographical area. Almost always following a dominant or powerful leader, they stressed the importance of religious experience, their worship usually being vibrant and they often had very strict codes of behaviour. Troeltsch called these groups 'sects' and he attempted to define 'sect' in the following way:

> The Sect is a voluntary society composed of strict and definite Christian believers bound to each other by the fact that all have experienced 'the new birth'. These believers live apart from the world, are limited to small groups, emphasise the law instead of grace, and . . . all this done in preparation for the expectation of the coming Kingdom of God.[2]

Troeltsch studied sixteenth-century European Christian Churches and the smaller groups which had separated from them. He noted in his definition that 'sects' were groups composed of 'strict and definite believers' who had experienced the 'new birth'. In other words, they demanded much more from their members in terms of their religious beliefs and feelings. It is of course the case that all the major world religions have these small vibrant 'sectarian' groups as well as their more established 'church' type communities. Islam, for example, is said to have seventy-two sects and Buddhism almost as many. Many of these groups also stress that salvation is experiential. It is a state of 'nirvana', 'enlightenment', 'bliss' or some other kind of inner tranquillity.

A number of 'sects' are orthodox in their beliefs. That is they have kept the same teachings of the older group from which they first separated. Others, however, have adopted quite markedly new doctrines. This book examines the teachings, worship and practices of some of those sectarian groups who have parted company with some of the teachings of the mainline Christian churches and some which have remained firmly attached to the orthodox creedal faith.

---

[2] E. Troeltsch, *The Social Teachings of the Christian Churches*, 993–4.

Since Troeltsch's time, quite a number of sociologists of religion and others have studied and analysed sects in greater detail. Roland Robertson observed that sects have several main attributes. They are voluntary associations where membership is on account of some claim to personal merit. There is a sense of eliteness and an ideal of perfection. Additionally, there is a strong commitment to the principle of the priesthood of all believers.[3] These findings have helped us to appreciate much more clearly how they understand and teach salvation, why they have particular codes of behaviour and what their attitude is to other religious groups and to the wider world beyond. Putting all their findings together it is clear that sects or sectarian groups can be identified by the following characteristics.

## Leaders are Dominant Personalities

Sects begin when a strong individual who is usually a member of an existing established religious group starts to attract a following. People begin to hang on their every word or to go to them for guidance and counselling. Such leaders are often self-educated laypeople who have natural gifts of charm and personality. As Bryan Wilson observed: Sects are normally lay movements, which practise their religion without an established ministry. They share very often, the central functions among the senior members (in the Christian tradition, often exclusively among the senior male members) and they often condemn the employment of a special ministerial order.[4]

This point about non-professional leadership is well illustrated by many Spiritualist groups where ministers are relatively few in number and function over wide areas. They do not have any authority over particular congregations and do not wear clerical dress or make use of ecclesiastical titles. Sects are essentially lay led and they emphasise the priesthood of all believers.

Sectarian leaders have a marked ability to lead others and to control and dominate their following. Joseph Smith, the founder of the Latter-day Saints, for example, not only claimed to have

---

[3] R. Robertson, *The Sociological Interpretation of Religion*, 130.
[4] B. Wilson, *Religion in Secular Society*, 180.

received visions of God, but was able to convey them to his followers, write the *Book of Mormon* and found his own movement in 1830. His successor, Brigham Young, despite the criticism concerning his allegedly having 48 wives, was able to lead 80,000 Mormons from Illinois to Utah where they finally established themselves in the Salt Lake Valley. Here Young exercised almost total control supervising the arrival of waves of new settlers and arbitrating in land, legal and family matters. A similar capacity to control her followers was demonstrated by Mary Baker Eddy, the founder of Christian Science. She had a hard childhood and little formal education. Her early married years were dogged by pain and sickness. She suffered from convulsive seizures in which she sometimes screamed out in agony. Yet in 1862 she was suddenly 'transformed' following a visit to a well-known mesmeric healer, Phineas Quimby. In 1870 she founded the 'Church of Christ Scientist' and by the turn of the century she had tens of thousands of loyal devotees all over America.

One of the most notable examples of a dominant sectarian leader in the twentieth century is that of Aimee Semple McPherson who founded The International Church of the Four Square Gospel. As a youngster she already had a strong sense of the dramatic and enjoyed playing religious games. Then when she was seventeen she was converted by a revivalist preacher, Robert Semple, whom she later married. Her fervent love for Robert brought to a sharp focus the three dominant driving forces in her life: religion, acting and ambition. After the death of Robert she married Harold McPherson. This marriage was destined to fail since Harold had no understanding of Aimee's ambitions to become an acclaimed evangelist. In 1922 she built the Angelus Temple in Los Angeles at a cost of $600,000. It had 5,300 seats, two sets of choir stalls which could seat a hundred singers, and the floors were covered with wall-to-wall red carpets. Aimee continued to have a love of the dramatic and would sometimes ride up the centre aisle on a motorbike, come to a screeching halt and then yell at the congregation: 'Stop, you are within a yard of hell!' In addition to her expansive sanctuary she set up a radio station and four years later she fell in love with her radio operator. She went off on a holiday with him although he was married. A court case followed but it did not reduce the boundless enthusiasm of her followers for their beloved

'Sister Aimee'. Further scandals followed including another marriage and a second divorce. Elmer Clark wrote of her:

> Thus 'Sister' grappled her followers to her with hoops of steel. Their devotion was not shaken by the many notorious escapades in which she was involved, family quarrels, lawsuits, alleged kidnapping and subsequent criminal prosecution, marriage, separation and so forth. Scandals which would have destroyed any decorous religious leader were used by this prophetess to strengthen her position . . . Her whole career was an interesting study in sexual charm and religious devotion.[5]

## Exclusive Salvation

Generally speaking many of the older, long-established churches are agreed that salvation is a lifelong process. It begins as individuals become aware that Jesus is the one who makes God known and they put their faith in him. But this is only a beginning. Salvation is a continuing lifelong process which involves acceptance and assent to the doctrines of the creeds, living out the teachings of Jesus and regular attendance at public worship. In contrast, in sects salvation is frequently instantaneous. The insistent call is: 'Now is the day of salvation.' 'Today is the day when things can be put right with God and your destiny made secure.' The American hymn writer Fanny Crosby (1820–1915), expressed the matter well in the following lines of one of her hymns: 'The vilest offender who truly believes that *moment* from Jesus a pardon receives.'[6] The great majority of sectarian conversion experiences are datable and individuals can often recall the day, the time and the place. Members of the International Church of Christ, for example, know that they are receiving the salvation which Jesus has promised to them in that moment when they are baptised.

Most sects, however, are adamant that they, and they alone, have the truth of salvation. The implication of this is clearly that salvation is only sure if you are a member of their group. Thus the Mormons claim to have 'the second testament' of Jesus Christ which contains

---

[5] E.T. Clark, *The Small Sects in America*, 116.
[6] The hymn was 'To God be the Glory' written in 1875.

his truth for the Latter Days. Members of the Latter-day Saints frequently begin their personal story when they 'testify' in public with the words 'I found the Church in . . .' Equally, Christadelphians believe that salvation is only possible for those who have been baptised into the 'one faith' which amounts to their founder John Thomas' understanding of Jesus' message. For the Jehovah's Witness salvation begins when 'you go to God in prayer through Jesus Christ and tell Jehovah that you want to belong to him'. In time past, Jehovah's Witnesses regarded all religious movements as 'a form of worship given to a false god and hence given to a creature'. Today Jehovah's Witnesses still regard themselves as 'the religion, the only pure religion'. Salvation for Jehovah's Witnesses involves faithfulness in door-to-door visiting and selling of the *Watchtower* magazine.

Sect teaching on salvation is set out in their own sacred texts which are used in addition to the Bible or the established scriptures of the religion from which they separated. Thus, for the Latter-day Saints, Joseph Smith's *Book of Mormon* and his second volume *Doctrine and Covenants* are all important, more so than the Bible. In the *Book of Mormon* the prophet Nephi warns against those who confine their authority to the Bible alone:

> And because my words shall hiss forth- many of the Gentiles shall say: A Bible! A Bible! We have got a Bible, and there cannot be any more Bible. But thus says the Lord God . . . Thou fool, that shall say: A Bible, we have got a Bible, and we need no more Bible . . . Know ye not . . . that I speak forth my words according to mine own pleasure. And because that I have spoken one word ye need not suppose that I cannot speak another; for my work is not yet finished; neither shall it be until the end of man, neither from that time henceforth and forever.[7]

For the Christadelphians, John Thomas' *Elpis Israel* is crucial to their understanding of salvation. Likewise, Christian Scientists believe the supreme truth of salvation to be set out only in Mary Baker Eddy's *Science and Health with Key to the Scriptures*. Spiritualists, while using the Bible in their worship, take as their main authority writings such as Emmanuel Swedenborg's (1688–1772) *Heavenly*

[7] Le G. Richards, *A Marvellous Work and a Wonder*, 56–7.

*Secrets* and *The True Christian Religion*. Similarly, Theosophists base their key beliefs on Helena Blavatsky's (1831–91) *The Secret Doctrine*.

## Organisation That Is Less Structured

In the traditional denominational churches organisation is usually bureaucratic and pyramidal. There is a complex hierarchy of buildings, officers, personnel and red tape. The Church of England with its extensive headquarters at Church House, Westminster, its Commissioners and diocesan organisations is a typical example. Its archaic officialdom is headed by two Archbishops and then graduates downwards with bishops, deans, canons, vicars and finally, at the bottom of the pile, curates. The Methodist Church is similar with a President of Conference at the top and then district chairmen, circuit superintendents, sector ministers and probationers all panning out in successive layers below.

In contrast, sects often have organisational structures which are much more dominated by their 'charismatic' leader. This is always the case when a sect is first established but even when it has continued its existence for many years its policy and structures often continue to be controlled by a dominant leader or a small group. Thus decisions tend to be made on the hoof and usually depend on what the leader feels that God is doing at any particular moment in time. The chief prophet of the Latter-day Saints, for example, still holds office for life and is believed to continue receiving direct revelations from God. The same is true of the Jehovah's Witnesses who are almost totally governed by a small group of senior leaders based at their Bethel House Headquarters in Brooklyn, New York. The organisation of Exclusive Brethren is still totally in submission to the dictates of their Australian leader, John Hales.

## Strict Codes of Behaviour

In what was the first attempt by anyone to define what is meant by a 'sect' Ernst Troeltsch noted that such groups were 'strict', 'they live apart from the world' and they 'emphasise the law instead of grace'.

In short, this means that sects always have rigid codes of behaviour. They practise what are often termed 'micro ethics'. These usually have to do with relationships, food, drink, entertainment and dress codes. Strong guidelines are often laid down by some sect groups with regard to relationships with the opposite sex, alcohol or tobacco. This type of rigid stance is typified in the preaching of Billy Bray, one of the leaders of a nineteenth-century sect called *The Bible Christians* which originated in Cornwall. According to his biographer:

> Billy frequently said that if God intended man or woman to take snuff, the nose would have been turned upside down: and that an architect who built a house without a chimney, so that all the smoke came out of the front door was in his opinion a very poor architect. And if the Lord intended man to smoke, He certainly would have made a little chimney at the back of the head for the smoke to pass through; but as he has not, I don't think he intended man to smoke for surely the Lord cannot be a worse architect than man.[8]

The following chorus sung by the children of a small inner city group in Boston, Massachusetts (near where we used to live) illustrates very well the stance of most sects on the matter of smoking and alcohol:

> My body is a temple,
> To God it doth belong.
> He bids me keep it for his use,
> He wants me firm and strong.
> The things that harm my body
> I must not touch at all.
> Tobacco is a harmful thing
> And so is alcohol.

It was in keeping with these sentiments that Joseph Smith ruled against the consumption of alcohol, tea, coffee and other hot drinks for the Latter-day Saints. In more recent times it was recommended that Coca Cola was to be added to the list, presumably because of its

---

[8]  F.W. Bourne, *Billy Bray* (Epworth Press, 1937), 104.

very high caffeine content. Christian Scientists may not drink alcohol or smoke and Seventh Day Adventists are forbidden to eat shellfish or pork.

Other aspects of strict behaviour in sects is seen in the denial of holidays, television, videos and fashion clothes. In the Jehovah's Witnesses, if a young couple develop a romantic attachment to each other and want to start dating, the elders or leaders of their Kingdom Hall appoint a chaperon to accompany them on their evenings out.

In very general terms, therefore, it is the case that sects keep a much tighter control over their members. In many instances would-be members are required to undertake introductory or commitment courses. These are often followed by a formally signed membership agreement in which the new recruit agrees to submit to the directives of the leaders or eldership and to tithe a tenth of their income to the group.

Individual members who fail to comply with the patterns of behaviour established by the sect are usually reprimanded, sometimes in public, and if 'rebellion' persists, expulsion procedures are resorted to. I have seen the minute books of a Latter-day Saints congregation which listed several members who were 'put out' for adultery and other forms of unacceptable behaviour. The conduct most guaranteed to end in excommunication from many sects includes marrying a non-member, 'worldly' behaviour such as cinema-going, inappropriate dress and failure to comply with the requests of the leaders.

## An Element of Separation

Most sects have a strong element of protest, particularly at the time when they were first formed. Not only do they 'protest' at what they see as the coldness of the more established churches, they also stand out strongly against certain aspects of wider social behaviour. Like most people in the churches, sects are very disturbed by violence on the streets, the collapse of marriage and family life and the breakdown of human relationships. Sects stand against these developments by persuading their members to keep themselves entirely separated from harmful activities and unacceptable company. Members of the Exclusive Brethren, for example, are not permitted to have television sets or radios. Nor are they allowed to take holidays on public beaches or to keep pets. In The New Testament Church of God, a Pentecostal sect, members are not allowed to wear bikinis, go to the cinema or straighten their hair. They often lay great stress on the home environment. For example, for members of the Latter-day Saints every Monday night is family night and husband, wife and children are expected to put aside all other commitments and be together to relax and enjoy family games. Some sects are much more demanding on their membership. Jehovah's Witnesses stand out strongly against anything which they regard as the concerns of the present world order. They will not acknowledge a country's flag and they do not celebrate Christmas or personal birthdays. For the same reason they do not campaign for political office, take part in electioneering or hold leadership positions in trade unions.

## A Literal Interpretation of Scripture

Sociologists of religion have observed that sects usually begin among poor and disadvantaged people groups. Sects provide these groups with a clear framework and straightforward answers to the fundamental questions of life. They also offer a secure, caring community and promise a blissful future in some form of heavenly or millennial Kingdom. For this reason sects still tend, even at the present time when their memberships are largely middle class and prospering, to interpret the Bible and other scriptures very literally. Many members of sect groups which have separated from Christian churches are therefore 'fundamentalists' in their attitude to the Bible.

The early members of the Society of Friends (Quakers), a seventeenth-century sect, tended towards biblical literalism. Shortly after James Nayler professed to have raised Dorcas Edbury to life in 1656 Susanna Pearson of Evesham attempted to raise a widow's child to life. Her method was to imitate the action of the Old Testament prophet Elisha who stretched himself out over the Shunamite widow's son. When this proved unsuccessful she restored the child to the grave from which she had exhumed it![9] For

---

[9] B. Reay, *The Quakers and the English Revolution*, 35.

many sectarians the world and everything in it was made in four literal days of 24 hours each; Noah constructed his boat, which was the size of the QE2, single-handed; women must not have their hair short, should avoid wearing jewellery, must have hats on during worship and play a subservient role in religious affairs. Some sectarians insist that everyone must have their feet washed after taking the Lord's Supper. If you visit the New Testament Church of God, for example, immediately following the sharing of the bread and wine at communion members wash one another's feet. First, all the women go out to the cloakrooms and remove their shoes and stockings and then return and wash each other's feet at the front of the sanctuary. Then when they have finished the men follow suit. On the occasion when I was present I recall there was plenty of lively music during the ablutions and a good deal of spilt water which was mopped up into buckets by the sidespeople. This kind of rigid literalism perhaps reached its height in the United States in the celebrated 'Monkeyville Trial' over the question of evolution in the 1920s. During the proceedings William Jennings Bryan declared that 'if the Bible had said Jonah had swallowed the whale he would have believed it'. Tim La Haye, a close associate of televangelist, Jerry Falwell, is a firm believer in the doctrine of the rapture which asserts that before Jesus finally returns in judgement believers will be plucked up into the sky to safety. This is based on a literal reading of Matthew 24:40–41 which speaks of two men working in a field, the one being taken and the other left; and two women grinding at the mill with one taken away and the other left behind. La Haye declared that when the rapture comes 'there will be airplane, bus and train wrecks throughout the world.' 'Who can imagine', he continued, 'the chaos on the freeways as automobile drivers are snatched out of their cars?'[10]

Other examples of the same kind of literalism are not difficult to find. Latter-day Saints, for instance, are baptised on behalf of their deceased friends and relatives for the reason that 1 Corinthians 15:29 says: 'If the dead are not raised at all, why are people baptised for them?' Certain sectarian groups dance with dangerous rattle-snakes in their hands when they worship because Mark 16:18 says: 'they will pick up snakes with their hands'. Candidates for adult

---

[10] F. Fitzgerald, *Cities on a Hill*, 184.

baptism in a London-based group are blindfolded for three days prior to their baptism in the sea for the reason that St Paul was blinded for three days before his baptism (see Acts 9:9). One other example may serve to reinforce the point. In the later 1980s a friend of mine belonged to the Bath City Fellowship which had strong links with Bryn Jones' sectarian Restoration network. At that time if a woman wished to speak during the service, or offer a prayer they had to have their heads covered. In order to do this they had to stand and raise their hand. A veil would then be passed to them in compliance with the instruction in Paul's first letter to the Corinthians 11:5 that every woman who prays or prophesies in the church must have her head covered. Only when the prescribed headgear was firmly in place could they speak out.

## Worship That Is Shared and Vibrant

One of the characteristics of sect groups, particularly in the early years when they were first founded, is vibrant and participatory worship. It frequently happens that once the sect becomes more established its worship becomes quieter and predictable, but almost always there remains a high level of congregational participation. A typical instance is the Latter-day Saints. In the early days charismatic phenomena were common. Both Joseph Smith and his successor, Brigham Young, often spoke out in 'loud tongues' and prophesied for extended periods. At their meetings there were also exorcisms and frequent prayers for people to be healed. These days, however, Latter-day Saints' worship is much like any nonconformist church Sunday service. Quite often the proceedings are led by a gently spoken, suited elder, with sedate hymns and carefully worded homilies. However, there is still a good deal of congregational participation. Members take part in offering prayers, readings, testimonies, reports and interviews. Equally, in the worship at the Kingdom Halls, Jehovah's Witnesses all take part in the Watchtower Bible studies and make contributions in readings and music.

In mainstream churches worship is very often a spectator sport with all the emphasis on the priest or pastor who 'conducts' the worship something after the style of an orchestra who simply follow his lead when invited to do so. In sectarian worship there are often much higher levels of participation from congregational members with testimonies, praying, prophecies, exorcisms and speaking in tongues. In the so-called Toronto movement of the mid-1990s other typically sectarian phenomena were observed including barking, jerking, roaring, pogoing, snaking and running on the spot. None of these more extreme manifestations were new. In fact they were all common in the life and worship of the early nineteenth-century sectarian movements.

In a number of sects active in contemporary Britain and in the West generally, vibrant worship is still a continuing feature. There is often an emphasis on 'singing the high praises of God' and 'getting the glory down'. I once attended worship of one such group with some students from my Sociology of Religion class. We sang one hymn 'Soon and very soon we're going to see the King', for twenty minutes. At the end of the service I remarked on this fact to one of the leaders. 'Yes', he said, 'that's right, we sing them till we feel them!' Other experiential aspects in the worship of the more revivalist sects include dancing, handclappings, shoutings and exorcisms. In many instances sectarian worship is highly animated. A close friend who attended the Sunday meeting of a large sectarian group in Birmingham described the worship as 'manic'. 'It was', she said 'as though the musicians were clockwork toys who had suddenly had all their buttons pressed.'

## A Strong Sense of the Spiritual Battle

The Bible and indeed the sacred texts of other major world faiths see the world as made by God and therefore fundamentally good. Despite this fact, most sects have a strong perception that the world is an evil place from which their members must separate and in some cases cut themselves off from totally. This is part of the reason why groups such as the Christadelphians and the Jehovah's Witnesses refuse to take any part in politics. It is also the explanation for members being urged to keep away from pubs, theatres, cinemas and other places of secular entertainment. Such buildings are regarded as the 'citadels of Satan' and people who visit them are likely to get hooked by wicked spirits. At the very least they will run into danger and fall victim to temptation and sin.

Coupled with this dominant feeling of evil in the world many sect groups have a vivid sense that they are engaging in spiritual war against Satan and his hosts. For this reason, sects often develop quite detailed demonologies as well as elaborate and specific ways of combating the devil and all his works. During a visit to a sectarian group in the Midlands I was somewhat taken aback when the leader said at the conclusion of a period of singing: 'devil this is for you'. Almost immediately the whole congregation were up on their feet again jogging on the spot, pounding the floor and slapping their legs above the knees. In a similar manner writer and journalist Roy Kerridge related how he visited a sect in a South London Primary School. At one point in their service the worship leader started the song.

> Lower, lower – stamp Satan lower! Lower, lower,
> Lower, lower, lower, lower!
> Higher, higher – raise Jesus higher . . .

This whole demonic issue has a number of associated dangers which will be highlighted in later chapters. Some sect teaching has produced a 'blame the devil for everything' syndrome. This has the danger of preventing people from facing up to their own actions and mistakes. It also, in some cases, leads to unhealthy preoccupations with 'evil spirits' and exorcisms.

## Lack of Self-Evaluation

The great majority of sects, as we have noted, believe themselves and no one else to have the truth of salvation. Only they have all the right answers, only they are the perfect group, only in their fellowship can true freedom be achieved. All of this leads to a general unwillingness on their part to examine carefully their values, beliefs, attitudes and practices. After all, if they have 'the truth', what is the point of their questioning or debating the fact? Sects therefore deal in certainties. The issues are clear-cut and the answers black and white. There is only one interpretation of the truth and one understanding of eternal realities and that is their understanding. All this means that whereas a more established church might set up a committee to look at its understanding of baptism or the role played by women, a sect is unlikely to consider such an exercise worthy of the time or effort.

Sectarian movements can therefore be marked out by a number of key characteristics, the most important of which have been discussed above. The Oxford sociologist of religion, Bryan Wilson, marked out a sect in the following way:

> (a) it is a voluntary association; (b) membership is by proof to the sect authorities of some special merit, such as knowledge of doctrine or conversion experience; (c) exclusiveness is emphasised and expulsion of deviants exercised; (d) the self-conception is of an elect, gathered remnant with special enlightenment; (e) personal perfection – however defined – is the expected level of aspiration; (f) there is ideally a priesthood of all believers; (g) there is a high level of lay participation; (h) the member is allowed to express his commitment spontaneously; (i) the sect is hostile or indifferent to the secular society and state; (j) the commitment of the sectarian is always more total and more clearly defined than that of the member of other religious organisations; (k) sects have a totalitarian rather than a segmental hold over their members, and their ideology tends to keep the sectarian apart from the world.[11]

It needs to be recognised that as with churches, sects come in all sorts, shapes and sizes. Many play valuable roles in providing a secure base and community for people who live on the margins of society or who find it hard to identify with official denominational church religion. Many are particularly strong on family issues and in the giving of aid and practical care. Sects emerge from a variety of different world faiths. Some are only found among specific people groups or in particular geographic locations. Others are strongly represented among particular social classes or occupational groups. More importantly, differing sects have very different concepts of salvation and of the way in which salvation can be achieved. The chapters which follow look in detail at particular sects and pick up on these issues. They will also explore key points of difference where they occur between sects and biblical creedal Christianity.

---

[11] Cited M. Hill, *A Sociology of Religion*, 77–8.

# Chapter 2

# The Variety of Sectarian Movements

Sects are not all of a piece. Within the general compass of sectarian movements there is a good deal of variety. In order to help the student of religious movements understand them more thoroughly, sociologists of religion have analysed a variety of different categories or types. They have attempted to make this classification from a variety of different standpoints.

Some sociologists have attempted to make distinctions between religious movements based on their styles of organisation. For instance, some religious groups have a democratic organisation. So for example, the Christadelphians insist that each of their 'ecclesias' or places of worship make all key decisions on the basis of a majority vote of their membership. In the Jehovah's Witnesses, many appointments to various posts are given on the basis of the democratic principle. Other communities, rather than being democratic, are in fact 'charismatic', that is, led by a strongly charismatic individual who is able to dominate the rest of the group and make decisions on their behalf. Here a typical instance would be Joseph Smith who in founding the Latter-day Saints made almost all the decisions concerning his following off his own back. Occasionally he sought the advice of other leaders but most often he formulated policy on a whim, often reinforcing it with new prophetic utterances, many of which were subsequently written down and incorporated in *Doctrine and Covenants*. On this way of examining the variety of religious sects other movements would be seen as monastic, colonial or communitarian in their organisational structure.

An alternative method of highlighting the variety of sectarian movements was put forward by Roy Wallis in his book *Rebirth of the*

*Gods*.[1] He attempted a classification based on attitudes to the world. Thus, according to his scheme, 'world denying sects' are those which emphasise the evil of the modern world. 'World denying sects' therefore tend to insulate themselves from their surrounding culture. In some instances they withdraw from it altogether and live on special reservations or in colonies. Two such groups which are considered in later chapters of the book, the Exclusive Brethren and the Jesus Fellowship, would both seem to fit into this category.[2] The Exclusive Brethren who emerged in a split away from the Open Brethren in 1848 almost immediately adopted a strong doctrine of separation. At the present time this has reached extreme proportions with members living in secluded neighbourhoods and having only minimal contact with those outside their own ranks. This is typified by their unwillingness to share a front door or bathroom with non-members and by their refusal to eat food prepared by people not belonging to their number. The Jesus Fellowship which was founded in the 1960s insulates a large section of its membership from the outside world by placing them in segregated houses where a fairly strict and puritanical regime is operated. This includes no televisions, newspapers or a number of sports and pastimes.

In contrast to 'world denying sects' are what Wallis terms 'world enhancing sects'. These groups actively seek to improve and enhance the quality of the life of their members so that in general they enjoy life to the full. The Latter-day Saints, the Spiritualists and certain elements of the Restoration movement house churches (now New Churches) most nearly fit this category.

Between these two contrasting attitudes Wallis placed a third category of 'world indifferent sects'. Such groups, he observed, tolerate the secular environment of which they are a part but try to encourage their adherents to see a purer and better way of life within the sect. Examples of this type would include the Christadelphians, a millenarian group, which originated in England and the United States of America in the mid-nineteenth century; and Christian Science, which emerged in Maine and Massachusetts in the same period.

---

[1] See R. Wallis, *Rebirth of the Gods*.
[2] For a full study of sectarian community see T.J. Saxby, *Pilgrims of a Common Life*.

Bryan Wilson preferred a third means of highlighting the variety among sectarian movements. He analysed them according to their concept of salvation. This analysis has the distinct advantage of focusing attention on the central religious issue which is always 'What must I do to be saved?' Using this analysis Wilson distinguished a number of clearly defined categories.[3]

## Conversionist Sects

Conversionist sects place a very high value on evangelism. Their aim is to impart a 'heart warming' emotional experience in their following. Most sects, as has been noted, believe themselves to be the sole possessors of the truth. They are convinced that only they have the message which can really transform society. It is therefore expected of members that they will devote a considerable amount of time proselytising by going from door to door or engaging in various forms of open-air evangelism. There can be few people in the Western world who have not come across the Jehovah's Witnesses going in pairs from door to door offering the *Watchtower* magazine and inviting householders to their local Kingdom Hall. Similarly members of the Latter-day Saints are encouraged to set aside two years of their life for a full-time missionary journey. Many young Latter-day Saints members undertake this after completing their first year of college or university. They then complete their studies on their return home. Members of the International Churches of Christ also fit well into the 'Conversionist' category. They are required to engage in evangelism on several nights each week. This is often in the form of issuing invitations to a 'Neighbours' Sunday Service' or engaging people in shopping centres or on public transport with the objective of interesting them in an exploratory Bible Study.

## Adventist Sects

A second type or category are 'Adventist' sects. The emphasis here is on the imminent return or advent of Christ. This is not of course to imply that mainline churches are unconcerned with the second

---

[3] See B. Wilson, *Religious Sects*.

coming of Christ. It is part of the historic creeds that 'He will come again to judge the living and the dead.' The difference is that Adventist sects make this coming an all-engrossing concern. In the Adventist sect it is not just a matter of Jesus coming; it is always Jesus coming *very soon*. Adventist sectarians are often carriers of sandwich boards with announcements such as 'Now is the End of the World' or 'Prepare to Meet Thy God'. Church history is littered with individuals who proclaimed the day of the Messiah's return only to see their hopes dashed.

One such group which all but ended in 1994 is Southcottianism. It takes its name from Joanna Southcott (1750–1814) who functioned as a prophetess from 1792 until shortly before her death in 1814. She dealt in dreams, visions and prophecies. Her message was straightforward: 'Amend your ways, or Napoleon, the Beast of Revelation, will prevail, whereas if you amend, he is doomed.'

Joanna was particularly impressed with the text of Zephaniah 1:14, 'The Great Day of the Lord is near . . . and hasteth greatly.' She lived with the expectation that the return of Jesus could be at any moment. She believed herself to be 'the woman clothed with the sun' described in Revelation 12:1. She was also the Lamb's Bride of Revelation 21:9 and 22:17. Just as Jesus had come to reverse the damage done by Adam, so she, Joanna, came to make good the deficiencies of Eve.

To all who studied and accepted her teaching and signed a document to that effect she issued seals. These were title deeds to the Kingdom of God and they were inscribed with Joanna's own wax seal. This was done to fit in with the 144,000 in the book of Revelation who, the Apostle John saw, were sealed before entering God's heavenly Kingdom. In general Joanna's teaching was markedly unorthodox. This was particularly the case in her treatment of the atonement and redemption. She declared, for example, that 'by her stripes all men must be healed'. This was a parody of Isaiah 53:5.

Southcottianism reached a crisis point when Joanna claimed to be pregnant by the Holy Ghost. The Spirit disclosed to her that she must make an earthly marriage to await the birth of a son. Although she was by this time in her mid-sixties a marriage was hastily arranged for her in 1814 with a certain John Smith, a yeoman aged fifty-six. From late 1812 until shortly before her death in December 1814 childbirth was confidently expected. He was to be a man child

– the Shiloh – prophesied in Genesis 49:10. In the event Joanna died childless. Clearly she had some doubts about what the Spirit had revealed since in her will she made provision that the many presents which had been given for Shiloh were to be returned.

Students of religious history often wonder how it is that Adventist sectarian leaders such as Joanna succeed in attracting adherents. The answer must be that individuals such as Joanna are seen as wise men and women. Although Joanna did not heal the sick and rarely visited them, she advised on dreams and visions. She counselled youth, commented on government bills and statutes, and reproved excesses. Perhaps above all was the fact that she had a phenomenal knowledge of the Bible and was an occasional and moving preacher.

Another Adventist sectarian who was to have great influence on the founders of Seventh Day Adventism, the Christadelphians, and the Jehovah's Witnesses was William Miller (1782–1840). In his early years, Miller was a deist and an enthusiastic supporter of Thomas Jefferson. He was converted in a local revival and soon became a keen Bible student. He spent considerable time delving into the chronology set out by Archbishop James Ussher who had earlier counted up all the 'begats' in Genesis and concluded that the creation began at 9 a.m. on 26 October 4004 BC. Miller began probing the Old Testament prophetic books focusing on Daniel in particular. Eventually he reached the conclusion that the second coming would take place between 21 March 1843 and 21 March 1844. Excitement reached fever pitch and huge tent meetings were held throughout New York State in such places as Albany, Utica and the Mohawk Valley. In Rochester the textile industry boomed in response to huge demands for ascension robes. On the predicted date many sat on the roofs of their houses clad in these white garments waiting to be whisked away in a heavenly rapture. 1844 came and went and William Miller was left crushed and despairing since he had pinned his whole ministry on this prediction. He wrote publicly after the event: 'I confess my error and acknowledge my disappointment.' He died, discredited and broken in 1849.

A significant group of his followers were not so easily put off by Miller's failed prophecies. In 1844 one of them, Hiram Edson, a farmer from western New York had a vision as he walked through a cornfield one day. He saw that 'the cleansing of the temple' had in fact taken place on the predicted day, not on earth but in heaven. A second man, Joseph Bates, had another solution. He was adamant that Jesus had not returned to earth in 1844 because the Lord's people were failing to keep the Sabbath. Instead they were observing Sunday in breach of the commandment. Prompted by the guidance of Ellen G. White (1827–1915) the Seventh Day Adventists were founded in 1855 with their headquarters at Battle Creek in Michigan. In addition to strict Sabbath keeping it was felt important for members to purify themselves by restricting their intake of meat. Significantly one of Mrs White's close supporters, Dr John Kellogg, had devised a special vegetarian diet of processed corn. As one commentator put it, 'Though Christ is still to come, Battle Creek remains the Breakfast Food Capital of the World.'[4]

Another more recent example of an Adventist sect are the Rastafarians who have become active in England since the 1960s and 1970s. The movement's origins lie in the preaching of Jamaican-born Marcus Garvey (1887–1940) and his 'back-to-Africa' campaign and subsequent ideas which were developed by Leonard Howell, who taught that Emperor Haile Selassie (Ras Tafari of Ethiopia) was the 'Living God'. Essentially Rastas look forward to a future salvation which will be inaugurated in Africa, the new Canaan, when Haile Selassie returns in triumphant messianic function.

A more recent instance of Adventism was seen in the prophet Bang-ik Ha's prediction that Jesus would come again in October 1992 to rapture believers away into the safety of heaven before the 'Great Tribulation' begins. In his publicity he was insistent that 'just as He called John the Baptist to prepare for His First Coming, now God has called Bang-ik Ha for His Second Coming'.[5] According to Bang-ik one of the signs that the end time is imminent is the rise of a ten-nation confederacy. In his own words:

> The Bible predicts the rise of the 10-nation Confederacy from Old Roman Empire that will dominate the world during the 7 years of Great Tribulation (Dan. 2:7, Rev. 13:17). One leader (the Antichrist) will rise in this Revived Roman Empire to whom the 10 Kings will

---

[4] M. Ruthven, *The Divine Supermarket*, 52.
[5] B. Ha, *Rapture in October 1992*, 4.

give their power. He will deceive the world by portraying himself as the awaited Messiah and will establish 7 years of peace treaty with Israel, but he will break it after 3 ½ years to start a massive persecution on both Israelites and Christians (Dan. 9:27). We are about to face the birth of this nation, the birth of the European Economic Community (EEC) in Dec. 31, 1992. The Rapture must take place BEFORE this unification.[6]

For Adventists salvation is predominantly future. It will be realised at some distant point after the advent of the Messiah. Adventist sects are therefore strongly orientated towards the future. Christadelphians, for example, have an evening meeting every Sunday night at which a talk is given on some aspect of the future coming Kingdom. On the noticeboard outside their meeting halls the preacher is always announced 'D.V.' which is short for *Deo volente* – God willing. Always in their thinking is that the advent may take place before the next week's gathering for worship in which case it will not be God's will for another proclamation to be made.

## Introversionist Sects

Another distinctive category of sectarian religious movements can be styled 'introversionist'. As the term implies these groups set high store on withdrawal from the surrounding world and its culture which are perceived as having a detrimental influence. Salvation is achieved by individuals keeping themselves 'unspotted from the world' and within the purity of their own community. Introversionists often have a heightened sense of the sacredness of their own community and a strong perception of the world as an evil place. Additionally, they frequently regard themselves as a gathered remnant of the faithful elect. Salvation is sometimes by 'inner illumination' or 'inspiration'.

The early Society of Friends typified this kind of introversionism. They lived sober lives, kept themselves to themselves, wore distinctive forms of clothing and refused to bear arms.

---

[6] Ibid. 4.

However, in the eighteenth century, particularly as a result of the revival under the Wesleys, the Quakers, as they became known, began to look outwards to the world around them and to engage in reformist activities. By the close of the twentieth century English Quakers were once again becoming rather more quietist and putting less emphasis on countering injustice and racism in the wider world.

Many contemporary sects have some introversionist traits but perhaps none are so comprehensively withdrawn from the outside world as the Exclusive Brethren. The 'Exclusives' parted from those who are now known as the 'Open Brethren' in 1848. Led by John Nelson Darby (1800–82) they came to have an overwhelming sense of their own sanctity. Darby and those who sided with him in the break, developed a strong doctrine of 'contamination' which was closely akin to the Old Testament ideas of holiness. Under the provision of the Mosaic Law, the Israelites were exhorted to 'touch no unclean thing' less they themselves should be tainted by it. In a similar way, Darby taught that even to listen to erroneous teaching or to 'fellowship' with those who were party to it was to become tainted. Only by 'separating' or 'departing' from such influences could salvation be considered secure.

With the passing of time a succession of dominant leaders followed in Darby's wake. By process of accretion they extended the founder's teachings into an even more rigorous degree of separation. John Stoney who later succeeded Taylor proclaimed that members should sever themselves from company where they were 'sure that the Lord had abandoned it'. Frederick Raven urged Brethren not to depend on worldly support or patronage. This included money and business alliances. In the twentieth century Exclusivism was dominated by the Taylor dynasty. James Taylor Snr adumbrated the doctrine that although salvation was 'in Christ' it was nevertheless in the church where Christ is honoured that salvation can be experienced. This meant that increasingly the entire life of exclusive brothers and sisters began to revolve around Brethren activities. Things reached a pinnacle during the ascendancy of James Taylor Jr, 'Big Jim', who dominated the Exclusives during the 1960s. He introduced 'the doctrine of separate tables' by which no one was allowed to eat with their own family members who were twelve years and older if they did not break bread with the Brethren. Later this was extended to the point where it was considered an offence to eat food of any kind if it had been prepared by those who were not Brethren.

Introversionist sects such as the Exclusives frequently practise 'endogamy', that is, marriage within the group. To marry 'outside' frequently carries the penalty of expulsion. Certainly within the Exclusives any person who contracted a relationship with someone outside would be visited by senior local leaders and then be 'withdrawn' from.

A number of black Pentecostal Holiness churches fit into this introversionist category. In the 1980s, for example, members of the New Testament Church of God in Coventry (with whom I have enjoyed friendship and worship on a number of occasions) were not allowed to date the opposite sex without permission from their elders. Jewellery was forbidden and young people were not allowed to go swimming with the opposite sex. Some of these kinds of puritanical attitudes emerged from American fundamentalists who denounce them as the stuff of liberalism. In 1979 televangelist Jerry Falwell published a book entitled *America Can Be Saved*. In it he wrote that 'the liberal churches are not only the enemy of God but the enemy of the nation'. He went on to describe as 'liberal' anyone who teaches evolution and anyone who does the foxtrot. He later said in reference to Carter's period of office:

> I don't know why every one of our Presidents thinks he has to wine and dine every drunk who comes over here from some other country and dance with his wife. It seems to me that if a President is a Christian, he can offer that foreign head of state some orange juice or tomato juice, have a good minister come in and read a few verses of Scripture, and if he doesn't like that, put him on the next plane home![7]

## Utopian Sects

Quite similar to introversionist sects are those styled 'Utopian'. Such groups seek to preserve their purity and sanctity by not only cutting themselves off from their surrounding culture but also

---

[7] F. Fitzgerald, *Cities on a Hill*, 173.

taking the further step of building their own colony or reservation. Such communities are often operated on the basis of a common purse. The importance is that the community is seen as essential to the experience of salvation.

One such early community were the Moravians who first emerged in Saxony prompted by Christian David, a pietist preacher, who urged his followers to cut themselves off from the wider world. Persecuted for their views they were given protection by Count Nicolaus von Zinzendorf in his estates at Hernhutt in Saxony. During a communion service in August 1727 the Holy Spirit came on the early members of the community in a remarkable way producing love, unity and a deep joy. It resulted in the group entering into a much deeper commitment to one another although there was no move towards establishing a common purse. Rather the principle was established in which members contributed to one another's needs out of their surplus as God blessed them.

With the passing of time groups of Moravians began to settle in other parts of Europe as well as in America before they established colonies in the townships of Bethlehem and Nazareth in the State of Pennsylvania. Here their objective was to become completely independent, self-supporting and self-sustaining communities. Moravians first established a community at Fulneck in Yorkshire in 1748.[8] Various businesses were established including a farm, shoe-making, tailoring and a glove factory. All the profits generated by these enterprises were held in common. Other Moravian communities were established at Fairfield near Droylsden and at Ockbrook near Derby.[9]

Utopian groups have not developed to any great extent in the UK partly for the reason that land is scarce and for the most part expensive. There are small communities in a number of places but the majority appear to be rather more 'churchly' than sectarian in character. One sectarian group which places a particularly strong emphasis on its own communes is the Jesus Fellowship discussed in a later chapter of this book. Emerging from the preaching of Noel Stanton at Bugbrooke, in Northamptonshire, more than sixty

---

[8]  See Saxby, *Pilgrims of a Common Life*, 127–30.
[9]  For Ockbrook, see E. Ring and M. Nelson, *Ockbrook Moravian Church and Settlement*.

communal houses have now been established in various parts of the country. The houses maintain strict segregation of men from women. Each house which is supervised by several male elders operates a strict code of conduct which includes all aspects of moral behaviour and major items of expenditure. Members pledge their allegiance to the Jesus Fellowship for life and there is a strong feeling that they need to be cut off from the wider world and its influences lest they are captivated by them and lose their salvation. Similarly the International Church of Christ with its principal UK congregations in London, Birmingham, Manchester and Edinburgh, encourages its young single members to live in Church houses or flats where they can be supervised in a highly structured environment. In this context they can be discipled and also disciple others, an aspect considered to be vital if they are to retain the salvation they believe they received at their baptism.

## Manipulationist Sects

Certain sectarian groups have been able to achieve salvation, as they perceive it, by utilising a particular insight or body of truth. Essentially salvation is achieved by 'manipulating' aspects of the outside world. The aim of manipulationist sects therefore is to help their members achieve a fuller and more meaningful experience of life. A number of these sects offer therapies of various kinds, some of which include exercises, special dietary arrangements and meditation. Among these are included Theosophy, Christian Science, Spiritualism and the Aetherius Society. The latter group offers solutions to those who are curious about cosmic phenomena – particularly UFOs. It does so by a mixture of methods including yoga and receiving radiations in specially selected locations.[10]

Theosophy was first taught by Madame Helena Petrovna Blavatsky (1831–91) who co-founded The Theosophical Society with Colonel Henry S. Olcott (1832–1907) in 1875. The word 'theosophy' is compounded from the Greek words *theos*, meaning God, and *sophia*, meaning wisdom. Although it encompasses a wide range of ideas its central concept is that the human race is still

---

[10] See Wilson, *Religious Sects*, 163.

evolving and each individual is progressing. The ultimate goal for each individual soul is to be united with the 'Universal Over-Soul'. In *When We Die* Geoffrey Farthing presents theosophical views on man's spiritual constitution, the afterlife, and issues relating to immortality.[11] These are based on a compilation of extracts from *The Mahatma Letters to A.P. Sinnett*, which he says theosophists believe to be authoritarian.[12] He explains that this is a different class of literature from that which has been written by mediums or psychics who have received knowledge passed to them by entities, because the authors of the Letters were living men. He has reproduced extracts from *The Mahatma Letters*, the originals of which are in the British Museum.[13] The letters in question contend that after death the soul goes into a state of gestation and can spend time in the edenic Devachan, a kind of heavenly resting place, before reincarnation. Theosophists see immortality as relating to consciousness and perception of Self.[14] Farthing says that an 'Adept' or initiate would be able to 'arrest the hand of Death at will' and would also have to be able to retain consciousness and perception of Self when obliged to leave the physical body.[15] No method of liberation is discussed in this book, only the idea that to be liberated, the mind should 'identify with the Infinite'.[16] The problem is that this ultimate condition is the state known in India as 'Samadhi' and 'only reached by the very few'. Its equivalent after death is called 'Nirvana'.[17] The problem, as theosophists perceive it, is the fact that the soul of man has become obscured by dense forms of matter so that the personality and lower mind is composed of a lower duality and animal soul which are clouded in ignorance. Mrs Blavatsky wrote in her second volume that 'we are at the bottom of a cycle' and in a 'transitory state' – one in which 'the divine intellect is veiled in man'.[18] The general theosophical idea is that we have but fleeting contacts with

---

[11]  Geoffrey Farthing, *When We Die*.
[12]  Ibid. 2.
[13]  Ibid. vii.
[14]  Ibid. 46.
[15]  Ibid.
[16]  Ibid. 49.
[17]  Ibid.
[18]  II, 74.

our higher Mind (Manas), Spiritual vehicle (Buddhi), and Spirit (Atma) which are referred to together as the Ego (individuality).[19] Our personality contains a shell (animal soul) which survives death. The 'Path of Discipleship' is a mystical progression Blavatsky believed all religions have in common. It also relates to the transformation of the self – with an emphasis upon knowledge or truth. Blavatsky's system appears as a cocktail which includes Spiritualism, hypnotism, mysticism and speculative astronomy. This may also be due to a mass of material written by mediums and psychics which has been incorporated into the Theosophical Society,[20] and to her 'Cosmogenesis' which she set out in Volume I of *The Secret Doctrine* published in 1888. Volume II, entitled 'Anthropogenesis', gives a full explanation of man's evolution. Some theosophists also believe that a hierarchy referred to as 'The Great White Brotherhood' intervenes in human affairs to influence mankind's evolution. Theosophists think of it being composed of elder brothers, who have taken the path of initiation upon which all devotees of Truth symbolically progress and have finally transcended the human nature at some time in history.

Following Madame Blavatsky's death in 1891, Annie Besant (1847–1933), a freethinker and early exponent of birth control, promoted the movement in England and other European cities. She later travelled to India where she promoted a young Indian boy named Krishnamurti as the forthcoming Messiah. This action caused widespread offence and in consequence Rudolph Steiner took the majority of German theosophists into his own Anthroposophical Society in 1912. Despite these defections Theosophy has persisted though its influence is diminished.

In contrast to Theosophy (God-Wisdom), Rudolph Steiner (1861–1925) developed 'Anthroposophy' (Man's Wisdom). His system is an esoteric form of Christianity. Paradise is a symbol of the ultimate unified consciousness of spirit-man with Elohim-Jahweh. This is the goal which the Cosmic Christ can enable each spirit-man to reach. Lucifer and Ahriman are two evil powers who operate to pull individual human beings back from achieving this end. Christ's life, death and resurrection, the 'three Cosmic Christ Events', were

---

[19] Farthing, *When We Die*, Table: 'The Principles of Man', 51.
[20] Farthing, *When We Die*, 1.

supremely important in helping men and women to overcome the downward pull and the distortions of Lucifer and Ahriman. By a series of meditations and study individuals can find their lost spiritual nature. Anthroposophy promotes personal growth in four key areas: the senses, imagination, inspiration and intuition. These faculties can be extended by various kinds of spiritualist channelling.

As Anthroposophy spread more widely its teachings were extended into various areas of life and in particular farming and schools. In the matter of agriculture Steiner stressed the importance of a spiritual and scientific philosophy. He stressed the importance of 'natural' seasons for sowing and harvesting and the avoidance of chemical fertilisers. In the matter of education Steiner was in the vanguard of a 'child-centered' approach. His great stress was on 'awakening what is in a child' rather than pressurising knowledge into a child. His methodology made especial use of music and movement and was particularly successful with retarded children. Over 500 schools now teach Steiner's principles. A number of these are residential communities and include worship and prayer.

A prominent example of a manipulationist sect is Christian Science. It was founded in the 1860s and 1870s by Mary Baker Eddy (1821–1910). Three times married, Mary suffered severe ill health for much of the early years of her life. Following a visit to Phineas Quimby (1802–66), a New England mental healer, Mary's condition rapidly improved. Later, in 1866, she slipped on the ice and it was felt that owing to the severity of her fall she would not recover. However, in a dramatic encounter she was instantaneously healed. Following this she developed her own system of healing which she termed 'Christian Science'. Undoubtedly she was influenced by Quimby's system, but she did not go along with all his methods. In particular, she rejected his notion of neutralising 'animal magnetism' by rubbing the head and other parts of the body to counteract its damaging effects. Additionally, where Quimby and others stressed the importance of attuning the human mind to positive influences, Mary underlined the necessity of the individual being open to the Divine Mind as the means to true wholeness.

In essence Mrs Eddy's teaching, which was decidedly Gnostic in character, was that man was created not as a material being but as wholly spiritual. The material man was therefore in a sense 'unreal' as was by the same token sin, sickness, disease and death. If a person could but realise this through openness to the Divine Mind by silent prayer and positive affirmation, healing could flow. This rectification of negative thinking Mary Eddy termed the 'divine principle'. Today most Christian Science congregations have several Christian Science practitioners among their number who seek to minister healing according to the principles set out by Mrs Eddy on page 476 of *Science and Health with Key to the Scriptures*.[21]

In essence Christian Scientists seek to reach out to the patient through divine love. If he or she does so the healing work will be accomplished and as Mary herself put it 'the disease will vanish into its native nothingness like dew before the morning sunshine'.[22]

## Reformist Sects

Some sectarian groups may be categorised as 'reformist'. According to Bryan Wilson such groups are comparatively rare and generally arise only in advanced societies.[23] Here salvation is evidenced by social activism or reformist agendas of various kinds. Wilson suggests that perhaps the best example is the Society of Friends or Quakers. Although they were very clearly introversionist in their early days, conscience became increasingly emphasised in their teaching and meetings. It was particularly marked in Quaker business dealings where they became noted for both shrewdness and integrity. As the Industrial Revolution progressed Quaker manufacturers such as Cadbury, Rowntree and Fry were noted for their high standards both in trading and in the treatment of their workforce. Quaker reformist activities included opposition to slavery, prison care stimulated by the work of Elizabeth Fry (1780–1845) and concern for the men and women who suffered under the harsh conditions of the Industrial Revolution. Men such as Joseph Rowntree (1801–59) and Henry Cadbury paid particular attention to the needs of their employees. Cadbury built model cottages for his labourers which were well above the general

---

[21] R. Peel, 'The Christian Science Practitioner', *Journal of Pastoral Counselling* 4.1 (spring 1969), 41.
[22] *Science and Health with Key to the Scriptures*, 365.
[23] Wilson, *Religious Sects*, 179.

standard of accommodation enjoyed by town workers in general. Furthermore he had a gymnasium built on his factory site so that his labourers could enjoy recreation during the day. Encouraged by Joseph Lancaster who formed what became The British and Foreign Schools Society, Quakers also took a keen interest in promoting education for younger children.

During the First World War the Quakers who were strongly pacifist did much work in tending to the needs of the sick and wounded. In the later years of the nineteenth century they were also noted for their strong opposition to nuclear weapons and for their concern for the environment.

In the later years of the nineteenth century the Salvation Army, which had been founded by William (1829–1912) and Catherine Booth (1829–90) in 1878, developed a strong reformist strategy in its attempts to reach London's 'submerged tenth' with the Christian gospel. Initially, Booth and his wife had proclaimed the simple black-and-white message reflected in their motto 'Blood and Fire'. The 'Blood' stood for the blood of the Cross and the Fire for the power of the Holy Spirit as individuals were overcome with the sense of God's presence at specially arranged holiness meetings.

By the later 1880s Booth was conscious that the membership of his army was gradually declining and he reached the conviction that his simple 'Come to Jesus' proclamation was insufficient to meet the needs of his hearers. As he put it on one occasion: 'No man ever got saved while he had tooth-ache.' In short he recognised that saving souls was no easy task when his hearers had cold feet and empty stomachs. Booth therefore put forward what he later described as his 'scheme for social salvation'. It was set out in detail in his book entitled *In Darkest England and the Way Out*, which he published in 1890. Booth's proposal consisted of a whole package of reformist measures. These included temperance crusades, hostels for the down-and-outs, rescue homes for fallen women and various systems to persuade working men to take the pledge. In addition Booth established various colonies to provide work for the unemployed. He also set up a Household Salvage Brigade to organise collections each week and gather up unwanted items from old furniture to food. These would then be redistributed to anyone who had need of them.

## Thaumaturgical Sects

Wilson proposed one further category of sect which he styled 'thaumaturgical'. The word derives from the Greek word *thaumaturgos*, which means wonder-worker. Here considerable emphasis is put on the miraculous or wonder-working. The ability of the membership to engage in miraculous acts is seen as part of the evidence of their salvation.

Perhaps the most notorious example of a thaumaturgical sect is the snake-handling Pentecostals of Tennessee and Kentucky. The practice is based on Mark 16:18 which states that believers 'will pick up snakes with their own hands'. The verse is taken literally as an injunction to engage in the practice on a regular basis in their times of public worship. At a certain point in the worship during the singing of choruses the worship reaches a climax and the tempo and atmosphere changes. At this moment dangerous mountain rattlesnakes are brought out and passed around. Those who are able to, dance with the snakes in their hands and pass them from one to another. The practice of snake-handling was first started in Tennessee by George Went Hensley in 1909. Handling the snake is held to be a test of genuine faith regardless of the consequences. Periodically the movement is brought into disrepute as a result of death from snake-bites. This included George Hensley himself in 1955. Bryan Wilson interpreted the practice of snake-handling as partly arising out of a strict puritanical ethic:

> Handling the snake is the test of faith, regardless of the outcome. The snake represents the devil but at an unconscious level it probably symbolises a capacity to dominate dangerous sexual desire among these ecstatic puritans. The idea of the snake as a primeval phallic symbol or as a pre-Judaic deity that had to be anathematised (in Genesis and Exodus) is probably quite unknown to snake handlers. These often semi-literate people in culturally retarded areas are concerned only with the manifestation of miraculous power.[24]

Despite the fact that some States including Tennessee, Kentucky and Virginia outlawed snake-handling, the practice continues in

---

[24]  Ibid. 175.

these States and elsewhere in the United States. In general the practice of snake-handling does seem to be largely located in rural and cultural backwaters.

In the UK the most widespread form of sectarian thaumaturgy is seen in the many active Spiritualist groups and churches. These are discussed in detail in a later chapter of this book. Modern Spiritualism is traceable to the writings and teachings of the Swedish mystic, Emanuel Swedenborg (1685–1772). Among other things he had a remarkable gift of clairvoyance and an ability to make future prediction. In its more popularised form, contemporary spiritualism takes its origins from the spirit rappings experienced by Kate and Margaret Fox at Hydesville in New York State. Although Spiritualists have a variety of different views, they are all united in the conviction that the universe is full of departed spirits who wish to communicate with and assist the living. These departed spirits can be contacted in a variety of ways including clairvoyance, trance-mediumship and rappings of different kinds. A typical Spiritualist worship service has two main components; devotion followed by demonstration. The occasion will begin with hymns, prayers, readings and a talk not unlike a nonconformist service. In the second part there is usually a medium who receives messages for some or all of those present. These are often words of comfort, reconciliation, forgiveness and guidance. They are frequently greatly reassuring to those who have been bereaved or are grieving. Sometimes the medium can provide answers to puzzling situations or convey a word of hope regarding the future. In addition, many mediums offer their services to individuals on a one-to-one basis, giving guidance and counsel.

Spiritualism enjoyed a resurgence of interest after the two world wars and particularly so following the 1914–18 war. It also appealed to women who were generally found to be more naturally suited to work as mediums. Furthermore, Spiritualism is essentially non-clerical and its lack of ritual in most places finds a much greater resonance with secularised Western society. Many of those who become members feel they have touched reality and it gives them great assurance.

A number of independent, small sectarian groups as well as some of the so-called New Churches developed a strongly thaumaturgical emphasis in the closing years of the twentieth century. The most obvious example is the so-called Signs and Wonders movement which emerged in the 1980s, particularly in the writings and teachings of John Wimber (1934–97) who presided over the Vineyard Churches from his headquarters at Anaheim in California.[25] He analysed the book of Acts and in a detailed chart noted that there are twenty-seven occasions in which church growth was directly related to signs and wonders. He commented: 'It seems clear from this survey of Acts that signs and wonders played a vital and integral part in the spread of the gospel. Has this stopped being the case? Surely NOT!'[26] As John Wimber read the New Testament he realised that the element missing from the contemporary church was the mighty Jesus who moved with power. He it was who gave the disciples power to expel demons, heal the sick, feed the hungry and set the captives free. What was needed was for people to see the works of Jesus, then they would more readily believe the words of Jesus. This led to a new emphasis on healing and prophetic gifts being seen as essential in the life of a growing religious community. There were some 500 Vineyard churches in the United States in 1999 and more than fifty in the UK.

## The Transformation of Sects

Almost all studies have shown that sects have a high death rate, that is, they only last for a comparatively short time. Either they 'evaporate' or they gradually become more like a denominational church. The term 'evaporation' is sometimes used by sociologists to describe the charismatic leader's loss of 'charisma' or power to dominate his or her following. This may happen as he or she 'runs out of steam' or becomes old or finds him or herself unable to cope with rival factions within the ranks. The American sociologist Richard Niebuhr, asserted that this process of becoming more churchlike usually happens in one generation.[27]

A number of writers have examined this course of sectarian change in more detail. Usually it begins with the need for better

---

[25] For a Study of John Wimber, see D. Pytches, *John Wimber: His Influence and Legacy*.

[26] J. Wimber, *Signs and Wonders and Church Growth*, 14.

[27] R. Niebuhr, *Sources of Denominations*, 19.

organisation. There comes a time where a sectarian movement swells in numbers to a point where the original leader can no longer cope with the organisation single-handed. There is therefore a need for other individuals to do the administration, to share the pastoral care and preaching and to assist in the management of the buildings and finances. The result is that a certain amount of hierarchy and structure are necessary and so an organisation starts to emerge.

Second, with the process of time the sect gradually begins to accommodate to the surrounding cultural environment. In this process of addressing its message to its locality it encounters other views and opinions which may well cause it to modify its original opinions and compromise its ethics.

Third, as the sectarian group prospers in economic terms it may well look for a more educated or formally trained ministry. Such leaders inevitably come with a less fundamental attitude to the Scriptures, which militates against the sect's early teaching.

Finally, social pressures gradually preclude frequent meetings of the sect. As members prosper they have other business and social commitments on weekday evenings. They are not therefore able to spend all their time in fellowship with one another with the result that their enthusiasm for the group's ideal is diminished.

The slowing-down process which most sects experience was termed 'routinisation' by Max Weber. By this he meant that the original enthusiasm of the leader is gradually put into a routine or a straightjacket. This of course makes it easier to handle and keep a check on, but for the participants it very soon becomes stale, dull and boring. Inevitably, they begin to look for something with more vitality in the near vicinity or if there is nothing which suits their tastes, further afield.

Not all sects do, however, experience this transformation. Some, particularly those with a high degree of introversionism, are able to insulate themselves sufficiently from the influence of the outside world. Such groups are sometimes referred to as 'persistent sects', the most obvious examples being the Exclusive Brethren, the Christadelphians and the Jehovah's Witnesses. Other groups remain markedly sectarian in character because they have unique, strongly held core beliefs which are difficult to modify or adapt. Most of the sectarian groups considered in the succeeding chapters of this book fit into one or other of these two categories.

# Chapter 3

# The Christadelphians

The Christadelphians are a Bible-based lay movement who, roughly speaking, follow the teachings of their founder, Dr John Thomas (1805–71). They do not describe themselves as 'Christian' since, as they perceive it, so many of the denominations deal in 'hierarchical priestcraft' and the 'traditions' of men. The name 'Christadelphian' was chosen by Thomas in 1865 and means quite literally 'Brothers [and of course sisters] in Christ'.[1] Thomas wrote at the time: 'I did not know a better denomination that could be given to such a class of believers, than 'Brethren in Christ'.[2]

Christadelphians have no paid ministry or priesthood and they eschew robes, rituals and ecclesiastical pomp and circumstance. Although in earlier times their movement was dominated by strong individuals such as Thomas and later Robert Roberts and C.C. Walker, there is no appointed 'head of the Church'. Christadelphians are active on most continents in the world and their presence is notable in Australia, New Zealand, Canada, the US and the UK, where the focus is on the Birmingham-based Christadelphian office. The Christadelphian place of worship is known as an 'Ecclesia', the New Testament word for a gathering of people. As in Apostolic times certain members are appointed as officers to manage the affairs of the congregation. These include a 'Recording Brother' who has a secretarial role and a 'Presiding Brother' who acts as chairperson for the year.

Each week there is a morning meeting for the 'breaking of bread' when there are hymns, prayers, readings from the Scriptures and an

---

[1] F. Pearce, *Who Are The Christadelphians?* 2.
[2] R. Roberts, *Dr Thomas: His Life and Work*, 237.

exhortation. The bread and wine are circulated among all the 'brothers and sisters' who are present. Non-members are not allowed to participate. In the evenings Bible lectures are held and members of the public are warmly invited to attend. Voluntary collections are taken at the breaking of bread and fraternal services to meet all expenses including those of visiting ministering brothers. The contributions are only made by members. As in the Christian churches, Christadelphians instruct their children in Sunday schools and youth groups. All Christadelphians are exhorted to a life of prayer and study and members follow a detailed yearly scheme of Bible readings.

Status as a Christadelphian is achieved only through faith and baptism in one of their Ecclesias. Faith is not an affair of the heart, rather it is seen as 'obedient faith' as in Romans 12:6. Such faith requires both submission to and an active carrying out of right doctrine. This can only be found in the teachings of Jesus, as expounded by John Thomas and to a lesser extent by his successor Robert Roberts. It is only on profession of this faith that baptism is regarded as valid and as being the 'one baptism' spoken of in Ephesians 4:5.[3]

## John Thomas

John Thomas was born at Hoxton Square on 12 April 1805. Of his mother little is known except that she was a mild, admirable lady of a religious turn. His father was recalled as 'a high-spirited, proud and talented man, with an active temperament and energetic mind, of eminently moral and intellectual tendencies'.[4] He held various posts including clerk in the East India Company, then successively Independent minister, keeper of a boarding school, Independent minister again, clerk in a London City Gas Office and then a Baptist minister at Brentford in Middlesex.[5]

---

[3] H.A. Twelves, *The Only Way of Salvation*, 18. This booklet was first published in 1946.
[4] Roberts, *Dr Thomas His Life and Work*, 4.
[5] See ibid. 4–5.

At the age of sixteen John became a member of his father's congregation in Chorley. After only four years his father returned to London but young John remained behind to continue his medical studies with a private surgeon under whom he had been placed two years earlier. When this assignment was completed he moved back to London and became a student at St Thomas's Hospital, qualifying three years later with an MRCS.[6] He practised medicine for a while in Hackney during which time he contributed a number of articles to *The Lancet*. He later recalled that during this period his mind was 'preoccupied with the world and his profession'.[7]

Early in the year of 1832 Thomas' father was seized with the American emigration fever. John decided to go with him partly because he had no particular prospects and partly because he had come to have an intense dislike for what he termed 'the priest-ridden society of England'. As a doctor he was able to secure an appointment as surgeon to a 500-ton passenger ship, the *Marquis of Wellesley*. They set sail from London to New York on 1 May 1832. The seas were heavy and after many days of storm the passengers became frightened and religious services were held. John who feared shipwreck prayed 'Lord have mercy on me for Christ's sake' and vowed he would devote himself to God's service if he survived.

Soon after disembarking Thomas set out for Cincinnati where he had letters of introduction to several people. On his arrival he was introduced to some of the followers of 'Campbellism'. They were an extreme Baptist group who followed the teachings of Alexander Campbell (1788–1868). One of their number, Major Daniel Gano, invited Thomas to his home. During the course of conversation the pastor, Mr Walter Scott, who was also present, succeeded in convincing Thomas of the need for a proper baptism by immersion. Having been convinced, Thomas was thereupon baptised by Scott at 10 p.m. in the light of the moon that same evening in the Miami Canal which passed in front of the house. People later jibed that Thomas had been 'moonstruck'!

After some months John Thomas left Cincinnati for the eastern States. During the course of his journey he met and stayed with Alexander Campbell who succeeded in persuading him to become

---

[6] Ibid. 6.
[7] Ibid. 3.

the editor of a new magazine which he proposed to establish under the title *The Apostolic Advocate*. After some initial reluctance Thomas accepted. The publication soon rang out with Thomas' anti-clerical sentiments. The very first article of the first volume began as follows: 'If one proposition be more self-evident than another, it is in this: that the religion of the disciples of Christ cannot be found among any of the popular religions of the 19th century, which divide among them the realms of the demesnes of Christendom.'[8]

The second article was on 'The Church of England' which he described as 'one of the daughters of a large family, descended from a parentage flagrant in crime, drunken with the blood of Christian heroes, and gorged with the spoils, and the woe, and the slaughter of men'.[9] Thomas found her origin in 'the Man of Sin, and his adulterous consort, the Mother of Harlots and of all the abominations of the earth'.[10]

In these early editorial days according to his biographer Robert Roberts, Thomas 'gloried in ignorance of other books, and in never having been cursed with the poison of a theological education'. One result of his study and writing was that Thomas changed his views in the matter of baptism. In October 1834 he published an article on Anabaptism in the sixth issue of the *Advocate*. In this piece he argued that no baptism was valid that was not based on an intelligent faith. Thomas was doubtless reacting against the lack of instruction given by many American churches, the Campbellites included, to those intending baptism. He wrote: 'The principle is this – that the terms of admission into the Baptist Church are not adequate to a reception into a Church of Christ.'[11] In one of his concluding paragraphs Thomas advocated rebaptism for such people:

My conviction is that all among us who have not been immersed upon the confession that Jesus is the Christ, and who did not *understandingly* appreciate the value of his blood, had better be re-immersed upon that confession; and that all from this time forth, who may wish to join us

---

[8]  Ibid. 26.
[9]  Ibid. 28.
[10]  Ibid.
[11]  Ibid. 35.

from the Baptist denomination (a few excepted, who can show just
and scriptural cause for exception) be required to make an intelligent
confession, and to be re-immersed.[12]

Controversy followed Thomas' publication in which he was
taken to task by Campbell. In his reply the doctor admitted the
charge of 'rebaptising the baptised' and went on to admit 'that I
have baptised the immersed, and continue to do so still, but cannot
the readers of the New Testament discern the difference between
an immersed and a baptised person?'[13] Thomas continued his
association with the Campbellites for a further decade but his
relationships with them were for the most part strained. The final
break was to come in 1847 when he reached the view that 'we are
saved by hope' (Romans 8:4) and that this hope is the coming of
the Lord in power and great glory to set up a heavenly Kingdom
on earth beginning at Jerusalem.[14] For Thomas simply to believe
that 'at death his congenital immortal soul would fly on angels'
wings to heaven "there to be with Christ and reign with him over
kingdoms beyond the skies" was insufficient'.[15] Such a hope was,
in his view inadequate and short of the full gospel which
demanded belief that 'this kingdom would be in the holy Land,
when it shall be constituted a heavenly country or paradise'.[16]
Once having reached this opinion that he was as yet unbaptised
Thomas therefore asked a friend to go with him to the water and
asked that he immerse him with the words 'Upon confession of
your faith in the things concerning the kingdom of and the name
of Jesus Christ, I baptise you in the name of the Father, Son and
Holy Spirit.'[17] Following this step of obedience Thomas published
a lengthy confession which included a further section on this
future hope: 'The kingdom is to be indestructible . . . it is to stand
for ever, that is, to be superseded by no other . . . the saints are to
take this kingdom and possess it for ever . . . with the Son of man,

---

[12]  Ibid. 37.
[13]  Ibid. 39.
[14]  Ibid. 151.
[15]  Ibid. 152.
[16]  Ibid. 162.
[17]  Ibid. 154.

to whom all nations will be politically and ecclesiastically obedient.'[18]

After his re-immersion Dr Thomas set out for Baltimore, Buffalo, and New York with the specific aim of sharing his perfected understanding of the gospel with Campbellites in those places. He met with a positive response in the first two places but his hearers in New York could not endure the idea of the restoration of the Jews.

In June of 1848 Thomas left his wife behind and sailed for Liverpool. On arrival he spent a day or two in Manchester and proceeded to London with the hope of gaining a hearing from the Campbellites. They were not however disposed to hear his proclamation that Jesus was expected to return within twenty years to set up the everlasting Kingdom with its seat of government in Palestine for at least a thousand years as a prelude to the eternal rest which remains for the people of God.[19] He was, however, well received at Nottingham in August where he spoke on several occasions to packed audiences in the Assembly Rooms. This opened the way for further speaking engagements in Derby, Birmingham and Plymouth. He was then very well received in Glasgow where he lectured on four occasions in the City Hall to crowds of between five and six thousand. After successful meetings in Edinburgh he returned to London where he shut himself away almost completely for four months and wrote *Elpis Israel: An Exposition of the Kingdom of God.*[20]

The doctor returned to New York in September 1850 and for eleven years busied himself by resuming publication of *Herald of the Future Age* under the new title of *Herald of the Kingdom and Age to Come.* At the outbreak of the American Civil War in 1860–61 Thomas was forced to suspend his literary work because postal communications were disrupted. In 1862 he accepted an invitation to England, visiting Huddersfield, Halifax, Leeds, Edinburgh, Birmingham, Nottingham and perhaps fifteen other places. It was during this visit that he first met with Robert Roberts (1839–98) who was later to succeed him as the dominant leader. Roberts who

---

[18] Ibid. 163.
[19] Ibid. 193.
[20] I. Collyer, *Robert Roberts*, 28.

already shared the Doctor's convictions about the future Kingdom was able to entertain him in the two rooms of his little lodging house in Huddersfield.[21] Thomas soon persuaded him that Birmingham was the best centre for the work in England and he suggested to his young host that he start a magazine. Roberts complied and moved with his young wife to the city where he began publication of *The Ambassador*.[22]

Thomas returned to America in 1862 where he devoted his time to completing *Eureka* , an exposition of the apocalypse. He also began communicating his views through Roberts' journal. One significant announcement in its columns concerned the name 'Christadelphian' in 1865. As Thomas travelled he found many of his supporters anxious to avoid conscription into the American Civil War. In order for their pleas to be accepted it was necessary that they should be identified. Thomas declared that he did not know a better denomination that could be given than 'Brethren in Christ'. Thus the transliterated Greek word 'Christadelphian' was adopted by his following not only in America but in England, Scotland and elsewhere. The certificate Thomas issued included the following paragraph:

> This is also further to certify that the undersigned is the personal instrumentality by which that Christian Association aforesaid in Britain and America have been developed within the last fifteen years, and that therefore, he knows assuredly that a conscientious, determined, and uncompromising opposition to serving in the armies of 'the powers that be' is one of their denominational characteristics.[23]

As a result of adopting this new title the movement's main periodical *The Ambassador* was changed to *The Christadelphian*.

In May 1869 Thomas returned to England accompanied by his daughter and proceeded to Birmingham where he received a warm welcome. The number of communities had expanded from about 12 at the time of his 1862 visit to 123. After studying in Birmingham a few weeks Thomas toured Britain and found that his preaching

---

[21]  Ibid. 31.
[22]  Ibid. 36.
[23]  Ibid. 237–8.

received a much more ready reception than was the case in America. This led him to determine to return to his native country. He left England on 4 May with the intention of winding up his affairs in America and returning in a few months with his wife. His plan was never fulfilled because on his return he was seized with a sudden attack of peritonitis from which he never sufficiently recovered to enable him to travel. He died suddenly on the 5 March 1871, the news appearing in a letter from his daughter in the April issue of *The Christadelphian*. He left strict instructions regarding his interment which included the following:

> I order that being dead, I myself be not deposited in so-called conse-crated ground; but in some portion of our common mother earth, undefiled by episcopal or presbyterial mummery of the harlot daugh-ters of Rome on either side of the Tweed; nor may any parson, popish priest, or non-conformist minister ordained or unordained – all of them dealers in the merchandise of the apostasy and traders in 'the bodies and souls of men' – to be permitted to read, pray, preach, or in any way officiate in committing me, myself not a fraction or part of me – to my temporary resting and sleeping in the ground.[24]

## Robert Roberts

Robert Roberts (1839–95) had been appointed by Thomas to look after affairs in the event of his death. He therefore hastened to New York with brother Bosher, 'a good little man with just that depth of character which many lacked'.[25] Roberts immediately made arrangements for the final interment of Dr Thomas, which took place at Brooklyn with reading of certain portions of Scripture and the address from an American, Brother Ennis, who spoke of 'the faith which had animated and directed his course through life – the one hope: the hope of Israel – which had sustained and buoyed him up through the deepest trials'.[26] Roberts regarded Dr Thomas as the best, the most Christlike and the most spiritually minded of all the men he had ever known. He wrote: 'In private life he reminded us

---

[24] Ibid. 243.
[25] Ibid. 61.
[26] Roberts, *Dr Thomas*, 249.

of Christ, by a gravity of deportment that was mixed with urbanity, and a dignity that was sustained by unfeigned humility . . . that was free and natural in all things connected with the truth.'[27]

Roberts, like Thomas before him, was a writer, preacher and traveller. He started life as a rope seller and later became a journalist working for the *Aberdeen Telegraph*. At nineteen he married Jan Norrie and the young couple moved south to Halifax and then to Huddersfield where he started a meeting for those who shared in the hope of Israel. As a young man of only twenty-three years he had published a series of lectures on the hope of Israel under the title *Christendom Astray*. These were read and approved by Thomas and have since become standard reading matter for Christadelphians everywhere. On his return to England Roberts busied himself with the publication of *The Christadelphian* giving first place to the writings of Thomas.

Christadelphian Ecclesias continued to grow in numbers and expand in the 1880s. Many of them were noted for their vigorous and joyful music – in some the singing was so good that people came to the meetings especially to hear it.[28] Roberts, unlike others active in Victorian times, was a great believer in musical instruments. He reminded doubters about the musical zeal of King David, pointing out the clear evidence that instruments will be used in the Kingdom of God.[29] In addition to fostering the work in Britain, Roberts set out on a number of extended lecture tours. In 1888 he journeyed to America and in 1895 embarked on a voyage to Australia where he delivered 130 addresses. He followed this with a visit to New Zealand and Tasmania before returning home via America. Reaching San Francisco on 21 September he lodged at the Cosmopolitan Hotel where, wearied with the accumulated troubles and long periods of separation from his friends and homeland he died unexpectedly two days later on the morning of 23 September. His body was taken to Brooklyn Cemetery and interred alongside Dr Thomas, the man whose teaching had so much influenced the course of his life.[30] Robert

---

[27] Collyer, *Robert Roberts*, 53.
[28] Ibid. 103.
[29] Ibid.
[30] Ibid. 172–3.

Roberts' assistant and successor, Charles Curwen Walker, hastened to America to officiate at the service.

The writings of both Thomas and Roberts are regarded by Christadelphians as foundational. Their understanding of the gospel message is seen as unalterable truth and all subsequent Christadelphian writing and literature is expected to cohere with Thomas' and Roberts' interpretation of the Bible. Roberts wrote: 'the knowledge of the Scriptures in the writings of Dr Thomas has reached a finality'. In 1872–73 Robert Roberts' own Ecclesia in Birmingham drew up *The Birmingham Statement of Faith* which was gradually adopted as their doctrinal basis by Christadelphian Ecclesias all over the world.[31] This document together with *A Declaration of the Truth Revealed in the Bible*, which was also formulated by Roberts in 1867, encapsulated the heart of Christadelphian beliefs.[32] What are regarded as 'first principle subjects' are not challenged, but minor issues of interpretation or prophetic understanding may change if subsequent evidence is seen to require it. Some books appeared subsequently which do not exactly accord with the views of Thomas or Roberts, particularly with regard to the book of Revelation. In general, however, there is a vetting process through the Christadelphian office in Birmingham which ensures a consistency on major doctrinal issues.

After Roberts' death there was a general tendency for Christadelphian Ecclesias to go their separate ways. In a sense this was to be expected since Christadelphians have never had any centralised council or organisation. One other important figure since Thomas and Roberts was John Carter (1889–1962), editor of *The Christadelphian* from 1937–62. By his speaking and writing he was able to bring together many of these diversified groups and draw them into a more cohesive movement.

---

[31] *The Birmingham Statement of Faith*, 1872–73, was amended by the insertion of one bracketed clause into section 24 on the appearing of Christ in 1898.

[32] Roberts, *Dr Thomas*, 222.

## Planned Scheme of Bible Reading

Within the Christadelphian movement there are no professional paid instructors of the Bible. Instead each individual member is encouraged to study its teachings for themselves with the aid of a carefully planned course of readings. These are set out in *The Bible Companion* published by the Christadelphian Office, which enables the reader to cover the Old Testament once and the New Testament twice every twelve months. Christadelphians are also encouraged to use commentaries which allow a certain breadth of interpretation. The Christadelphian office markets a range of 'suitable' commentaries, most of them written by authorised members of the movement. Many Christadelphians do also make use of commentaries written by those from outside their movement.

All Christadelphian doctrines are rooted in the Bible. Roberts wrote of the Bible as 'a book of Divine authorship' and on another occasion: 'Outside the Bible all is speculation. Our safety lies in holding hard and fast to God's word.'[33] Christadelphians regard the Bible as the only authority in all matters of faith and practice. Both Testaments are held to be 'without error in all parts of them except such as may be due to transcription or translation'.[34] Regarding the interpretation of the Bible Roberts is clear that with 'certain qualifications, the Bible means what it says'.[35] He made the further point that 'the Bible as written revelation from God, must be written in language capable of being understood by those to whom it is sent'.[36]

## Doctrine of God

The Christadelphians in company with most historic Christian churches regard God as a person not as an abstract principle or energy. Roberts wrote: 'It is impossible to mistake the tenor of these testimonies: they plainly mean that the Father of all is a person who exists in the central "HEAVEN OF HEAVENS" as He exists

---

[33] R. Roberts, *Christendom Astray*, ch. 1, p. 2.
[34] *Statement of Faith* (Leicester Ecclesia, 1902).
[35] Roberts, *Christendom Astray*, 8.
[36] Ibid. 39.

nowhere else.'[37] Again he wrote: 'The testimony before us is, that God is the only underived and self-sustaining existence in the universe. All other forms of life are but incorporations of the life which is in him . . .'[38] Similarly, in a more recent publication, John Carter wrote:

> There is only one God, the eternal God, who created heaven and earth and whose spirit is everywhere. The Spirit of God is his power emanating from Himself, and is the basis of all things that exist . . . when this power is used for particular purposes it is described as Holy Spirit meaning that which is set apart for divine use.[39]

Christadelphians reject the creedal doctrine of the Trinity, asserting in the words of Roberts that it is 'a contradiction – a stultification – an impossibility'.[40] Roberts continued that 'it professes to convey an idea, and no sooner expresses it than it withdraws it, and contradicts it. It says there is one God, yet not one but three, and that the three are not three but one. It is a mere juggle of words, a bewilderment and confusion to the mind.'[41]

One of the arguments Roberts brought forward against the Trinity was the Old Testament assertion of the unity of the Deity as the One Father out of whom all things have proceeded, and who is supreme above all, even above Christ. This supremacy and unity of the Father would not be affirmative in his view if there were three co-equal personalities in his one personality. Historic Christianity accords with the Christadelphian assertion that there is only one God but it also affirms that this God reveals himself in three co-equal ways as Father, Son and Holy Spirit. Interestingly the very text which Roberts cited, Deuteronomy 6:4, to assert the supremacy of the Father is regarded by orthodox theologians as endorsing the Trinity. In the Hebrew it reads as follows: 'Hear O Israel, the Lord (Jehovah, singular) our God (Elohim, plural).' Hebrew scholars point out that the word for God in the Old

---

[37] Ibid. 79.
[38] Ibid. 81.
[39] J. Carter, *God's Way*, 47–48.
[40] Roberts, *Christendom Astray*, 77.
[41] Ibid.

Testament occurs 2,579 times in the plural and only 314 in the singular.

## Christ

In rejecting the Trinity Christadelphians necessarily oppose the traditional doctrine of Christ. They believe that before his birth Jesus did not exist except as a thought in God's mind. Jesus came into existence at a specific point in time. In *Christendom Astray* Roberts argued the matter by saying that God could not be called 'Father' unless he brought the Son into existence. He speaks of Christ having a derived existence and 'not God himself'.[42] In another paragraph Roberts wrote: 'The simple appellation of "Son", as applied to Christ, is sufficient to prove that his existence is derived, and not eternal. The phrase "Son of God" implies that the one God, the eternal Father, was antecedent to the Son.'[43]

During his earthly ministry Roberts regarded Jesus as being essentially 'man' or 'flesh' but anointed with God's spirit from the time of his baptism. 'If he were "very God" in his character as Son, why was it necessary that he should be "anointed" with spirit and power?'[44] Roberts in fact did not see Jesus as becoming 'very God' until the moment of his ascension: 'When raised from the dead and glorified, he was exalted to "all power in heaven and earth"; his human nature was swallowed up in the divine; the flesh changed to spirit. Hence, as he now exists, "in him dwelleth all the fullness of the godhead bodily" (Colossians 2:9).'[45]

This understanding of the glorified Jesus is altogether different from that of the Council of Chalcedon of AD 451 which reached the conclusion that Jesus is fully divine, at one with the Father in his divinity; and fully man, at one with us in his humanity.

Christadelphians assert in the words of John Carter that Christ 'being found in fashion as a man, and yet being sinless, was a perfect sacrifice'.[46] However, they stress that Jesus died as a 'representative'

---

[42]  Ibid. 93.
[43]  Ibid.
[44]  Ibid. 94.
[45]  Ibid. 95.
[46]  Carter, *God's Way*.

rather than as a 'substitute'. Christadelphian writers point to the fact that there is a great difference between a 'representative' and a 'substitute'. A representative, they hold, is not disconnected from those represented, whereas a substitute performs a role instead of those for whom he or she is substitute. Carter stated it as follows: 'Christ suffering as the representative of his people is one with them, and they are one with him.'[47] Additionally, *The Birmingham Statement of Faith* speaks of 'the offering of the body of Jesus once for all, as a propitiation to declare the righteousness of God, as a basis for the remission of sins'.[48] This understanding of the atonement is not far removed from that of the orthodox creedal Christian churches who would want to affirm that Jesus died both as a representative in that he represented the entire human race to God and as a substitute in that he personally met and bore the punishment which the sin of every individual merits.

## Doctrine of Salvation

Unlike many groups active in the contemporary Western world Christadelphians do not believe in an immediate and instantaneous conversion. For them salvation is a progressive affair which will only be completed in the millennium or thousand-year, end-time period. They do, nevertheless, stress the point that salvation cannot be earned by service or good works. There are two basic conditions for salvation: obedience to the teachings of Jesus and immersion baptism on profession of faith in the future coming Kingdom. On this matter Robert Roberts wrote in *Christendom Astray*: 'Nothing will save a man in the end but an exact knowledge of the will of God as contained in the Scriptures and faithfully carrying out the same.'[49] Three essential aspects of this knowledge are the name of Jesus, the things concerning the Kingdom of God and baptism by immersion. Roberts derived this from the summary of Philip's preaching in Acts 8:12 where he proclaimed to the Samaritans 'the things concerning the Kingdom of God and the Name of Jesus Christ'.

---

[47] Ibid. 100.
[48] *The Birmingham Statement of Faith*.
[49] Roberts, *Christendom Astray*, 231.

The things concerning the name include his crucifixion as a sacrificial offering for sin, his resurrection and future return. The way in which Christadelphians take the name of Jesus upon themselves is through baptism 'the divinely appointed formula' which according to Galatians 3:27 'introduces into the name of the Father, and the Son and the Holy Spirit'.[50] H. Twelves, a more recent Christadelphian writer, puts the essential nature of baptism as follows: 'Baptism, then, is the means of putting on the new man, Christ, of clothing ourselves with the righteous garment of Christ, so that in God's sight we are covered and our sins do not appear. Thereafter we are in Christ, but we still and every day have to put on bowels of mercy that are the mark of Christ's character.'[51] The one Baptism, Twelves points out, can only be valid if the subject has right belief.[52] A major aspect of this, as has been noted from John Thomas' own baptism, is a declaration of belief in a future salvation to be realised on this earth.

An obvious concomitant of this view of baptism is the Christadelphians' strong rejection of infant christening which Roberts described as 'religious foolishness'. The Christadelphian writer Harry Tennant has a detailed section on baptism in his standard text on the movement in which he emphasises that 'baptism was to be preceded by faith'.[53] From this position it becomes obvious that baptism is for adults who can make a 'mature decision'.[54] Of paedobaptism Tennant writes: 'There is no record anywhere in Scripture of the baptism of babies. The practice of Christening was introduced gradually from the second century A.D., and became the accepted practice much later on; but it has no place in the Gospel as Christ and the apostles preached it.'[55] Tennant underlines the Christadelphian conviction that 'there is no guilt attaching to new-born babies from which they can or need to be freed'.[56] In his view no one can be held to be guilty until they have

---

[50] Ibid. 229.
[51] H.A. Twelves, *The Only Way of Salvation*, 14.
[52] Ibid. 18.
[53] H. Tennant, *The Christadelphians: What They Believe and Preach*, 204.
[54] Ibid.
[55] Ibid.
[56] Ibid.

choice in the matter. Children do, he maintains, share the consequences of that sin but they do not bare blame for it. There is, he
points out, therefore 'no original sin' which christening, or adult
baptism for that matter, can remove.[57]

Baptism preceded by right belief is seen as that which 'translates
us into an entirely new set of relationships. We become members of
the household of God, and are enrolled as citizens of the Kingdom
of God'.[58] It is the conviction which led Robert Roberts to
proclaim the somewhat controversial teaching that neither infants
nor the mentally deficient can be saved. He put it as follows in
*Christendom Astray*:

> The second class of those who do not attain to life, are those who,
> never having seen the light, have never rejected it, what is to be done
> with them? . . . Paul answers the question in Romans 2:12 – 'As many
> as have sinned without the law shall also perish without the law.'
> Paganism, heathenism, idiocy, and infantile incapability are amenable
> to no law. Therefore, resurrection does not take place in their case.
> Death has passed upon them . . . and they sleep never to be disturbed.[59]

## The Holy Spirit

Christadelphians tend to speak and write of 'the spirit' rather than of
the 'Holy Spirit'. They view the spirit as God's agent or active force
by which he accomplishes his purposes. Robert Roberts saw the
outpouring of the Holy Spirit on the early church as God's way of
validating their preaching and ministry. This was, in his words, 'the
power granted to the apostles for the confirmation of their testimony'.[60] The apostles had power to bestow the spirit wherever the
truth was received. However, this ability has long since ended and
since the passing of the New Testament era 'the spirit operates
through the written word. This is the product of the Spirit – the
ideas of God reduced to writing by the ancient men who were

---

[57] Ibid.

[58] Ibid. 210.

[59] Roberts, *Christendom Astray*, Lecture 4, 52–3.

[60] Ibid. 84.

moved by it.'[61] Roberts rejected as hype the outpourings of the Holy Spirit at their revivalistic meetings. They bore 'no resemblance to those of the apostolic experience, and, therefore, must be rejected'. He continued: 'But the fact is, it is not the Holy Spirit at all. It is the mere spirit of the flesh worked up into a religious excitement, through the influence of fear – an excitement which subsides as rapidly as the agency of its inception is withdrawn.'[62]

Christadelphians are therefore 'cessationists' who believe that gifts of the Spirit have been withdrawn. Harry Tennant stressed that glossolalia, or speaking in tongues, and 'the supposed gift of healing' are 'widely different from those of New Testament times'.[63] Echoing Thomas he wrote of speaking in tongues as 'religious excitation' and referred only to the 'supposed' gift of healing which he regarded as 'the power of the mind of the healer upon the mind and will of the person who has come to be healed'.[64] There are apparently some Christadelphians who do maintain that the gifts of the Holy Spirit are still in operation but they usually end up joining one of the evangelical churches.

## Strict Ethical Behaviour

For the Christadelphian, sin represents anything that opposes God and his commands. They see this in relation to behaviour, rather than emotional feelings of guilt. The world beyond the Ecclesia is seen as being in opposition to God and therefore sin is very often seen in terms of 'worldly behaviour'. For this reason Christadelphians are 'introversionists', that is, they are a religious movement which seeks to separate as far as possible from the outside world. They are not, however, totally exclusive and where their conscience permits they will engage in conversation and friendly relations with members of other denominations.

In their early days Christadelphians adopted a strict avoidance of public amusements, sporting pastimes and the popular press,

---

[61]  Ibid. 86.
[62]  Ibid.
[63]  Tennant, *The Christadelphians*, 128.
[64]  Ibid.

novels and glossy magazines. Robert Roberts in an article in *The Christadelphian* denounced 'betting, races, sports, comic papers and novel reading'.[65] Public houses and the theatre were to be avoided as was also tobacco.[66] Roberts described smoking as 'the heathenish practice of the gentiles'. Today it is still regarded as unacceptable but it is tolerated. Drinking alcohol is not practised in Christadelphian homes but most members will have wine on special occasions. *The Christadelphian* of 1902 said: 'There is little hope for a community given to betting, races, sport, comic papers and novel reading – things which frivolise, demoralise and harden the heart.'[67] Cinemas, public houses, and dances are not generally seen as places for Christadelphians because they are 'of the world' and therefore 'not loved by the brethren'. These days there is a growing acceptance of entertainments and television and the media are generally accepted.

Marriage between a Christadelphian and a non-Christadelphian is not accepted and leads to 'disfellowshipping'. If such an offence takes place, the Ecclesia will signify its disapproval but the offending member will usually be allowed to retain their place if they acknowledge their offence.

Certain occupations are closed to Christadelphians. These include the police force, politics and the military. Christadelphians have been from the very beginning 'conscientious objectors' believing sincerely that this is Christ's call on their lives. In fact they avoid all employment in which there is violence of any kind.[68] They also avoid homage to the flag, maintaining that their 'honour and allegiance are first to the flag of Christ'. Regarding their pacifist stance Alfred Norris wrote as follows in a Christadelphian publication entitled *The Things We Stand For*:

We must altogether deny that 'it is lawful for Christian men at the command of the magistrate to wear weapons and serve in the wars', and to abstain from warfare is one of the principles of our body: 'the servant of the Lord must not strive, but be gentle unto all men, apt to

---

[65] *The Christadelphian* 33 (1896), 261.
[66] Ibid. Vol. 28 (1891), 32.
[67] Tennant, *The Christadelphians*, 235.
[68] *The Christadelphian* 39 (1902), 401.

teach and patient (2 Timothy 2:24). Our Lord himself will direct His Servants' duties when He returns, but since His Kingdom is not of this world, we will not now fight'.[69]

Christadelphians seek always to foster a positive attitude rather than a negating attitude to life. They seek to be considering, caring, compassionate and good neighbours. At the same time they try to recognise modern civilisation is transient and can offer no abiding hope. Rather it is the gospel of the Kingdom of Christ which provides an anchor in the present life and offers an unshakeable future security.

## The Millennial Kingdom

The great Christadelphian hope lies in the future coming Kingdom which will be inaugurated when Jesus returns. He will establish a thousand-year reign on the earth. This millennial period will be a time of intense happiness before the final end. It is often described as the 'Sabbath' or 'rest' of the world. During it the divine purpose for the creation will be fulfilled. A key aspect of the Christadelphian millennial scheme is that it will take place on this earth, not in some distant renewed planet. Robert Roberts wrote in *Christendom Astray*:

> Men are now trying to cure depravity and ignorance by various agencies: educational works, Blue Ribbon movements, Mechanics Institutions, Temperance Societies, Missionary Societies, 'Salvation Armies', Home Missions etc., are among the instrumentalities by which reformers hope to improve the world and bring about the millennium. The idea is vain. The regeneration of the world is be-yond human accomplishment . . .

But how is this result to be practically attained? The machinery of the Kingdom of God is the answer. When the governments of earth have been overthrown, and divine authority established with

---

[69] A. Norris, *The Things We Stand For*, 18.

a firm hand . . . Jerusalem, once more the centre from which divine illumination will irradiate, will be so this second time, on a larger and grander scale, and with more glorious results.[70]

The coming return of Jesus to inaugurate this millennium will be preceded by a devastating conflict on the plains of Armageddon. Harry Tennant in *The Christadelphian* believes that a confederation of nations, led by either Turkey or Russia, will invade Israel from the north. Further, based on his exegesis of Ezekiel 38 and 39, he asserts that they will be assisted by Iran, Ethiopia and Libya.[71] Before this can happen, the promise made to Abraham concerning the land of Canaan will be fulfilled: 'And I will make you a great nation and I will bless you' (Genesis 12:12). The Jews will be gathered in Palestine and the Kingdom of Israel will be restored. Alfred Norris, an accepted Christadelphian authority, wrote of their belief that 'He will, as he must, conquer, and take over the rule of the Kingdom of the world for himself (Daniel 2:44; Revelation 20:4). We believe that Israel, brought back to Palestine from all nations, will see him there in his glory and be invited to repent from its former wickedness in crucifying him (Zechariah 12:10).'[72]

Early Christadelphians followed the progress of the Jews very carefully. For a time they called their meeting houses synagogues and donated money to help the restoration of Jews in Palestine. In earlier times Thomas had confidently expected the end to come in 1866–68 and the final subjugation of the nations to be complete by 1910.[73] However, present-day Christadelphians avoid setting dates on these events and emphasise the need to live out Jesus' teaching faithfully in the expression of being found ready and prepared for his coming. The Kingdom ultimately to be established will be worldwide, but with its administrative centre at Jerusalem. The temple will be rebuilt and the city will become the capital of the earth. Before this, the dead will be resurrected and be judged according to their deeds, whether good or bad. Only true believers will become immortal.

---

[70] Roberts, *Christendom Astray*, Lecture 10.
[71] Tennant, *The Christadelphians*, 275.
[72] Norris, *The Things We Stand For*, 14.
[73] Roberts, *Dr Thomas*, 263–4.

This great Christadelphian emphasis on a future Kingdom and a future salvation has led sociologists of religion to speak of them as a millennial movement. Millenarians are those who not only stress a salvation which will only be realised at some future point, but additionally that it will be located on this earth and accomplished by supernatural means. Christadelphians are essentially passive millenarians who, rather than seeking to hasten the day of Christ's return by reformist social action, seek instead to withdraw from worldly involvement waiting for divine intervention.

## Christadelphian Constitution and Adherents

Christadelphianism is a lay movement. There are no full-time paid pastors, special officers or priestly leaders. Most of this emphasis dates back to Thomas who came from a Congregational Church background and held a particular dislike for priestcraft and ritual. Each group of Christadelphians is organised into a gathering known as an Ecclesia which is entirely self-governed. There is an office at Shaftmoor Road in Birmingham from where *The Christadelphian* and other books and literature are published, but it has no jurisdiction over any district or local group. Sunday morning worship is focused on the breaking of bread and only members are allowed to attend. On Sunday evenings there is a public meeting with a Bible lecture on some aspect of the Kingdom. The general atmosphere is much like that of a nonconformist service with hymns, reading, prayers and notices.

All the offices of the Ecclesia are elected annually. There are five presiding brethren who take it in turns to preside at the Ecclesia's meetings. There are seven managing brethren who decide all matters in connection with the general running of the Ecclesia, while the Recording Brother takes minutes and deals with matters of correspondence. A variety of minor officials include Sunday school teachers and the President of music. It is clear therefore that Christadelphians are strictly democratic in their organisation and character. In general women play a fairly subservient role in the public affairs of the local Ecclesia. They do not lead public worship or speak at the meetings, though they do have a role with the children.

## Membership

Worsley saw millenarian sects as arising primarily among the lower classes. Studies by Cohn have led him to the view that millenarianism is more likely to find rest in expanding areas of urbanisation,[74] while Wilson and others have pointed out that Christadelphianism was particularly well received in the Black Country and Birmingham. In the 1860s these were certainly areas of poverty and harsh living conditions. Wilson proffered the following explanation as to why early Christadelphianism flourished in this area: 'Poverty and poor conditions certainly existed, the domestic industrial system persisted longer here than in many parts of the country . . . Trade Unionism was retarded and less aggressive than elsewhere perhaps leaving more room for a discontented and revolutionary sect. The area had a reputation for immorality and degradation.'[75]

A reading of Roberts' biography of Thomas, and Collyer's biography of Roberts, suggests that most of the people they moved among were essentially lower middle-class tradespeople and entrepreneurs. It would seem unlikely that the unlettered manual workers would have embraced the complex biblical teachings of these two founding leaders. Certainly today the movement is for the most part dominated by well-healed, middle-class professionals. There are approximately three hundred Ecclesias in the British Isles and membership is estimated to be of the order of 20,000. Circulation of *The Christadelphian* was set at 7,000 copies per issue in 1998 with a slightly rising demand. The following table suggests that membership has been fairly static for a number of years and is declining very slightly.

---

[74] See Hill, *A Sociology of Religion*, 211.
[75] B. Wilson, *Sects and Society: A Sociological Study of Three Religious Groups in Britain* (Heinemann, 1961), ch. 12.

**Christadelphians**

| Year | Church Members | Churches or Congregations |
|------|------|------|
| 1970 | 21,000[1] | 379[1] |
| 1975 | 25,500 | 400 |
| 1980 | 22,000 | 360 |
| 1983 | 21,000[1] | 345[1] |
| 1985 | 20,000[1] | 330 |
| 1987 | 20,000[1] | 330[1] |
| 1990 | 20,000[1] | 320[1] |
| 1991 | 20,000[1] | 320[1] |
| 1992 | 19,500[1] | 318[1] |
| 1993 | 19,500 | 310[1] |
| 1994 | 19,500 | 300 |
| 1995[1] | 19,500 | 300 |
| 2000[1] | 19,500 | 300 |
| 2005[1] | 19,500 | 300 |
| 2010[1] | 19,500 | 300 |

[1]Christadelphians' own estimate

Source: *UK Christian Handbook 1996–1997* (Marc Europe, 1995), 278.

# Chapter 4

# Jehovah's Witnesses

There can be few people in England who are unfamiliar with the Jehovah's Witnesses. They are perhaps best known for their very active missionary work which puts most of the denominational Christian churches to shame. They have also achieved notoriety on account of their pacifist stance in the two world wars when many of their number suffered imprisonment on account of their refusal to bear arms. Many witnesses endured severe suffering in Hitler's concentration camps and in more recent times others were persecuted in Russia and some of the eastern bloc countries. JWs also sometimes hit the headlines over their unwillingness to celebrate Christmas or birthdays and their refusal to accept blood transfusions. Regardless of people's popular perceptions, however, they are a rapidly expanding movement in many parts of the world. In 1998 they were at work in 233 countries with 5,888,650 active members ('publishers'). In 1997 they were at work in 232 countries with 5,353,078 publishers. There were 316,092 baptisms in 1998 compared with 375,923 baptisms in the previous year. Among the countries where they have a large following are Brazil, Mexico and the United States where they have 1,040,283 active publishers.[1]

Jehovah's Witnesses distinguish between committed members, designated 'publishers', who aim to spend at least ten hours a month going from door to door seeking to share their faith and handing out the *Watchtower* magazine, and others who merely worship at the Kingdom Halls and attend the Annual Memorial Communion

---

[1] *1998 Yearbook of Jehovah's Witnesses* (Watch Tower Bible and Tract Society, 1998), 31; *1999 Yearbook of Jehovah's Witnesses* (Watch Tower Bible and Tract Society, 1999), 31.

service. In Britain in 1998 there were 131,981 publishers and 214,351 people attended the Memorial service. In 1997 there were 124,623 UK publishers but 223,301 people attended the Memorial service.[2]

## Early History

Religious movements rarely originate in a vacuum. Rather they are shaped by the culture, politics and the religious environment in which they emerge. Such was the case with the Jehovah's Witnesses whose beliefs and practices were moulded in a climate of revivalistic millennial preaching and later by the uncertainties of the First World War and the great Wall Street crash of the 1920s. Indeed the later years of the nineteenth century witnessed a continual stream of preachers who predicted the time of Christ's return and the coming of the Kingdom of God on earth. Among them were the Campbellites, the Millerites and the Seventh Day Adventists.

The early development of the Jehovah's Witnesses is closely linked with the life and teaching of the first four leaders and presidents of the movement. The first of these was Charles Taze Russell (1852–1916), the son of a Pittsburgh draper. He was born in the town of Allegheny on 16 February 1852 and was brought up in his parents' Presbyterian church. By the time he was fifteen he had entered into partnership with his father and together they managed a chain of clothing stores. As a young man he had begun to feel uncomfortable in his parents' religious environment and joined the Congregational Church which, for a while, he found a little more to his liking. There were frequent sermons on hell and Russell began to have severe doubts about the doctrines of predestination and eternal punishment and this led to his discarding his faith altogether. He described his state of scepticism in the following words:

> Brought up a Presbyterian, indoctrinated from the Catechism, and being naturally of an inquiring mind, I fell a ready prey to the logic of infidelity, as soon as I began to think for myself. But that which at first

---

[2] Ibid. 1999, 33; and ibid. 1998, 33.

threatened to be the utter shipwreck of faith in God and the Bible was, under God's providence, overruled for good, and merely wrecked my confidence in human creeds and systems of the Bible.[3]

On a day when he was still in this state of doubt he went to hear an Adventist preacher by the name of Jonas Wendell speak on the second coming of Christ. The message he heard brought him back to faith in Christ. Russell later wrote: 'Though his Scripture exposition was not entirely clear, and though it was very far from what we now rejoice in, it was sufficient under God, to re-establish my wavering faith in the Divine inspiration of the Bible.[4] What he heard excited in Russell a deep interest in Adventism and he soon gathered together a small Bible study group which met in Pittsburgh from 1870 to 1875. However, Russell and his circle differed from the Adventists in one important respect. They were convinced that Jesus' second coming would be spiritual and invisible rather than a physical, bodily return. Russell set out his views in a pamphlet entitled *The Object of Our Lord's Return* and 50,000 copies were printed. In 1876 Russell came into contact with a small group based in Rochester, New York, led by Nelson Barbour who also maintained that the second coming was invisible and spiritual. The two groups joined together and Barbour's magazine *The Herald of the Morning* became a joint publication. In 1877 Russell and Barbour co-authored a booklet in which they asserted that Christ's second presence began invisibly in the autumn of 1874. They also set the year 1914 as the end of the gentile times.[5]

After a year or two Russell broke with Barbour, on account of the latter's denial that the death of Christ was a ransom for sin, and set up independently. In 1879 he established his own journal under the title *Zion's Watchtower and Herald of Christ's Presence*. By this time his enthusiasm had spread and he had organized more than twenty study groups in eastern States of his homeland. In 1881 he constituted his following as Zion's Watchtower Tract Society with himself as manager. In December 1884 his group was given a legal charter and officially recognised as a public corporation. Thus

---

[3] *Jehovah's Witnesses in the Divine Purpose*, 14.
[4] Ibid. 9.
[5] *Qualified to Be Ministers*, 300, cited ibid. 11.

began the religious organisation which has since become known as the Jehovah's Witnesses. Its aim was simply to publish Bible truths in different languages in tracts, pamphlets and books. As a major part of this strategy Russell began what subsequently turned into a seven-volume work which was later entitled *Studies in the Scriptures*. These books were in wide demand and the first volume which appeared in 1886 eventually achieved a circulation of more than six million copies.

In 1889 the society purchased premises in Allegheny which served as the official headquarters until Joseph Franklin Rutherford, Russell's lawyer, secured substantial buildings in Brooklyn, New York. In 1891 Russell began to travel overseas, which resulted in branch offices being established in Germany, Australia and the British Isles, where small groups of Russellites had been in existence, some of them since the 1870s.

In 1879 Russell married Maria Frances Ackerly who was known as a well-educated, intelligent woman who had been one of his Bible students. For fifteen years she shared her husband's vision and was a strong supporter of the work. For a time she acted as secretary-treasurer of Zion's Watchtower Society and with Russell co-authored several books and pamphlets. In addition, Maria addressed a number of women's meetings where she gained a considerable following. Beneath the surface, however, everything was not as it appeared and in 1895 Russell asked for a separation and offered to give his wife the house if she would agree to a settlement. There followed a long drawn-out public struggle which consumed both the tabloids and the broadsheets of the day. Much of the titillation revolved around an alleged quotation on the part of his adopted daughter that he was like a 'jellyfish' where the opposite sex was concerned. Despite the *Washington Post* referring to him in one of its articles as 'Rev Jellyfish Russell' no evidence was ever brought before the court that he had behaved with impropriety and even his wife did not accuse him of adultery. In 1913, however, Mrs Russell divorced Charles on the grounds of 'his conceit, egotism, domination and improper conduct in relation to women'.[6] Even then little evidence of cruelty or immorality was ever brought to the court and it seems most likely that the marriage broke up because of Russell's

---

[6] H.H. Stroup, *The Jehovah's Witnesses*, 9–11.

incompatibility and his expressed desire to live a celibate lifestyle. Russell denied ever having engaged in any compromising behaviour and took a vow never to be alone in a room with someone of the opposite sex.[7]

Russell had great confidence in his understanding of the biblical text and this was well illustrated by what he wrote in the *Watchtower* concerning his own *Scripture Studies* publications:

> Not only do we find that people cannot see the divine plan in studying the Bible by itself, but we see, also, that if anyone lays the 'Scripture Studies' aside, even after he has used them, after he has become familiar with them, after he has read them for ten years – if he lays them aside and ignores them and goes to the Bible alone, though he has understood his Bible for ten years, our experience shows that within two years he goes into total darkness. On the other hand, if he had merely read the 'Scripture Studies' with their references and had not read a page of the Bible as such, he would be in the light at the end of two years, because he would have the light of the scriptures.[8]

As the Campbellites, Millerites, Adventists – and even orthodox Christians – had done, Russell also predicted the date of Christ's return. His first chosen date was 1874 and when it failed to materialise, his followers, like those of the earlier adventists, were inevitably disillusioned. However, they went on to teach that just as Jesus had preached for the three and a half years so his second presence would be for a corresponding period. This meant that the Kingdom would be set up in 1878 and that then the faithful witnesses would be taken away to heaven. Like the Millerites before them, some of Russell's followers purchased white robes and eagerly awaited the coming rapture. Inevitably disappointment followed and Russell returned to re-examine the biblical text concluding that he had miscalculated. He began to teach instead that Christ had in fact returned in 1874 but invisibly and that the elect would be taken up into heaven in 1914. Further disillusionment followed but 1914 did prove to be a year of major significance with the outbreak of the First World War. It was then that the key doctrine of the active rulership of

---

[7]  Cited R. Tucker, *Strange Gospels*, 121.
[8]  *Watchtower*, cited Hoekema, *Christian Science*, 13.

Christ was first enunciated. At that point in time he commenced his judgement 'assigning full control of all his earthly interests to "a faithful and discreet slave class" and factually, giving ultimate authority to its ruling body'.[9] Russell died on 31 October 1916 while journeying home on the Santa Fe train from a speaking engagement in California. According to the movement's official history, 'C.T. Russell served Jehovah's Witnesses for thirty-two years . . . travelled more than a million miles as a public lecturer, preached more than thirty thousand sermons and wrote books totalling over 50,000 pages.'[10] At his funeral service Joseph Rutherford paid this tribute to him: 'With strong physique, a fertile brain, and a brave heart, wholly devoted to the Lord, he consecrated and used all of his power, to teach man the great Message of Messiah's Kingdom and the blessing which it will bring to the world.'[11]

## Joseph Franklin Rutherford (1869–1942)

After a short but bitter struggle 'that threatened the very existence of the organisation'[12] Joseph Franklin Rutherford was unanimously elected by the corporation as the new president of the Watch Tower organisation. Rutherford who had served as the movement's legal adviser was born at Booneville, Missouri, of Baptist parents. He studied law and at the age of twenty-two began to practise jurisprudence, subsequently serving for four years as public prosecutor in his home town. At a later point he was appointed as a special judge for one of the districts of Missouri and occasionally served as a substitute judge when the regular judge was absent on account of illness. Hence he came to be known as 'Judge' Rutherford.

Rutherford first came into contact with the Watch Tower Society in 1894 but did not dedicate his life to Jehovah God until 1906 when a poor woman came into his office and gave him some of Russell's books. Rutherford later reflected:

---

[9] R. Franz, *Crisis of Conscience*, 343.
[10] *Jehovah's Witnesses in the Divine Purpose*, 343.
[11] Ibid. 62.
[12] Ibid. 64.

She was modest, gentle, and kind. I thought she was poor, and that it was my privilege and duty to help her. I found she was rich in faith in God. I bought the books and read them. Up to that time I knew nothing about the Bible; I had never heard of Pastor Russell. I did not even know that he was the author of the books at the time I read them ; but I knew that wonderfully sweet, harmonious explanation of the plan of God thrilled my heart and changed the course of my life from doubt to joy[13]

Rutherford was a strong character and a number of his followers reacted against his leadership. Rutherford met with particular opposition from P.S.L Johnson whom he sent to oversee the work in England and who then attempted to wrest control of the entire branch. When he was summoned back to New York he succeeded in persuading four of the seven members of the Board of Directors to side with him against Rutherford. It was not until 1917 that Rutherford's presidency was finally endorsed by the membership who had been invited through the columns of the *Watchtower* magazine to register their votes of confidence. By this point Johnson and the four other rebel directors had left the society together with about 4,000 individual members. The majority joined one or other of two newly founded groups, 'The Pastoral Bible Institute' and 'The Laymen's Home Missionary Movement'. Attendance at the Memorial Communion in 1917 was registered at 21,274, and in 1919, following the separations, at 17,961. The Society had 813 congregations at the close of 1917.[14] Rutherford soon began to make a number of major changes in the doctrine and running of his Watch Tower following. His major objective was to take a much tighter hold on the organisation and running of all the activities including both pastoral care and publishing. Travelling representatives of the society known as 'pilgrims' were increased in number from sixty-nine to ninety-three. Their main responsibility was to visit and strengthen the more than one thousand congregations of Jehovah's witnesses at that time. Rutherford also recognised the need for qualified speakers to represent the movement on public platforms and to this end he instituted the V.D.M. arrangement.

---

[13] *Watchtower*, December 1917, cited Tucker, *Strange Gospels*, 125.
[14] *Jehovah's Witnesses in the Divine Purpose*, 72.

These letters stand for 'Verbi Dei Minister' or Minister of the Word of God. There was a stringent system of assessment and those who passed were recognised as public speakers on particular issues.

The Great War brought the society into conflict with governmental authorities in both Canada and the United States. In 1917 the seventh volume of Russell's *Studies in the Scripture* was published posthumously under the title *The Finished Mystery*. It contained four pages printed as a tract under the title 'The Fall of Babylon', which was distributed in great quantities. It predicted imminent doom to the historic Christian churches, both Catholic and Protestant. A graphic cartoon depicted stones marked 'Romanism', Popes, Cardinals, doctrine of the Trinity ($3 \times 1 = 1$) and the like, falling from an ecclesiastical structure into the sea. What made matters more difficult was the fact that the book asserted that not only would the churches be destroyed but additionally all the masses of the people, 'the great Babylon', would perish and be forgotten for ever. This resulted in accusations that the society were anti-war and undermining the security of the allied war effort. The book and other Watch Tower literature were banned in Canada and anyone caught with it in their possession was liable to a fine not exceeding $5,000 and five years in prison. The Winnipeg-based *Tribune* newspaper stated:

> The banned publications are alleged to contain seditious and anti-war statements. Excerpts from one of the recent issues of 'The Bible Students Monthly' were denounced from the pulpit a few weeks ago by Rev. Charles Paterson, Pastor of St Stephen's Church. Afterward Attorney General Johnson sent to Rev. Paterson for a copy of the publication. The censor's order is believed to be the direct result.[15]

The US also adopted a strong tactic against the society and in May 1918 Rutherford and seven other key leaders were arrested on charges of conspiring to dissuade men and women from joining the country's armed forces. They were found guilty and sentenced to twenty years' imprisonment in the Atlanta Federal Penitentiary. It appears that they took their sentence well, the *New York Tribune* of 22 June reporting that the Federal Court rang out with the strains of

---

[15]  Cited in ibid. 76.

'Blessed be the Tie that Binds' and Rutherford stating that this suffering for his faith made it the happiest day of his life.[16] In the event their sentences did not last long and shortly after the war had ended their convictions were overturned and they were released.

Rutherford at once set about the task of influencing the future shape of the movement's doctrine. On 1 October 1919 a new magazine, *The Golden Age*, was launched which, in the words of their official history, 'proved indeed to be a valuable and powerful instrument in exposing false worship and deeds of darkness of the rulers of the world, as well as providing comfort and hope for the masses of the people'.[17] This was followed by *The Harp of God* in December 1921. Written by Rutherford it recounted the plan of God beginning at the creation and working through to the Lord's return and the final Restoration. This was merely the start of a whole series of writing on the part of the second President who proved to be an even more fertile author than his predecessor had been. Despite a punishing schedule of travel and speaking engagements he averaged a book a year. Inevitably Rutherford's works soon began to replace Russell's as the official teachings of the society.

In 1920 Rutherford published his most famous book *Millions Now Living Will Never Die*,[18] which ushered in an outreach and publicity campaign lasting two years. The book was translated into many languages and many thousands of copies were sold. In his teaching about the end times Rutherford now moved away from 1874 or even 1914 as key dates in the economy of God's Kingdom. Instead he focused on 1925 as the time when the rule of God would be established on earth. He reinterpreted the battle of Armageddon which preceded the Kingdom as a global conflict in which all those outside the Watch Tower movement would be destroyed. As a further prelude to the inauguration of this millennial period he taught that the patriarchs Abraham, Isaac and Jacob would reappear on this earth. So certain was he about it that he built a mansion, 'Beth-Sarim', in San Diego for their use and put a car in the garage. In the interim he lived in the house and made good use of the car! When he died his followers tried to bury him there but the city

---

[16] Cited in ibid. 80–81.
[17] Ibid. 89.
[18] Ibid. 98.

council refused to grant permission. 1925 was a year of great disappointment for many Bible student farmers in both Canada and America who refused to sow their spring crops and scorned some of those who did.[19]

Rutherford made sure that the movement would henceforward remain under much tighter control than was formerly the case. In 1922 he took the step of requiring that the *Watchtower* magazine be studied both in congregational groups as well as individually. As an aid to members, questions to be discussed were also printed.[20] To this day the *Watchtower* carries the text for Sunday Bible study in all Kingdom Halls throughout the world. In the following year a regulation laid down that the first Tuesday of each month was to be set aside as 'service day' when class workers were to meet with the person appointed to oversee the field service. As a stimulus to this witnessing it was decided that half the Wednesday night prayer meetings should be devoted to sharing testimonies arising from encouraging door-to-door visiting. Additionally in America members were encouraged to distribute bound books and booklets on Sundays for a contribution.[21] In general there was a tightening up of the responsibility to participate in witness and from 1920 onwards everyone in the congregation was required to submit a weekly report of their personal visits.

During Rutherford's presidency the Brooklyn-based Governing Body began to be spoken of as a 'theocracy' and to take progressively more control over the movement. One of the first steps in this process was to invite congregations who wanted to be involved in the campaign of public witness to register with the head office. They then 'theocratically' appointed one of the local members to be the director of the congregational outreach. Unlike the other local elders he was not elected on an annual basis. This move was not uniformly well received and a warning was issued not to follow leaders who had their own personal agendas and wanted to exert their own influence over local congregations. This 'theocracy' was further strengthened in 1926 when a prophecy was given that God's sanctuary would be cleansed in 2,300 days' time. This was

---

[19] M.J. Penton, *Apocalypse* Delayed, cited Tucker, *Strange Gospels*, 12.
[20] *Jehovah's Witnesses in the Divine Purpose*, 104.
[21] Ibid. 123.

interpreted to mean 'the cleaning out from God's congregation those called elective elders', who had been elected to office in democratic fashion. The *Watchtower* in its issues of 15 August and 1 September carried a two-part article entitled 'Jehovah's Organisation' which exposed the whole system of elected elders as not in accordance with 'the Great Theocrat'. The article concluded by presenting a resolution that it be adopted by all congregations. The decision was taken up by congregations of Jehovah's Witnesses all over the world. The announcement of this acceptance and hence the cleansing of God's sanctuary was printed in the *Watchtower* magazine of 15 October 1932 at the exact end-time period mentioned in Daniel's Prophecy.[22]

During Rutherford's presidency in the year 1931 the name 'Jehovah's Witnesses' was first adopted. Up until that time outsiders generally referred to them as 'Millennial Dawn People' or 'Russellites'. A resolution was passed which called attention to the confusion this created and went on to state that 'we desire to be known as and called by the name, to wit, "Jehovah's Witnesses" – Isaiah 43:10–12; 62:2; Rev. 12:17.'[23]

During the run-up to the Second World War Jehovah's Witnesses in both Italy and Germany suffered harsh punishments for their faith. Despite active protests from Rutherford, many died in Nazi concentration camps at Flossenberg and elsewhere. Hitler's war offensive also brought to the fore the issue of saluting the flag. The Nazis sought to dragoon the peoples of Europe to salute the swastika. For Jehovah's Witnesses this conflicted with their allegiance to the Supreme Sovereign God and in consequence they suffered terribly. In Third Reich camps Jehovah's Witnesses who refused to make ammunition cases were sentenced to eight weeks' solitary confinement in cells without windows, and many hundreds of other members with great courage endured torments on account of their continuing to profess their faith.

It was when the Second World War was at its height in the dark days of 1942 that Rutherford finally died according to his expressed desire 'fighting with his boots on'. Like his predecessor Russell his personal life was often marked by controversy. He was separated

---

[22] Ibid. 126–7.
[23] Ibid. 126.

from his wife who was reported to be 'a semi-invalid who could not render the judge his marital dues'. He also had too much of a fondness for alcoholic drink and a penchant for gracious living which partially worked itself out in his luxury New York City apartment, his palatial residence on Staten Island and his two-hundred acre estate in California.[24] Nevertheless Rutherford had proved himself to be in the words of one writer 'a human dynamo' who during his twenty-five year period of office had carried the movement forward in a strong and forceful manner. The *Yearbook of Jehovah's Witnesses* for 1942 showed that in the previous year the distribution of books and booklets reached 36,030,595.[25] Rutherford had written twenty-two books and many pamphlets and tracts. He had made great use of radio broadcasts to publish the movement's message and had also made a large number of phono-graph recordings. Perhaps the most significant development of his period in office had been to change the society from what was essentially a democratic organisation to a 'theocratic one' where the field directors and congregational elders were chosen by the Brooklyn-based governing body rather than elected locally.

## Nathan Homer Knorr (1905–77)

Nathan Homer Knorr was born in Bethlehem, Pennsylvania, in 1905, and graduated from Allentown High School in June 1923. At the age of sixteen he resigned his membership in the Reformed Church and joined the Allentown Congregation of Jehovah's Witnesses. In 1923 he was invited to become a member of the head-quarters staff at Brooklyn Bethel. During his early days in this position Knorr travelled a good deal at weekends giving Bible lectures and encouraging local groups of Witnesses. He became a trusted official and in due course was appointed co-ordinator of all the Society's printing programmes. In 1932 he was chosen as general manager of the publishing office and plant. This was followed in 1934 by his appointment as one of the directors of the Society's New York corporation. In 1940 he was made a director

---

[24]  Penton, *Apocalypse Delayed*, 72–4, cited Tucker, *Strange Gospels*, 127.
[25]  *Jehovah's Witnesses in the Divine Purpose*, 194.

and chosen as vice-president of the Watch Tower Bible and Tract Society.[26]

Knorr did not have quite as high a public profile as Rutherford, but a number of important developments took place during his presidency. In 1943 the Watch Tower Bible School of Gilead was opened in the Finger Lakes section of New York State close to the city of Ithaca. The aim of the school was 'solely for the purpose of training men and women to be more efficient servants as ministers of the Lord in certain fields'.[27] Those entering the school were trained for full-time work with a view to serving in foreign mission fields. They were required to have completed two years' pioneer service before entrance. No tuition was charged and travelling and living expenses were covered by the society. In addition to advanced biblical studies, the course included English grammar, arithmetic and international law. Shortly after the start of this programme a further development, the Theocratic Ministry School, was inaugurated. This aimed to provide a more effective training for all local ministers in their door-to-door publishing activities. To facilitate this the Bethel headquarters produced a textbook entitled 'Theocratic Ministry', which consisted of fifty-two lessons, one to be covered each week. The project was received with enthusiasm and the schools began to run a one-hour session after one of the other weekly meetings.[28] Within a relatively short space of time a number of additional books were published as additional reading for the course. These included *Theocratic Aids to Kingdom Publishers* which was released in 1945 and *Equipped for Every Good Purpose* which followed in 1946. Another valued book *Qualified to Be Ministers* was released to coincide with a series of 'Triumphant kingdom Assemblies' in 1955 in which 403,682 people gathered together in thirteen separate locations.[29] In these schools Jehovah's Witnesses were trained 'to speak in modern conversational manner and not in the affected, oratorical manner of the religious clergy'.[30]

---

[26] Ibid. 196–7.
[27] Ibid. 203.
[28] Ibid. 214.
[29] Ibid. 274.
[30] Ibid. 214.

As well as the publications specifically designed for witness training, a number of other specifically doctrinal books were produced. Unlike those of the Rutherford era most of these had multiple authorship, although, according to an interview with his personal secretary, Knorr was the primary author.[31] One of the most significant of these books was *Let God Be True*, first published in 1946 and revised in 1952. It is a basic doctrinal summary of Jehovah's Witness teaching, of which it is claimed more than 17,000,000 copies have been printed in 50 different languages. *Let God Be True* was described in an official Watch Tower publication as 'our most effective Bible Study aid for use in a home Bible study'.[32] *Make Sure of All Things*, which appeared in 1953 and was re-issued in 1957, provides scriptural passages on seventy topics which can be used for ready reference when visiting.

A major project which was carried out during Knorr's presidency was the production in 1950 of The New World Translation of the Christian Greek Scriptures. This was published in separate volumes until finally The New World Translation appeared in 1961 in a one-volume edition. It has become a standard translation which is used by all Jehovah's Witnesses alongside what are regarded as secondary versions such as The American Standard Version and The King James. The names of the translators are not disclosed in the preface but Frederick Franz is known to have played a major role in the work. Although the New Testament is based on the Westcott and Hort text, the rendering of the Greek is not altogether objective and tends to follow interpretations which support Jehovah's Witness doctrines. Thus, for example, where most translators of the first chapter of John's Gospel render 'the Word' (Jesus) was God, the The New World Translation has 'the word was *a* God'. Witnesses had previously been attached to The American Standard Version on account of its 'commendable feature of rendering God's name "Jehovah" at the 6,823 places where it occurs in the Hebrew Scriptures'.[33] The The New World Translation followed this procedure justifying it on the ground that the tetragrammaton, JHWH, had been read as 'Jehovah' since the

---

[31] Hoekema, *Christian Science*, 18.
[32] *Jehovah's Witnesses in the Divine Purpose*, 295.
[33] Ibid. 256.

twelfth century and been popularised in that form in the Christian churches. Also during Knorr's presidency new hymn books were published, *The Kingdom Service Song Book* in 1944 and a further volume in 1950. Singing has from the earliest days always been a popular feature of the Jehovah's Witnesses. In 1890 the Watch Tower Society had produced *Poems and Hymns of the Millennial Dawn* which contained '151 choice religious poems and 333 select hymns'.[34]

Like his predecessor Knorr placed great emphasis on mission and he himself travelled widely. In 1951 he launched the 'Clean Worship' Assemblies at London's Wembley Stadium. At the final session 36,315 attended and listened to his address on 'Will Religion Meet the World Crisis?' During the conference a mass baptism of 1,123 was held at Ruislip Lido. Further assemblies in this series were held in Paris, Frankfurt, Stockholm, Helsinki and Copenhagen, where 2,259 people were baptised.[35] Alongside this emphasis on mission and pure worship there was a general strengthening of moral standards. Timothy White in his book *A People for His Name* enumerates some of them:

> The witnesses are specifically forbidden to practice gambling, hunt or fish for sport, tell lies among themselves, laugh at dirty jokes, wear mourning clothes for long after the death of a relative, justify themselves, masturbate, become an officer in a union or picket, go out on a date without a chaperon, throw rice at a wedding, display affection in public except momentarily at greetings and partings, become a member of, or frequent a nudist colony, participate in prayer led by one not dedicated to Jehovah, give free rein to unbridled passion whilst having allowed sexual intercourse, use profanity, or do the twist.[36]

Under Knorr's leadership the Bethel-based governing body became much more powerful and the role of the president was correspondingly reduced.

---

[34] Ibid. 258.
[35] Ibid. 261–2.
[36] T. White, *A People for His Name*, 385–6, cited Tucker, *Strange Gospels*, 129.

The major blow in Knorr's presidency was the failure of the prediction that the world would end in 1975. This had been predicted in the 8 October 1966 issue of *Awake*, the companion magazine to the *Watchtower*, on the basis that the date of the creation was in fact 4026 BC. This meant that 6,000 years of creation would have been completed in 1975. Thus that year would inaugurate the final seventh millennium. By means of the year–day mechanism all this fitted well into the creation scheme of Genesis 1 with the six days of creation being followed by the Sabbath day of rest. After the end of the world failed to come in 1975 large numbers of men and women, including some senior leaders, left the movement.

This decline continued for a while during the presidency of Knorr's successor, Frederick Franz (1893–1992). Franz took a liberal arts degree at the University of Cincinnati where he applied himself to the study of Greek, intending to become a Presbyterian minister. He won a Rhodes Scholarship qualifying him for entry to Oxford University but before he took it up his brother Albert introduced him to the Witnesses. He was baptised on 30 November 1913 and immediately became a pioneer. He became a member of the Bethel headquarters staff in June 1920 and was elected to the office of President on 22 December 1977. In 1978, the first year of Franz's presidency, decline continued with the number of publishers worldwide dropping from 2,117,194 to 2,086,698.[37] Eventually in 1980, following a 15 : 3 vote of the Governing Body Members, in the *Watchtower* of 15 March 1980 the organisation publicly acknowledged their error. In the years immediately following 'the great disappointment' of 1975 there was a considerable tightening up within the Governing Body or Bethel Family as it is sometimes called. In particular, members of the 'writing committee' were investigated with inquisition-style tactics in which other witnesses were set up, tape-recorded and made to report that they held views contrary to those of the society. In essence these claims appear to have been based on comments made at informal Bible study groups and private conversations in members homes.[38] The most celebrated victim of this Governing Body purge was Raymond Franz, the nephew of the new President.

---

[37] R. Franz, *Crisis of Conscience*, 212.
[38] Ibid. 248–70.

He had moved into the Bethel headquarters shortly after the death of Nathan Knorr. Raymond Franz spent more than forty years as a full-time representative and served at every level of the movement's organisational structure. The last fifteen of these were spent at the international headquarters and the final nine as a member of the worldwide Governing Body. His particular responsibilities were as a member of the Writing and Service Committees. In his capacity on the former of the two bodies, Franz was charged with the over-sight of a number of publications which were eventually printed in millions of copies in many languages. Among the wrong teaching with which he was alleged to have been implicated were the following: that Jehovah does not have an organisation on earth, that its Governing Body is not being directed by Jehovah, that everyone baptised from Christ's time forward should have the heavenly hope, and that all these should partake of the emblems of bread and wine at Memorial Communions. In addition the 144,000 mentioned in Revelation 7:4 is to be taken as symbolic and not understood literally; we are not now living in the 'last days' which in fact started 1900 years ago and that Christ Jesus was not enthroned in 1914 but his return is yet to come in the future.[39]

There was a long series of interrogation sessions by a small committee which was chaired by Albert Schroeder during which secret tape recordings of his conversations with others were played back to him and long-standing friends and colleagues accused him of disloyalty and unorthodox views. Raymond Franz later wrote: 'As in the Inquisition, all rights were withheld by the inquisitors, the accused had none. The investigators felt they had the right to ask any question and at the same time refuse to answer questions put to them.'[40] In the event those seeking to disfellowship Franz failed to achieve the two-thirds majority needed, with the result that chairman Schroeder asked him to resign. After a two-day break Franz did this by letter dated 22 May 1980.[41] Shortly after this he and his wife retired to East Gadsen, Alabama, and associated themselves with the worship of the local Kingdom Hall. For a while this proved

---

[39] Letter of the Chairman's Committee to the Governing Body 28 April 1980, cited ibid. 266.
[40] Ibid. 271.
[41] Ibid. 284.

a beneficial move but then, almost out of the blue, the local elder-ship disfellowshipped Franz on the ground that he had eaten a meal with Peter Gregerson who had earlier been put out of the society.[42]

The purges which took place following the events of 1975 marked a reduction in the powers of the President and a strengthen-ing of the power of the Governing Body over the *Watchtower* movement. Raymond Franz wrote that much of this policy was 'es-sentially the product of the writing of Fred Franz, and much of the policy regarding "disfellowshiping" issues likewise his'.[43] Frederick Franz died in 1992 and was replaced by Milton Henschel who had been exercising a powerful influence in the Governing Body during his last years. After the internal traumas of the late seventies and early eighties the Jehovah's Witnesses have seen a steady growth both in membership and in the number of active publishers.

## Daily Life and Worship

The Jehovah's Witnesses are under the direction of their Governing Body which consists of twelve men and a President. It is regarded as a theocracy or the means through which Jehovah God carries out his Kingdom work on earth. They decide on all matters of doctrine and public policy. They also have oversight of all writing, including books, tracts and, above all, the *Watchtower* which prints out the Bible studies which every congregation throughout the world must follow at their Sunday meetings. The 232 countries in which Jehovah's Witnesses are at work are arranged in branches which are directly accountable to the governing body. The branches' books and finances are regularly scrutinised by zone overseers and sometimes by higher officials. In a given locality individual congregations are formed into circuits and, as in the Methodist church, a number of circuits form a district. Congregations are under the direction of local elders who in turn relate to the district officials. The local eldership is structured in such a way as to prevent any of their number establishing a personal hold over the congregation. There are five

---

[42]  Ibid. 320–27.
[43]  Ibid. 342.

eldership positions: Presiding Overseer, Theocratic Overseer, *Watchtower* Overseer, Bible Study Overseer and Field Service Overseer. On 1 January each year each of the five officials change position, the Presiding Overseer moving to the position of Theocratic Overseer and the others following suit.

The Kingdom Hall is the local church building of the Jehovah's Witnesses. It is reserved for specifically church activities and only congregational meetings, weddings and funerals are ever held in them. The buildings are plain and simply designed, often having the appearance of a doctor's surgery or a village library. One Kingdom Hall is often shared by two or perhaps three local congregations which meet at different times during the day. There are no full-time pastors or clergy and all the meetings are led by one of the local elders. The main Sunday meeting is in two parts. There is a public talk given by one of the male members or possibly by a visiting member of another congregation. One or two songs are sung accompanied by a piano or occasionally by tapes sent out from headquarters. After the talk is ended the second half of the meeting, an hourlong study of the *Watchtower*, follows. This is highly structured and the *Watchtower* article has printed questions at the foot of each page, the answers to which are in the text of the article. The questions are read out and various audience members give answers. This is continued until the right response has been made. Only then do they move on to the next question. Women are not permitted to hold any leadership roles and so do not take part in the meetings publicly. However, as in many other modern religious movements, they form the backbone of the Witnesses' outreach programme. From time to time women are reminded of their place and role within the movement. In 1951 the *Watchtower* underlined the fact that they were not to cut their hair, for to do so would 'remove this natural, God-given sign of Woman's subjection to man'.[44] Again in 1960 the same magazine urged that all women wear hats at Kingdom Hall activities because it 'alerts Christian men against succumbing to female influence'.[45]

---

[44] *Watchtower*, 15 February 1951, cited Tucker, *Strange Gospels*, 138.
[45] *Watchtower*, 15 March 1960, cited Tucker, *Strange Gospels*, 138.

## Distinctive Teachings

Jehovah's witnesses are well known for their insistence on 'Jehovah' as the personal name for God. Unlike most translators who render the Hebrew letters YHWH as 'Lord' or 'God', The New World Translation keeps consistently to 'Jehovah'. A key text for the movement is Isaiah 43:10 and 11 which states: 'Ye are my witnesses, saith the Jehovah, and my servant whom I have chosen; that ye may know and believe me, and understand that I am he: before me there was no God formed, neither shall there be after me. I, even I, am Jehovah; and besides me there is no saviour.' Jesus, 'the faithful and true witness', came to bear witness to the truth' (John 18:37; Revelation 3:14), and Jehovah's Witnesses now regard themselves as those who have been commissioned to take up his mantle.

In all their witnessing, members use their own New World Translation of the Bible which differs in its interpretation of certain key texts from other Bibles used by Protestant and Catholic Christians. Additionally in their private devotional study some Witnesses do use other versions of the Bible. Like most Protestants, Jehovah's Witnesses take the Bible to be the supreme basis of all they believe and teach. It is, in the words of the author of *Let God Be True*, a book of 'unmatchable value' containing 'principles of truth and righteousness which never change'. In another place in the same book it is stated that 'The word of God is the dependable basis for faith.'[46] However, Witnesses differ significantly from the denominational churches in their interpretation of certain crucial passages on which important doctrines are based. The reason for this lies in their various hermeneutical methodologies. Most importantly the interpretations given by Presidents Russell, Rutherford and Knorr have become a basic starting point for interpretation. Over a period of thirty years Russell wrote six volumes of *Studies in the Scriptures* which continue to underlie much of Jehovah's Witness theology. Russell affirmed that anyone who studied the Scriptures without the aid of these would soon be in darkness. From 1918 onwards the movement has accepted that the light of God's truth has come from the

---

[46] *Let God Be True*, 104 and 121.

'anointed class' of 'Jehovah's Theocracy', that is, the movement's Governing Body.[47]

On a number of issues such as the Trinity and the status of Jesus, the Witnesses have followed the understanding of the Unitarians and the Arians of earlier times. In some cases, however, a very literal interpretation of particular texts has been taken. An obvious example of this is Leviticus 17:4, 'I said unto the Children of Israel, You shall eat the blood of no manner of flesh', and the injunction of Acts 15:20 'to abstain from blood'. In contrast to the traditional interpretation that this means that the blood should be drained from meat before it is eaten, these verses are taken to be a prohibition of blood transfusions. On this basis a Witness would feel it right to let a loved one die rather than consent to a blood transfusion. It should be noted, however, that in more recent times a number of proven blood substitutes have come on to the market which are effective for the purpose and are not precluded by their understanding of the biblical text. Another example of a literal interpretation is the contention that 1914 was the year when Christ's Kingdom was established. This is based on passages from the books of Daniel and Revelation which together indicate that the Kingdom would be established 2,520 year-days from the time of Daniel.[48]

## The Doctrine of God

Jehovah's Witnesses are believers in one God whom they call 'Jehovah'. His name is interpreted to mean 'He causes to be'. They believe him to have been the sole agent in creation. They see the creation as both an argument for the existence of God and as a testimony to his nature and character. The writer of a recent publication entitled *Jehovah's Witnesses in the Twentieth Century* wrote:

> Just as the works of men and women reflect their qualities, so do the works of Jehovah God. The Bible tells us that 'his invisible qualities are clearly seen from the world's creation onward, because they are

---

[47] Ibid. 200.
[48] Ibid. 125–9.

perceived by the things made.' Also, without voice or words, 'the heavens declare the glory of God.' – Romans 1:20; Psalm 19:1–4.[49]

Following the mainstream Christian churches Witnesses believe that God is the eternal ruler and sustainer of the universe. He is self-contained and therefore not alone. Because he is spirit, God is and ever will be invisible to human eyes. As creator, Jehovah is the source of all life, power and goodness. He is the author of all the provisions for the saving of humankind from sin. Although he has allowed his chief adversary and his servants a hold over the world there is coming a time after the battle of Armageddon when he will establish his theocratic rule under his Messiah or Anointed King.[50]

A major point of difference between Witnesses and historic Christian churches is the doctrine of the Trinity. Creedal Christianity asserts that God reveals himself in three ways: as a loving, gracious and generous Father who cares for his people, as a Son who stands alongside and fully identifies himself with the human race, and as Holy Spirit, the divine unseen personal presence, who lives within the lives of God's people.

## Jesus Christ

The early Christians who lived and worked with Jesus came to the conclusion that he was much more than a mere man. As they worked alongside him, heard his teaching and witnessed his miracles, they were convinced that he was, as he claimed to be, equal with God and had the power to extend God's forgiveness to men and women who were truly repentant and wanting to turn away from their sin. When after his resurrection Jesus appeared to Thomas, he fell at his feet and said: 'My Lord and my God.' Jesus very readily acknowledged his worship and in so doing declared himself to be nothing less than God. John who recorded this incident in his Gospel had no doubts that Jesus is God in all his fullness. It is John who recorded Jesus' words 'I and the Father are one' (John 10:30) and that to have seen him is to have seen the

---

[49] *Jehovah's Witnesses in the Twentieth Century*, 12.
[50] See *Let God Be True*, 25–32.

Father (John 14:9–11). He begins his Gospel by declaring that Jesus, the Word, was not only *with* God from the beginning but he also *was* God (John 1:1). Towards the conclusion of this prologue to his Gospel John categorically affirms the incarnation that 'the Word became flesh and lived for a while among us' (John 1:14). Others of the apostolic community made similar affirmations. Paul in his letter to the Philippians spoke of Jesus as 'being in very nature God' and not therefore needing to 'grasp' at equality with God (Philippians 2:6). He in fact concluded his hymn in praise of Jesus by declaring that there is coming a time when 'every tongue will confess that Jesus Christ is Lord' (Philippians 2:11). Significantly the word translated 'Lord' is *kurios* which is the Greek equivalent of 'Yahweh' or 'Jehovah'. The historic Christian churches see these statements as the basis of the Nicene Creed which asserts that Jesus is 'of one substance with the Father' and is also 'very God of very God'.

Jehovah's Witnesses take a different view of the biblical material. They hold that Jesus was 'not Jehovah God', but was existing in the form of God 'as a spirit person'. He was 'a mighty one but not almighty as Jehovah God is'.[51] In essence therefore they deny the essential deity of Jesus. As mentioned above, this is reflected in their New World Translation of John 1:1 which reads: 'Originally the Word was, and the Word was with God, and the Word was a god.' Witnesses happily accept that Jesus had a prehuman existence but he did not, in their view, think of himself as ' "equal in power and glory" with Almighty God'.[52] Although he existed before his coming to earth he was nevertheless a created being. In the words of one author: 'He was the first of Jehovah God's creations.'[53] Further evidence for this position is, they assert, found in two texts in particular, Colossians 1:15, which speaks of Christ as 'the first born of creation', and Revelation 3:14, which refers to him as 'the beginning of God's creation'. Everything, however, depends on the interpretation of these two texts. The traditional view held by Catholics and Protestants alike is that 'first born' is simply a common Jewish title of great and special honour. In Jewish

---

[51] Ibid. 34.
[52] Ibid. 37.
[53] Ibid. 35.

tradition 'the first born' was the head of the household. The phrase 'first born' should therefore be taken to mean that Jesus is the sovereign Lord of all creation and that he is held in the highest honour by all of creation. The 'first born' was also the heir and so the emphasis here is held to be that Jesus is the heir of the entire created order. The early Church Fathers and other biblical commentators have underlined the fact that the whole emphasis of this Colossians passage is Jesus' total superiority over and above the created order. The Revelation text which speaks of Jesus as 'the beginning of creation' is seen by the church's commentators as simply indicating that Jesus was the one through whom God's creative work began. From the earliest Christian centuries the church has held that these texts cohere with the rest of the New Testament, teach that Jesus was eternally God, and that he was in no sense a created being. The main denominational churches are united in the view that the Bible teaches that not only is Jesus fully God, he is also fully man. The early church council of Chalcedon ruled in AD 451 that the Bible taught that in his being Jesus is fully at one with God the Father in his deity and fully at one with us humans in his humanity, and that these two natures, the human and the divine, are not in any way mixed or diluted by virtue of their existing together.

Witnesses are clear that Jesus died on the cross to ransom men and women from their sins. The author of *Let God Be True* states:

> The scriptural doctrine of the ransom is that in sending his Son Christ Jesus to earth Jehovah God through him and his death provided a redemptive price. Thereby men who have faith in his provision may come into harmony with God, and, serving him faithfully, they may receive the gift of life, being freed from inherited sin and from eternal death as a result of sin. To this effect it is written, at Romans 6:23, 'For the Wages of sin is death: but the gift of God is eternal life through Jesus Christ our Lord.'[54]

While the writer does not lay any emphasis on the cross as the means of deliverance from the present guilt and power of sin, he does go on to stress that those who continue trusting in this

---

[54] Ibid. 95.

provision 'will find Christ Jesus to be their "everlasting Father" '
(Isaiah 9:6) and they will have a certain destiny of 'eternal life on this
earth under God's kingdom'.[55] The most recent Jehovah's Witness
publication *Knowledge that Leads to Everlasting Life* stresses also
present forgiveness of sins: 'So even if we have committed a serious
sin, we can ask God for forgiveness in Jesus' name.'[56] Jehovah's
Witnesses with whom I have spoken, have a strong belief that if
they were to die at this moment their sins would be forgiven and
that they would be resurrected to live for ever on this paradise earth.

Witnesses do not believe that Jesus rose bodily from the grave.
Rather they assert that 'Jehovah God raised him from the dead, not
as a human Son, but as a mighty immortal spirit Son, with all power
in heaven and earth under the Most High God'.[57] In contrast to the
creeds which assert that Jesus ascended bodily into heaven,
Witnesses take the view that he 'did not take his human body into
heaven, because, had he done so, that would have left him ever
lower than the angels'.[58]

## The Holy Spirit

Not only do the Jehovah's Witnesses not believe that Jesus is God,
they take the same view where the Holy Spirit is concerned. The
Holy Spirit is not regarded by them as a person but rather as God's
active force which enables God's people to live for him. As one
writer put it: 'When a man has the spirit of God upon him it means
that he has been authorised to do a certain work, whatever that
work may be. The Holy Spirit is the invisible active force of
Almighty God that moves his servants to do his will.'[59] Sections
written on the Holy Spirit in Jehovah's Witness literature tend to be
rather more brief than is the case in systematic theology books
produced by church theologians. This suggests that the Holy Spirit
does not play quite so significant a role in the lives of Witnesses as is

---

[55] Ibid. 104.
[56] *Knowledge That Leads to Everlasting Life*, 68.
[57] *Let God Be True*, 43.
[58] Ibid. 44.
[59] Ibid. 181–2.

the case in many sections of the Christian church. As Jehovah's Witnesses understand it, the Holy Spirit's main function is to make the commandments come alive in God's people giving them a heart to be ministers or servants under the new covenant.

## The Trinity

In view of their teachings on the Father, Son and Holy Spirit, it will be clear that the Witnesses do not subscribe to the doctrine of the Trinity. This teaching they believe to be rooted in pagan thinking of the early Roman Empire. Indeed the *Watchtower* of June 1882 saw the doctrine as 'an apostate form of Christianity endorsed by Roman emperors in the fourth century C.E.',[60] and the issue of July 1883 said: 'More Bible and less hymn-book theology would have made the subject clearer to all. The doctrine of the trinity is totally opposed to Scripture.'[61] The writer of *Let God Be True* considers many of the texts which Protestant and Catholic biblical scholars have used in support of Trinitarian theology but he interprets them differently. Commenting on those texts which suggest the oneness of Jesus and the Father he writes: 'They are all one in agreement, purpose and organisation. If this were not the logical conclusion Jesus would never have said: "My Father is greater than I" (John 14:28)'[62] The problem with this interpretation, as early church leaders such as Tertullian and generations of the church's theologians since have seen, is that it implies that there are three separate gods. Put another way, unless the Father, Son and Holy Spirit are ontologically one the result is tritheism or belief in three gods.

## The Last Things

Raymond Franz was adamant that the one feature above all others which distinguishes Jehovah's Witnesses is not their rejection of eternal torment, the inherent immortality of the soul, of the Trinity, nor their use of the name Jehovah or their belief in a paradise earth.

---

[60] *Jehovah's Witnesses: Proclaimers of God's Kingdom*, 125.
[61] Ibid.
[62] *Let God Be True*, 86.

All of these teachings can be found in other religious organisations. In his view the one unique tenet centres on 1914 as the date when Christ's active rulership began.[63] 1914 was the key date because it was before October in that year that Russell had predicted that Christ would return to gather his church for glory. When this did not happen Russell struck a positive note that they could be thankful because there was now time for perfecting holiness as well as preparing for survival during the coming cataclysm of Armageddon.[64] 1914, however, was not drained of all significance; it came instead to be regarded as the date when Christ turned his full attention to directing the earth's affairs. It was then that his 'invisible presence' on earth began, marking the beginning of the last days.

In his early days Russell was much influenced by the Adventist N.H. Barbour, and shared his belief that Christ would return in 1874. When the year passed by uneventfully they were left in a state of disillusionment, but Russell came to the view, which he subsequently expressed in a booklet entitled *The Object and Manner of Christ's Return*: that the Lord's 'unseen presence' had returned to earth and that his physical return would be in 1914. In 1877 he co-wrote a booklet saying that the living believers would be 'caught away bodily' in 1878 in what other adventists termed 'the rapture'. 1881 was then put forward as the time by which 'the bride' would be gathered into the place of safety. Following this, everything became focused on 1914 as the time when Christ would return to establish his Kingdom on earth. When this failed to happen, Rutherford took the view that his predecessor was mistaken in his calculations regarding 1914, and after some further study he moved the date forward to 1918. In his book *The Finished Mystery* he contended that the Scriptures 'prove that the Spring of 1918 will bring upon Christendom a spasm of anguish greater even than that experienced in the Fall of 1914'. Rutherford continued that 'also, in the year 1918, when God destroys the churches wholesale and the church members by millions, it shall be that any that escape shall come to the works of Pastor Russell to learn the meaning of the downfall of Christianity'.[65]

---

[63] Franz, *Crisis of Conscience*, 343.
[64] C.T. Russell, *The Time is at Hand*, preface, cited Franz, *Crisis of Conscience*, 165.
[65] J. Rutherford, *The Finished Mystery*, 24, cited ibid. 168.

In fact 1918 proved to be relatively uneventful with signing of peace treaties at the end of the war. Rutherford then published a further booklet in 1920, *Millions Now Living Will Never Die*, a unique document which tied the date of the prediction to 1925. Although Witnesses still firmly hold this belief, as the years pass by, the millions are gradually diminishing in number, and the movement no longer offers predictions or time scales for these events. The recent teaching manual *Knowledge That Leads to Eternal Life* states: 'Warning them not to speculate about the matter, Jesus said: "It does not belong to you to get knowledge of the times or seasons which the Father has placed in his own jurisdiction." '[66]

## Armageddon

The great future hope all Witnesses are looking forward to will only be realised after the cataclysmic end-time conflict known as 'Armageddon'. In this worldwide and last great struggle, which will involve peoples of every nation, God will make for himself a name. According to their most recent history 'the peoples of every nation, kindred and tongue will learn that Jehovah is the all-powerful, all-wise and just God'.[67] This is not a battle in which Christians should engage in the conflict, for the battle is God's. In this Jehovah's Witnesses, in company with the Christadelphians, are 'passive millenarians' believing that the millennium will be achieved solely by divine intervention.

Unlike some other millennial movements, Witnesses do not believe that God will restore the Jews to Palestine. What is currently taking place, in their view, is not motivated on the part of the Jews 'out of any love for God or desire for his name to be magnified by fulfilment of his Word'.[68] Their position on Zionism is that it is a political and human movement and as such will not accomplish God's heavenly Kingdom. They take the restoration of Israel to refer to 'spiritual Israel', 'the Israel of God'. By the same token, the exaltation of Jerusalem does not have reference to 'a mere earthly city, but, rather, "heavenly Jerusalem" where

---

[66] *Knowledge That Leads to Everlasting Life*, 96.
[67] *Jehovah's Witnesses: Proclaimers of God's Kingdom*, 140.
[68] Ibid. 141.

Jehovah installed his Son, Jesus Christ, with ruling authority in 1914 – Hebrews 12:22.'[69]

## The 144,000 and the 'Other Sheep'

After the conclusion of Armageddon, faithful Witnesses will enjoy God's promised salvation. There will be two categories of the saved, the 'little flock', or 144,000, and the 'great company', or 'other sheep', to whom Christ referred in John 10:16. The smaller elite company will experience full salvation in heaven while the great company will enjoy the blessing of a renewed earthly paradise. The remnant of 144,000 will lead the other sheep through 'the great tribulation' and Armageddon to begin the work of establishing the paradise on earth. They will then go to heaven where they will be priests of God and of Christ and will rule as kings with him for the thousand years. Only those who feel in their hearts that they are among 'the anointed' are permitted to take the bread and wine at the annual Memorial Communion which is celebrated on 14 Nisan. In 1997 only 8,795 partook of the sacrament out of a total worldwide attendance of 14,322,226.[70] It will be clear from this that the number of the elite is almost complete and the majority of current Witnesses do not expect to go to heaven. The denominational churches interpret this biblical material differently, most taking the view that the 144,000 of Revelation 7 are to be interpreted symbolically. The John 10 passage is seen as referring to those gentile Christians who have yet to believe and who anticipate a heavenly destiny.

## Life in the Millennium

Life on earth for the great company will be a state of ageless perfection and harmony. The writer of *Let God Be True* described it in the following terms:

> Here then, is a 'new earth'! A new, visible governing organisation created at the hand of God (Isaiah 66:22). What a contrast with the

---

[69] Ibid. 142.
[70] *1998 Yearbook of the Jehovah's Witnesses*, 31.

wicked, Devilish 'earth' that rules to-day, shall the 'new earth' be (2 Peter 3:10, 13)! Justice, goodness and uprightness will mark every move of the 'princes', as they work in perfect accord with their King-Father, Christ Jesus . . . And when may we expect the setting up of this 'new earth'? Every shred of evidence in fulfilment of Bible prophecy points to . . . the immediate future, in this very generation – Luke 21:25–32.[71]

The same writer goes on to underline the fact that in this new world 'aches and pains will die out, as radiant health, unmarred by cancer, or influenza, or even toothache implants itself in every soul'. There will also be a dissolution of old age, 'with its wrinkled skin, its grey hair, and feebleness'. It means, he continues, 'that vigorous, energetic youth, so fleeting to-day, shall be the eternal lot of every human'.[72] A more recent publication entitled *You Can Live for Ever in Paradise on Earth* paints a very similar picture: 'Think of it. People of all races will learn to live together as one. They will love one another. None will be unkind. No more sickness, old age or death. Truly, it will be a paradise.'[73] The author of another Watch Tower publication also stresses the coming future perfection:

> Just think! No more eyeglasses, no more crutches and canes, no more medicines, no more dental clinics or hospitals! Never again will emotional illness and depression rob people of happiness. No childhood will be blighted by disease. The ravages of ageing will be reversed (Job 33:25). We will become healthier, stronger. Each morning we will wake from a refreshing night's sleep with renewed energy, filled with vigour and eager for a new day of vibrant life and satisfying work.[74]

## Final Destiny

As the *Watchtower* for September 1989 put it, 'only the Jehovah's Witnesses, those of the anointed remnant and the "great crowd"

---

[71]  *Let God Be True*, 259.
[72]  Ibid. 263.
[73]  *You Can Live For Ever in Paradise on Earth*, 163.
[74]  *Knowledge That Leads to Everlasting Life*, 183–4.

have any scriptural hope of surviving the impending end of this doomed system dominated by the devil'. For those who reject the teaching of the Jehovah's Witnesses one thing is certain: they will not suffer everlasting punishment in hell, but will simply be annihilated. Russell's view was that death is death and that when our loved ones die, they are neither with the angels nor with the demons in a place of despair. After a public debate with the Rev Dr E.L. Eaton, a Pennsylvania minister, another clergyman approached Russell and said: 'I am glad to see you turn the hose on hell and put out the fire.'[75]

## Encountering Jehovah's Witnesses

There is much in the life and teaching of Jehovah's Witnesses which is both appealing and challenging. They stress the importance of marriage and family life. Those who commit adultery and are unrepentant are disfellowshipped. Witnesses view divorce with great concern and urge it as a very last option. Teaching is given about loyalty, respect and faithfulness between husbands and wives. When young couples are courting, chaperons are appointed to accompany them during their early meetings. Stress is also placed on setting an example and the importance of disciplining children and teaching them respect. Prayer has a high priority in the lives of individual Witnesses. Most will pray in their homes with their families and children and also at mealtimes. In addition there is a regular weekly meeting at each Kingdom Hall when there is intercession for individual and local needs as well as support for the publishing activities. Their latest teaching manual states: 'Prayer is not an empty ritual, nor is it merely a means by which to gain something. A major reason for approaching God is to have a close relationship with him.'[76] Witnesses take a strong line against smoking and no user of tobacco can be a member or even an appointed representative of the headquarters' staff. Since 1973 no one who smokes has been accepted for baptism. Alcohol is used in moderation despite the fact that Russell was a total abstainer. Witnesses stand strongly

---

[75] *Jehovah's Witnesses: Proclaimers of God's Kingdom*, 130.
[76] *Knowledge That Leads to Everlasting Life*, 150–51.

against abortion and blood transfusions, believing both to be prohibited by the Scriptures. Members also stand aloof from politics, neither standing as candidates nor taking part in elections. Witnesses are not pacifists, but they do not bear arms in war. One of the reasons why Witnesses were so brutalised in the Nazi concentration camps was their avowed political neutrality. Jehovah's Witness sources in Germany reported that 2,074 of their members ended up in such places of torture.[77] Basing their practice on Daniel and his three friends' refusal to bow before the image, Witnesses refuse to salute any flag or stand in homage before one. Witnesses do not celebrate birthdays or the festivals of Christmas, Easter, New Year's Day, May Day and Mother's Day because of their possible association with pagan gods. For the Witness the key to everything is knowledge of God which comes through the careful, daily study of the Scriptures. It is this knowledge which enables them to live holy lives now and above all in the future will enable them to pass through Armageddon to enjoy a future of perfection and happiness.

As already observed Jehovah's Witnesses differ from the historic Christian churches on a number of the creedal doctrines. The most significant of these is their rejection of the doctrine of the Trinity and its concomitants that Jesus and the Holy Spirit are less than fully God. Witnesses do not take the view held by many denominational Christians that Jesus ascended into the heavens as a man. Rather they assert him now to be a wholly divine spirit-being. Many teachers in the Christian churches find it hard to accept that Jesus could be the ransom for sin and offer God's forgiveness, as Witnesses assert, if he was not fully divine to represent God and not fully human in order to be the representative of the human race. Orthodox Christians, like Witnesses, aim to enter into a personal relationship with God, but for them his Holy Spirit's presence within them is the vital ingredient in this process. Witnesses with whom I have spoken have a strong belief that when they die they have a sure destiny on God's paradise earth. They appear, however, not to share the assurance of many Christians that as a result of their faith they have eternal life here and now.

---

[77] *Jehovah's Witnesses: Proclaimers of God's Kingdom*, 19.

# Chapter 5

# The Exclusive Brethren

## Early Days

John Nelson Darby was born at Westminster, the youngest son of John Darby of Leap Castle, Kings County, Ireland. His uncle, Admiral Sir Henry Darby, commanded HMS *Bellerophon* in the battle of the Nile. His grandfather was Admiral Lord Nelson. He trained in law at Trinity College, Dublin and was called to the Bar in 1822. On being 'converted', much to his father's annoyance, he then relinquished the law and took Orders in the Anglican Church of Ireland. In 1826 he took up the post of curate of Calany, a remote country parish in County Wicklow. Here in his own words he later recalled, 'As soon as I was ordained I went amongst the poor Irish mountaineers, in a wild and uncultivated district, where I remained for two years and three months, working as best I could.'[1] The young minister who had a restless and inquiring mind, as well as a real desire to 'save souls', was soon also recognised for his saintly living. In the spring of 1827, however, he suffered a riding accident and was taken to Dublin in order to recuperate. Here he encountered a group of discontented evangelicals who were meeting together to pray, to read the Bible and encourage one another. In November 1829 a group of about a dozen of their number held a simple freestyle communion service at 9 Fitzroy Square. Thereafter a regular weekly breaking of bread was established and numbers soon began to grow. This necessitated the group having to move to a large auction room at 11 Aungier Street. Of those times Dr Cronin later wrote, 'We had the master's smile and sanction' and

---

[1] N.L. Noel, *The History of the Brethren*, I, 35.

'seasons of joy never to be forgotten'.[2] Some of those involved expressed concern about this step fearing that it would result in their becoming a separate church. Such indeed eventually proved to be the case. The first Brethren Meeting in England was held at Plymouth in January 1832.

The backdrop to this formation of the Brethren or the 'Saints' as they are sometimes called, focused on the uncertainties and the political turmoil of the 1820s. This was also a decade of rising unemployment following the end of the Napoleonic Wars. Food prices were high and across the countryside men and women were expressing their discontent by rick burning in the name of the legendary Captain Swing and destroying machinery under the auspices of the fictitious Ned Ludd. As so often happens in times of hardship and political uncertainty people begin to believe the end of the world was near. They readily welcome apocalyptic preachers who proclaim the nearness of the coming of Jesus to set up a thousand-year period of bliss on earth. It was not only Darby who emphasised an imminent millennium, other groups such as the Catholic Apostolic Church, the Christadelphians, the Millerites and the Seventh Day Adventists all came to share this same emphasis.

## Early Leaders

The first 'brother' of this new movement is generally reckoned as Edward Cronin (d. 1882). It was his view that all true Christian believers of whatever denomination should be invited to share in the breaking of bread at the Lord's table. The movement which reached a membership of 6,000 by 1855 achieved a significant impact on account of its inner core of leaders who had both gifts and social influence. Prominent among them was Anthony Norris Groves (1795–1853), a dentist, who had been a missionary in both Syria and India. In 1825 he had been instrumental in the conversion of Michael Solomon Alexander (1799–1845), who later became the first Bishop of Jerusalem.[3] Groves' ideas captivated the thinking of the inner circle. Speaking to John Gifford Bellett (1794–1864), a

---

[2] Ibid. 25.
[3] For Solomon Alexander see entry in *Dictionary of National Biography*.

Dublin lawyer, he said: 'This I doubt not, is the mind of God concerning us, that we should come together in all simplicity as disciples, not waiting on any pulpit ministry, but trusting the Lord will edify us together by ministering to us, as He sees good from ourselves.'[4]

John Nelson Darby (1800–82), destined to become the leader of the 'Exclusives' following a major rift in the movement in 1848, became prominent in this inner circle from the earliest days. Darby was an inveterate traveller and early visited both Cambridge and Oxford where, among many others, he met with Benjamin Wills Newton (1807–99) and George Vicesimus Wigram (1805–79). Both men became ardent supporters of his views. Wigram, whose brother Joseph later became Bishop of Rochester, was the twenti-eth son of Sir James Wigram MP and was a man of considerable independent means. Forsaking a commission in the army he entered Queen's College, Oxford, where he was the only under-graduate to keep a closed carriage. He had intended to become a clergyman of the Church of England but Bishop Blomfied refused to ordain him on grounds of his extreme evangelical views.

Darby also visited Plymouth from which town Newton also hailed and a Sunday meeting for the breaking of bread was soon established. Plymouth was the centre from which most of the early publications originated and for this reason the early gatherings for worship were often known as 'Plymouth Brethren'. Newton was a serious and dedicated brother with an inquiring and restless mind. Under his earnest and forthright leadership the Plymouth meeting expanded rapidly.

Bristol became another prominent centre of early Brethren activity. Here George Müller (1805–98), later famous for his orphanage homes and many faith ventures, co-pastored Bethesda Chapel with Henry Craik (1805–66). Müller was the brother-in-law of Anthony Groves and, possibly for this reason, he and Craik led their congregation to adopt Brethren principles.

Membership grew relatively slowly in the 1830s. Unusually for a group which was to become so sectarian in its attitudes the great

---

[4] John Gifford Bellett was born in County Dublin, matriculated 3 April 1815, graduated BA in 1819 and called to the Irish Bar in 1821, *Alumni Dublinensis*, 57.

majority of early leaders were men of fortune, intellect and influence. This incidentally has been a continuing feature of the movement right up to the present time. An analysis of forty-four early Brethren leaders revealed the following. Twelve were Anglican clergymen or were training for the Anglican ministry when they joined the movement. Five were nonconformist ministers, four were lawyers, twelve owned land or had income from family funds, four were doctors or teachers, five were in business and there was one actor and one artist.[5] N.L. Noel gives biographical details of thirty-six early principal Brethren. Four were from the aristocracy, five were Free Church ministers, two were Anglican clergy, five were army officers, five were doctors, five were businessmen and the rest followed middle-class occupations such as publishing and the foreign service.[6]

However, this upper middle-classness of the leaders later enabled the movement to spread more rapidly. It is also the probable explanation for the quashing of speaking in tongues at Plymouth and the rejection of other phenomena which are based on biblical literalism such as foot washing and the kiss of peace. One of the Anglican clergymen who took up membership with the early Brethren was James L. Harris (b. 1793), a graduate of Exeter College, Oxford.[7] He edited *The Christian Witness* to which Darby, Bellett, Newton and others all contributed lively articles which set out the Brethren doctrines with appetising vitality. A tract department was established and a steady flow of pamphlets and other literature began to attract the attention of the gentry and well-healed sections of society. Among them was Lady Powerscourt with whom Darby established a close rapport. She initiated prophetic meetings at Powerscourt Castle in Ireland in 1829 and 1830. 'Learned men,' according to Noel, 'profound students of the scriptures, were thus found at Powerscourt Castle in Ireland.'[8]

---

[5]  B. Wilson, *Patterns of Sectarianism*.
[6]  Noel, *The History of the Brethren*, I, 95–149.
[7]  Rev James Lampen Harris matriculated at Exeter College, Oxford, 2 December 1811, BA 1815, Fellow of Exeter College 1815–29, curate of Plymstock, Devon, before seceding.
[8]  Ibid. 32.

The early Brethren had no place for an ordained ministry or specially prepared Sunday homilies. Instead everyone was expected to share their faith whenever the opportunity arose. Preaching in the open air and in meeting houses and drawing rooms was expected of everyone in fellowship. The Sunday breaking of bread meetings were simple and unadorned. Hymns were sung without musical accompaniment and the brothers who felt prompted to do so, offered their insights on a chosen biblical passage before the communion elements were passed round.

Gradually, almost imperceptibly, the newly emerging assemblies began to emphasise the need for 'separateness' from the world. The 1830s and 1840s were a time when 'end time expectancy' was running high; the Lord was at hand, and everyone, above all the Brethren, must be ready to meet Him at his coming. So what had begun as a movement with a Communion table which was open to all believers was transformed into one which eventually excluded all save the elite of the Brethren.

The leading spirit in all of this was Darby. During the later 1830s and 1840s he rose to a position of total ascendancy over the many assemblies which were being established. Darby was constantly on the move, a skilled organiser, a persuasive debater and, perhaps above all, a gifted and inspiring preacher. Indeed even in the 1970s evangelists such as Canon David Watson were making reference to his writings and sermons. Darby's preaching tours frequently took him to London, Ireland and the Continent where he focused his energies on France, Germany and Switzerland. Here some seventy Brethren meetings were established.

## The Split of 1849 and the Formation of the Exclusive Brethren

Virtually the only place in England where Darby did not hold sway was Plymouth. While he was overseas in the early 1840s Benjamin Newton had remained in his home town and took almost total control over the Ebrington Street Assembly. Darby who was quick to recognise his own traits in others returned and protested at his 'clericalism' which he maintained quenched the work of the Holy Spirit. A conflict of some kind was inevitable.

The clash that was waiting to happen was occasioned in 1847 when Newton gave some unorthodox explanation on the person of Christ to a small invited group. In essence he taught what Brethren later termed 'the tainted Christ'. His contention was that Jesus had, like the rest of the human race, been born and lived under the curse of God until the time of his baptism in the river Jordan. This was quite simply a version of 'adoptionism' which maintained that Jesus did not have any divine status until God 'adopted' him as his beloved son. This doctrine has found a steady flow of advocates through the centuries, notably in the writings of Bishop David Jenkins of Durham. Most of those who had sat at Newton's feet soon admitted to having been taken in by 'the delusion of Satan'. Even Newton himself confessed to the error of his ways and subsequently moved away to London.

Far from this being the end of the matter, however, it proved to be only the beginning of what was to be an irreparable rift among the Brethren. Some of those who had listened to Newton in Plymouth went to Bethesda in Bristol where they were allowed to break bread. There was no evidence that any of them had taken on board Newton's recent teachings but, notwithstanding, calls were made by Darby and others for Bethesda to exclude them. In response the Bethesda leaders issued a celebrated document known as *The Letter of the Ten*.[9]

At the beginning of this letter the leaders 'utterly disclaim the assertion that the blessed Son of God was involved in the guilt of the first Adam' or 'ever . . . had the experiences of an unconverted person'. Most crucially of all they refused to admit that merely by hearing erroneous teaching Christians are contaminated by it: 'For supposing the author of the tracts were fundamentally heretical, this would not warrant us in rejecting those who came from under his teaching until we were satisfied that they had understood and imbibed views essentially of foundation truth.'[10]

This paper committed Bethesda to the original Brethren position of keeping the communion table 'open' to all who share the historic biblical Christian faith. However, Darby and George Wigram had by this time already separated themselves from

---

[9] *Letter of the Ten*, 29 June 1848.
[10] Ibid. 3.

Newton's assembly and set up a rival meeting at Raleigh Street. Müller and Craik did their best to keep open the hand of friendship with them and invited Darby to speak at Bethesda in April 1848. He declined this well-meant gesture and instead embarked on a tour of the north in July and August following which he issued his celebrated *Bethesda Circular*. In this he maintained that to associate with evil in the way that Bethesda had done 'is opening the door now to the infection of the abominable evil from which at so much cost we have been delivered'.[11] Darby also stated a little later in the same paragraph that 'by receiving persons from Bethesda, those doing so are morally identified with the evil'.[12] Thus began the overarching and principal doctrine of the Exclusive Brethren, namely separating from evil.

From 1849 onwards the 'Exclusives' emerged as a separate group. Frequently they were referred to as 'Darbyites' on account of Darby's total domination. Far from declining as a 'faithful remnant', however, the next thirty years proved to be a period of expansion and prosperity. One early writer referred to it as 'the flowing tide of the Exclusive Movement'. Between 1848 and 1878 Darby visited and preached in many places including Switzerland, France, Holland, Canada and the US on six separate occasions.[13] Andrew Miller in his book *The Brethren, Their Origins, Progress and Testimony*, published in 1878, charted some of the results of Darby's endeavours:

> In the United States, ninety-one meetings of the Brethren have sprung up of late years . . . In Canada, there are a hundred and one meetings. In Holland, thirty-nine; in Germany, a hundred and eighty-nine; in France, a hundred and forty-six; in Switzerland, seventy-two; in the United Kingdom, including the Channel Islands, about seven hundred and fifty; besides twenty-two other countries where the meetings vary from one to thirteen.[14]

In 1849 George Wigram employed his academic talents by editing a separate Journal under the title of *The Present Testimony*. It

---

[11] J.N.D. Darby, *The Bethesda Circular* (1848), 3.
[12] Ibid.
[13] Noel, *The History of the Brethren*, I, 57.
[14] A. Miller, *The Brethren, Their Origins, Progress and Testimony*, 163.

continued for thirty years and ran to eighteen volumes. To it Darby contributed his 'Synopsis of the Books of the Bible', and others produced well-written articles on key doctrinal issues.

## The Character of Exclusive Brethren

Darby's teaching on 'separation' from evil was essentially rooted in the Old Testament notion of holiness of 'touch no unclean thing!'[15] The fear was that if a person associated with evil in any shape or form they would be 'contaminated' or, at the very least, tainted by it. The matter is symbolically illustrated by Jesus' parable of the Good Samaritan, though it is probably not a parallel the Exclusives would make. The Priest and the Levite were both unwilling to come into close proximity with the man who had been robbed lest he should be dead, since to have touched a corpse would have left them ritually unclean.

From Darby's time onwards the Exclusive Brethren have become steadily and increasingly withdrawn from the outside world, which is regarded as a place of evil and corruption. Darby progressively taught a sharp distinction between the true Church, that is the assemblies of the Exclusives, and the rest of Christendom which had apostatised. In theory Darby believed a saint could exist outside the Exclusive Brethren, but in practice it was only within the fellowship of the saints that people experience and work out their salvation. For the 'Exclusives' their assembly and their community is the only safe place.

As in many areas of life one person initiates a new doctrine or teaching and others run with it with more enthusiasm and to considerably greater extremes. Such was the case with the Exclusives. Darby expressed his views in a paper entitled *Separation from Evil, God's Principle of Unity*. In it he wrote: 'Separation from evil becomes the necessary and sole basis and principle of unity . . . for God can have no union with evil . . . He separates the 'called' from evil. Come out from among them and be ye separate, and I will receive you, and ye shall be my sons and daughters, saith the Lord Almighty.'[16]

---

[15]  See Isaiah 52:11.

[16]  J.N. Darby, *Separation from Evil, God's Principle of Unity*.

When Darby died in 1882 the movement was dominated for a brief period by James Butler Stoney (1814–97). Stoney had been associated with the Brethren from the earliest days. Like Darby he had given up the prospect of the Bar so that he could take Orders. He later wrote, 'I felt the immensity of the step of leaving the established order for the unsightly few in Aungier Street.'[17] The decade which followed Darby's death witnessed the emergence of a number of other smaller factions, each taking the name of their most prominent teacher: Grant, Kelly, Stuart and Lowe.[18] The descendants of most of these groups are still active today. Stoney's teaching of 'separation' emphasised the need to sever all connection from people if it is clear that the Lord has abandoned them.

After a short period Stoney was succeeded by Frederick Raven (1837–1903) who lived in Greenwich, England. His profession as a lecturer gave him added respect among the Brethren, which enabled him to become dominant over the London meetings. The extent of his popularity was attested by the fact that nearly 1,500 Brethren attended his funeral service at Nunhead cemetery. Raven's ministry was the cause of major ructions within the Exclusives in 1890. Raven taught, as Apollinarius had done in the second century, that Jesus did not have a human spirit and that his impulses were therefore solely those of the divine Son of God. He also contended that eternal life is not a life conveyed to a believer but rather a sphere of life which the believer enters into when he or she fellowships within the assembly. In this he was opening the door of separatist teaching a little wider than had previously been the case. He stressed the importance of not relying on or depending on sources outside the Brethren. 'If you want to go with the gospel', he declared, 'you must go with it perfectly independent of all worldly support. You must not look for patronage or support from man.'[19] He wrote in another place: 'Holiness is the obligation of the people of God. It is almost the first principle of relationship with God . . . Israel had to be separate from material things; with the Christian separation is

---

[17] Noel, *The History of the Brethren*, I, 32.
[18] See D. Tinder (ed.), 'The Brethren Movement in the World To-day', *Christian Brethren Fellowship* 25 (September 1973), 12.
[19] F.E. Raven, *Ministry* I, 313.

moral.'[20] This is still a prominent trait among present-day Exclusives who only work in Brethren companies and borrow money solely from within their own fellowship.

On the death of Raven, James Taylor Snr (1870–1953) took the reins of the movement. Born in the small County Sligo village of Coolaney, Ireland, he emigrated first to Newfoundland and then a year later to New York City where he established a linen business. His commercial activity, which involved a good deal of national and international travel, enabled his rise to prominence among the Exclusives. In his early ministry at Chicago on the subject of 'The House of God and the Gospel' he propounded a new teaching in which he asserted that while salvation was in Christ, it was also in the church, 'since it was in the Church that Christ was honoured'.

The years 1918–20 saw the beginnings of a theological justification for separation. It was all a matter of 'dealing with evil'. A key passage in this teaching was in 2 Timothy 2:19–22, where Paul teaches that the man who has 'purified himself' will 'separate himself to be a vessel to honour'. The crucial text which all Exclusives still underscore is verse 19: 'and let everyone who names the name of the Lord withdraw'. Thus the way to deal with evil is to 'withdraw' from it.

Another controversial aspect of Taylor's teaching emerged in the summer of 1929 when he began a ministry series on 'The Eternal Sonship of Christ' in which he rejected 'the eternity of the son of God'. Taylor stated categorically: 'I do not know that there is such a term in scripture as eternal sonship . . . The son of God is announced in scripture *after* the Lord Jesus was here. In Luke it says, "The holy thing which *shall be* born also which *shall be* called the son of God" ' (italics mine).[21]

The implication of this teaching is quite clearly that Jesus was not fully God at the moment of his birth but rather that he became flesh. Taylor suggests that this was either when he was twelve years of age when he was found in the temple asking questions or at the time of his baptism. This view stands in contrast to the creedal faith of the mainstream churches which teaches that Jesus is eternally God and eternally man.

[20] Ibid.
[21] A.J. Gardiner, *The Recovery of the Truth*, 249–51.

After the death of James Taylor Snr there was a period of some six years when it was not clear who would be the leader. During that time most regarded G.R. Cowell as the main leader. However, in 1959 James Taylor's son, James Taylor Jr (1896–1970), made a bid for power and Cowell was sidelined. Taylor accused him of moving too slowly to separate the Brethren from such evils as 'serving on boards of directors' or other 'unequal yokes'. James Taylor Jr, otherwise known as 'Big Jim', assumed overall control of the movement. There is some evidence that in the early years of his leadership he enjoyed a certain amount of popularity. Interviewed in August 1964 he was asked, after addressing a mass rally of supporters in Aberdeen's City Music Hall, how members of his faith regarded him. 'They obviously regard me as something of a nice fellow', he remarked, and young girls in straw hats and clutching Bibles cheered.[22] In his public ministry entitled 'The Foundations of the Gospel and Other Readings' he introduced the doctrine of 'separate tables'. This forthright injunction required that no one was allowed to sit at table with their own family members of twelve years and older if they did not break bread with the Brethren. Later the doctrine was extended more widely. Members were not allowed to eat with unbelievers in their home or at their office or place of work. Children were no longer allowed to eat school dinners; instead they had to take a packed lunch or go to a Brethren home during the midday break. Things reached paranoid extremes when Taylor declared that the Brethren were not allowed to eat any food which had been prepared by an 'unbeliever', that is, a person other than a member of the Brethren. Taylor's notion of separation provoked some bizarre incidents. In the north-east of Scotland many Exclusives were involved in the fishing industry. In order for them to avoid sitting at table with fellow crew members who were unbelievers, galley tables were sawn down the middle so that there was an eighth of an inch gap. Brethren fishermen ate their food at one end and the rest of the crew at the other. However, even this was outlawed when it reached Big Jim's ears![23] It is estimated that about 8,000 people left the Raven-Taylor fellowship over the edict.

---

[22] *Aberdeen Press and Journal*, 6 August 1964.
[23] Ibid. 25 May 1961, and 11 September 1961.

## Brethren Life Today

From Big Jim's era to the present day little has changed in the restricted lifestyle of the Exclusive Brethren. If anything the many harsh and often banal injunctions which he laid down have been both tightened and extended. As with most strongly controlled religious communities, marriage arrangements are closely legislated. From much earlier times Brethren were required only to marry within the movement. This is a common practice among sect and cult groups, known as 'endogamy'. In the Taylorite era Brethren were required to marry young. Many girls wedded at sixteen or seventeen and boys about the same. Since college or university was not an option and employment was guaranteed with the Brethren there was no reason to delay. Taylor made it clear that to remain single was unacceptable. Young men were to take the initiative and propose to any sister they felt drawn to. There was to be no refusing and all wedding ceremonies were to take place on Tuesdays. James Symington produced an official sounding marriage contract to be read at weddings. In it the bride and groom undertake to raise any children born to them within the fellowship. When a young man makes a proposal to marry and the woman agrees the wedding must be approved by the 'man of God'. Engagement rings are not given and the couple are encouraged to marry as soon as possible. In the 1970s and 1980s Taylor further insisted on large families as a way of increasing the membership. At the present time it is now generally accepted that it may be better for couples to marry when they are a little more mature, perhaps having reached nineteen or twenty years of age.

Under Taylor's leadership, restrictions were brought in regarding education and professional qualifications. Children in primary and secondary schools were not allowed to play for school teams or take part in after school activities. They were only to socialise with other Brethren children and that off the school premises. Pupils were withdrawn from morning assemblies and Religious Education. A child could not participate in any school religious exercises which involved reading the Bible or the discussion of religion. When such things take place Exclusive children are expected to stand outside the classroom or in a hallway. In 1961 a ban, which has continued to the present time, was placed on university and college education. Newspapers listed the names of undergraduates who had quit Oxford and Cambridge Colleges to 'avoid fellowship with unrighteousness'.[24] In the 1960s increasing numbers of Brethren opted to have their children home-schooled. This trend has continued largely on account of the growing use of computers in the state school curriculum.

About this time a rule was introduced which forbade anyone to be a member of a trade union or a public body of any kind. This meant that Brethren were forced to give up the practice of medicine, pharmacy and all occupations requiring professional validation. Almost overnight men who had held positions as scientific researchers, company directors and solicitors were forced to take up manual and shop-floor jobs. In my home town of Cheltenham, one man who was a researcher at the National Coal Research Station was compelled to become a counter assistant with Sharpe and Fisher Builders Merchants. He continued in this position for a number of years until retirement. One escapee reported that he had finally left the Exclusives because he was banned by the sect from being a member of the 'unholy Automobile Association'.[25] During his time as leader, Symington encouraged Brethren only to work for companies owned by the Brethren or to employ fellow Brethren. Separation was to be extended to anyone not in fellowship, including business contacts. A job such as a representative, which entailed a sales conference with a meal following, was forbidden.

Brethren inevitably keep themselves aloof from party politics and local government. They steadfastly avoid any entanglement with 'the powers of this world'. Historically because of their commitment to private enterprise and managing their own affairs Brethren have had an in-built suspicion of Socialism. Occasionally they have sought to lobby Parliament as, for example, in June 1964 when representations were made on their behalf in the Commons debate on the Pharmacy Bill. This proposed to allow members of the Brethren to practice pharmacy without being members of the Pharmaceutical Society. In more recent times the Tory MP Teddy Taylor has spoken on their behalf on one or two occasions.

---

[24] *Daily Express*, 29 April 1961.
[25] *Daily Mail*, 11 July 1962.

There are 188 cities in which the Taylorite Exclusives have assemblies. In some large conurbations there may be anything up to twelve gatherings. There is one central administration for each city whether it contains one meeting or several. Membership in Britain has been estimated at between 7,000 to 10,000.

Women play a very subservient role among the Taylorites. They are forbodden to cut their hair and they must let it hang down to its full length. Women are also exhorted to wear 'comely' clothes, the meaning of which is defined by the Brethren leaders. Women must not wear slacks or jeans, and jewellery is used sparingly. Men must not have long hair or long sideburns, nor must they wear a beard or a moustache.

Perhaps hardest of all for the Brethren, and particularly for their children, is the fact that they are compelled to live a very restricted lifestyle. Quite apart from the prohibition to eat with non-members, the Brethren may not share a bath or a front door with them or even have a common sewage pipe or main drainage. Saturday is now regarded as a holy day along with Sunday and any type of work is forbidden on penalty of expulsion. Exclusives are prohibited from having any contact with family members who are not in full membership. Margaret N., a friend of mine, was not even informed when her father died. In fact it is standard practice that funeral arrangements are kept secret in order to prevent unbelieving family members from attending.

Generally speaking it is expected that the Brethren will not make friends with people who are not in the fellowship. They will, however, be good neighbours in the minimal sense. Brethren generally move into quiet private housing areas. Cul-de-sacs are particularly popular. If members want to purchase a house a loan is taken out from the assembly or from other members of the Brethren. To take out a policy with a mortgage company is strictly forbidden. This means that many individuals are financially tied in with their local meeting for periods of thirty or forty years. For employment these days Brethren work only for Brethren or for Brethren companies and businesses.

Personal travel by the Taylorites is very restricted and must be approved by the leading man in the city in which the brother or sister concerned is resident. Usually travel to visit friends and relatives is not permitted unless it combines with a Fellowship meeting which happens to be in the area in which they live. Because of these restrictions Brethren set a particularly high value on their Fellowship meetings. Family trips to the scenic areas are not usually permitted. Brethren are not allowed to take holidays on public beaches, are not allowed to possess a radio or television set, and the cinema and dance hall are regarded as 'citadels of Satan'. Cats, dogs and other domestic pets are not to be kept. In general, Brethren have few hobbies, although photography is actively encouraged. In fact in the early 1990s it became an Exclusive practice to photograph all the members attending meetings. Children often spent their spare time making collages of their local fellowship. Part of the thinking behind this was to help the younger ones choose marriage partners. However, the practice was abandoned by the end of the decade because some of these albums had fallen into the hands of those who had escaped from the movement.

One area where the Exclusive Brethren do hold together is in the matter of hospitality. At weekends Brethren families come together in quite large numbers. Perhaps twenty or thirty people will sit down to a meal after which there will be games, homespun music and fun activities. One surprising aspect of Brethren socialising is that the use of spirituous liquor, especially whisky and gin, is encouraged. This practice also dates back to a Taylorite edict. Big Jim, it seems, had a great liking for his Johnny Walker so he exhorted his members to follow him. Indeed it was strongly insisted among the Brethren that to limit the use of whisky was 'a criticism of the way of life of the Man of God'. Bryan Wilson of All Souls College, Oxford, observed that 'The Brethren make their family life their central concern. Since they eschew other social involvements, the family, and the reinforcing involvements of the community, constitute their social world. Harmonious family life is the norm for which all Brethren strive.'[26] Again, Wilson continued, 'Relationships at work and school are kept to the minimum of what is necessary, and whilst the Brethren conduct themselves with integrity, responsibility and courtesy, they do not look to these external involvements to provide them with any social life.'[27]

---

[26] B. Wilson, 'The Brethren: A Current Sociological Appraisal', 9.
[27] Ibid.

Up until the early 1970s Brethren funerals were carried out by 'worldly' undertakers at which time James Symington announced that they should make their own arrangements from 'inside'. So brothers who had carpentry skills were asked to make coffins and deal with laying out dead bodies. As with the Muslims they now have one of their people in each area who embalms the body, buys the coffin and transports it to the cemetery. Funerals are held with as little public attention as possible. Often young boys are left to fill in the hole above the casket when the burial prayers have been completed. This produced one or two unforeseen complications in the early days and there was one reported instance where a coffin became snagged in a hole which had not been made sufficiently long. A brother actually jumped up and down on the lid in an effort to make it sink into the grave. It sometimes happens that Brethren who have been excommunicated have nevertheless left a request in their wills to be buried by the Exclusives. On occasion some such individuals have received what is known as an 'Ass's funeral' where the casket, instead of being carried, is dragged over the grass to place of burial. It is likely that this procedure is based on Jeremiah 22:19 where it is said of Jehoiakim, the son of Josiah, king of Judah, that 'they will not mourn for him . . . He will have the burial of a donkey – dragged away and thrown outside the gates of Jerusalem.' Such a grotesque practice, where it has happened, reveals something of the contempt in which those who have been 'withdrawn from' are held.

## Exclusive Brethren Worship

Only those who are in good standing are allowed to attend the meetings. When everyone has arrived the doors are locked. A child must be baptised before coming to the meetings. Children, usually baptised at about eight days old, are expected to be present at all the meetings, and there is a meeting every night of the week and on Saturdays. Exclusives use only the J.N. Darby translation of the Bible. The worship of the 'Saints' has always been plain and unadorned since the earliest times. What takes place on a given Sunday today is little different in basic ethos from the early beginnings in Dublin in the 1830s. Essentially the congregation is seated in two circles with men in front and the women behind. Hymns are sung unaccompanied by any musical instrument as this is felt to 'hinder the freedom of the Spirit'. The women wear headscarves and are not allowed to speak or sing at the meetings, since according to the New Testament, they are to keep silent in church. They do, however, always suggest the hymns. The meeting is usually focused on an elaboration of a particular Bible passage. The leading brother will introduce this for a few minutes after which the men who are present are free to ask questions. Brothers only stand at large gatherings such as Fellowship Meetings. The discussion which takes place on the Scripture which is read is always what the 'Man of God' or 'Universal Leader' or 'Our Beloved Brother' has written or said about the passage. No room is given for any fresh insights to be brought by the Brethren at the meeting. There is no prepared sermon, order of service or set prayers. Since Taylor Jr's time 'breaking of bread' services have been held at 6 a.m. Everyone is required to take the bread and wine, even children who are too young to be intelligent believers. Babies receive the elements as soon as they are old enough to digest solid foods. On Sundays there is usually a further service at 9 a.m. This will include all members of the city. Here again a leading brother introduces a passage and men who are present are encouraged to ask questions. Again the sisters play little part in this. At some point later on the Sunday there will also be a gospel preaching at which three men will give short gospel messages. In addition there are 'Fellowship Meetings' which are held from time to time on other days of the week. These are one-day gatherings for Bible study. Additionally there are occasional Three Day Bible Conferences with addresses. A further somewhat quirky regulation was Big Jim's requirement that men do not wear ties at any of the meetings because 'all worldly ties must be cut'! A man always removes his wristwatch on entering the meeting room though boys and women are allowed to wear theirs. The reason for this is that the Brethren do not believe that the length of a meeting should be governed by a clock. Exclusive Brethren often preach in the open air on Saturday mornings, although they find themselves at a loss when people start to engage them in conversation to find out more. Most assemblies hold a Gospel service, although these are often during the Sunday lunch hour period when few people are likely to want to attend.

## Big Jim: A Man out of Control

At one level the tightening restrictions in the Brethren in the 1960s are understandable against the background of freedom and liberalisation which was taking place in society. However, as the decade progressed the power which Taylor exercised over his following went well beyond reasonable limits. The absolute power he had in his hands began to corrupt him absolutely. Three things in particular were to cause his downfall. He became increasingly engrossed in money-making activities, his gin drinking led to his becoming an alcoholic and his salacious appetite led him to an increasing obsession with women and sex.

It had long been the custom for the acknowledged world leader of the Brethren to give public Bible teaching in England. These gatherings were often held at major venues such as Westminster Central Hall and attended by several thousand members. Called 'Readings' the teaching was, and still is, given in a dialogue format. A nationally recognised brother speaks out the question and then the leader answers. In the early days these readings were deeply spiritual expositions of biblical passages which were related to the issues of daily living. All readings were and continue to be published in small paperback volumes and treasured as God's Word.

By the late 1960s and early 1970s Jim Taylor was clearly a man out of control. Many of the readings were punctuated with crude innuendoes and cheap hurtful jibes which made little sense to anyone. Speaking at Nostrand Avenue, New York City, he addressed one member of the congregation as follows: 'You are a man of action too you fat there, don't forget your cheque. We will take cheques, we will take anything, but we do not want them to bounce.' Turning to a lady he said: 'Ah, it occurs to me about that dear sister over there, Mrs. B. have you changed your will? Well if not do it, you must do it.'[28] Later he confronted another gentleman: 'Do you hear that you Toronto man, what in the world is your name, you baldy? But you are not a baldy like L. you have not got the brains he has got.'[29] At the celebrated meeting in Aberdeen in

---

[28] J. Taylor, Jnr, *Readings at Nostrand Avenue and Other Ministry* 4 (October 1970), 105.

[29] Ibid. 108.

August of the same year the rhetoric was even worse as Taylor denounced devout believers as 'bums', 'bastards' and 'sons of a bitch'.[30] But this was comparatively mild fare compared with what followed. Shattered and exhausted, Taylor retired to his room at the home of James Gardiner on the outskirts of the city where he was staying. Among the visitors were Alan and Madeleine Ker from Harrow. 'Madey' Ker offered to wash Taylor's feet and followed up with some gentle massaging of his neck. 'I find that very soothing', Taylor later confessed to a *Daily Express* reporter. The therapy completed Madeleine got into the bed beside Taylor only to be discovered a short time later by Gardiner and some of the other local leaders.[31] Despite Taylor protesting his innocence the national press carried headlines the following day with a large picture 'The Woman in Big Jim's Bed'.[32]

Once the news broke, it was sufficient to shake substantial numbers free of the abusive and emotional hold Taylor had over them. Following the incident about eight thousand members parted company with the Exclusives over the next two years.[33] Whatever had taken place, Taylor was clearly compromised. 'Mrs. Ker was in the same bed', he told one reporter, 'but she wasn't lying with me, and I wasn't lying with her, if you see what I mean.' Escapees with whom I have spoken, take the view that obsessed with sex as he was, Taylor was probably incapable of committing adultery. A few days after the event at Aberdeen Big Jim changed his storyline. It had all been deliberately staged to see who were the 'real saints' who would remain faithful to him. Then at the beginning of October just when moves were afoot to oust him from the leadership altogether the papers reported: 'Big Jim Taylor, the Archangel of the Exclusive Brethren, the fanatical religious sect, has died in New York.'[34]

After the Aberdeen affair those Brethren who remained in the Raven-Taylor Brethren were known as 'Jimites' or 'Jimmies'. For a brief period after Taylor's death there was a three-way power

---

[30] See N. Adams, *Goodbye Beloved Brethren*, 120–33.
[31] *The Sunday Express*, 23 August 1970.
[32] *The Sunday Mirror*, 16 August 1970.
[33] *Daily Mail*, 16 October 1970.
[34] *New York Times*, 17 October 1970.

struggle between James Taylor III, Dr Maynard and James Symington for overall control. This continued for some months until James Symington (1914–87), a pig farmer from Neche in North Dakota, eventually gained the ascendancy. He was highly regarded in America and Taylor himself had publicly said to him: 'You will take over when I go.' According to ex-Exclusive, Dick Wyman, 'J.H.S. turned the fellowship into a cash machine, earning a reported US $1.5 million per year from the contributions he exacted from the Brethren.'[35] Non-Brethren reported busloads of Brethren who would come to Neche to hear the Symington ministry. It was inevitable that, as one of Big Jim's toadies, he would maintain the regime with more of the same. It is axiomatic among the Exclusives that their leader can do no wrong, hence it becomes difficult for a successor to reverse his predecessor's edicts. This meant that all the extremes, including 6 a.m. Sunday worship, separate tables, total isolation from the outside world, and even the exhortation to drink whisky and spirituous liquor, have continued down to the present time.

Symington remained at helm until the early 1980s. When he died he is alleged to have designated Lloyd R. Paskewitz of West Minnesota to succeed him. However, John Hales succeeded in persuading the Brethren at a universal gathering in Winnipeg that he should be their international leader. John Hales (b. 1922) is the older brother of Big Jim's Australian son-in-law, Bruce Hales. Bruce, who had been noted in the 1960s as a 'very ambitious young man', was highly motivated in business and came to England on a number of occasions in an effort to mobilise Brethren companies to make more money. He married Taylor's daughter, Consuella ('Consi'), a move which doubtless increased his prominence in the later 1960s when he held power for a period of three years while his father-in-law was hospitalised. However, as things turned out it was his older brother, John, who succeeded in taking up the reins and who retains the position at the present time.

John Hales was born and brought up in Thirroul, a small seaside town 42 miles south-west of Sydney. He graduated from the University of Sydney with a BSc in economics and then qualified as

---

[35] D. Wyman, 'Plymouth Brethren: Exclusive Raven/Taylor Sect' (http://cloudnet.com/~dwyman/pb.htm), 2.

a chartered accountant. He is married and has three sons and a daughter and still lives in Sydney.

The Exclusives are currently reckoned by those who have recently left to have a membership of about 27,000 members worldwide, and possibly as many as 7,000 in the British Isles.

The government of the Brethren is in the hands of an assembly of elders called 'priests', which is a strange term in view of the fact that the early Brethren eschewed clericalism so strongly. Each region has a priest over the assemblies of its area but all of them remain very much under the overall and total control of the 'Universal Leader'.

## Present Features of the Exclusive Brethren

There can be no doubt that the leadership of the Exclusive Brethren has become increasingly controlling and dominant. On this point recent escapees from the movement are unanimous. The Exclusives, it seems, have many of the characteristics of what sociologists of religion designate New Religious Movements (NRMs).

From the earliest days of John Nelson Darby there has been a dominant figurehead over the Exclusive Brethren, but since Big Jim's time such leaders have come to exercise total control. They are known as the 'Universal Leader' or the 'Man of God'. Big Jim cultivated the notion that as the 'Man of God' he was shielded from error. James Symington developed the idea that the principal leader should approve all significant decisions. He came to exercise enormous power, approving marriages, permitting people to relocate, and determining who should be 'shut up' or 'withdrawn' from. He taught that computers were evil and Exclusives were forbidden to use them. By the late 1990s the Brethren were of the opinion that John Hales was 'the Lord's Elect Vessel', a conviction they derived from Isaiah 42:1, 'Behold my servant, whom I uphold; mine elect.' Schoolchildren in Australia apparently told their teachers that Mr Hales can see right through them and read the labels on the backs of their shirts. Dick Wyman was present at a conference meeting where Hales was publicly called 'the personification of the Holy Spirit'.[36] Their major public teachings are

---

[36] Ibid.

conveyed at 'readings' and are then printed in book form. They are required to be acted upon without question even though they have devastating consequences, including the separation of husbands from wives and children from parents. These have resulted in a trail of divorce, broken homes and suicides. Many who escaped the movement in the 1970s and 1980s, some of whom I know personally, remain severely emotionally damaged.

The Exclusive Brethren operate a totalitarian regime. Only those in absolute agreement with the doctrines and practices are allowed to be members. At the time of the Aberdeen affair members in most cities had to declare their total commitment to Taylor. Government is from the top and passed down through area leaders who are also 'ministering brothers'. Taylor instituted what is known as the monthly 'Care Meeting' to which any member who has failed to comply with the movement's pronouncements is summoned. Additionally the 'Assembly Meeting' can be called at any time, usually on a Tuesday evening and it is 'in Assembly' that matters of discipline are usually dealt with.[37] Deviants who have engaged in such activities as visiting non-Brethren family members or eating with work colleagues are either 'shut up' (confined to their own home) or 'withdrawn from' (not spoken to) for designated periods of time. The concept of 'shutting up' is derived from the book of Leviticus where instruction is given that if a person was suspected of having leprosy they were to be confined to their house. Priests would visit them from time to time to see if the leprosy had spread. In Exclusive practice this means that if a person is believed to have sin (leprosy) operating in their lives they are 'shut up' in their homes and not allowed to attend meetings or have any contact with the fellowship. A person could be shut up for days or even months. In a given area faltering or lapsed members who are 'shut up' are visited by the local leaders who remonstrate with them about the error of their ways, deciding when it is right for them to come out of their houses. There are many accounts by recent leavers of abusive questioning including extracted confessions of affairs, masturbation, lust and cinema-going. Most co-operate with the directives of their 'priests' because they sincerely believe their

---

[37] Written information received from Mr D. Shorto in May 1999.

fellowship is the one true church on earth. If a person refuses to respond they are put out of the fellowship altogether.

The chief characteristic of the Exclusive Brethren, as their name suggests, is separation from evil. In general they are expected to refrain from any friendships or dealings with anyone who is not in the fellowship. They find the justification for this in the book of James: 'Know ye not that friendship with the world is enmity with God? Whoever therefore is minded to be the friend of the world is constituted the enemy of God' (James 4:4). For this reason an Exclusive brother or sister must not

- Be a member of any other religious group.
- Visit any other place of worship.
- Be a member of a trade union or professional association.
- Join any association where it involves them in membership with any person not in the fellowship.
- Live in the same building as a person who is not in fellowship. A semi-detached residence is not acceptable.
- Have their business in the same building or share a common wall with another business whose owner is not in fellowship.
- Share a driveway with neighbour.
- Share a sewer with a neighbour if they connect before reaching city property.
- Own shares in a company with any person not in the fellowship.
- Share profits in any profit-sharing scheme.
- In business share advertising costs with either a supplier or a distributor.
- Be in any group benefit arrangement with employees or employer.
- Marry someone not in the fellowship.
- Live in the same house as a mate who has been put out of fellowship. They must be legally and physically separate from their mate to be allowed to participate in the fellowship.[38]

---

[38] Ibid. 7.

In addition to separating from people, Exclusives are also required to be separate from worldly things. They are not allowed to watch television, movies or video, listen to a radio, read newspapers or novels except approved school books, go to places of entertainment such as Disneyland, own or operate a computer, or have or use a cellular telephone or CB radio. In fact any device which uses the airwaves, including garage door openers, are forbidden because Satan is 'the Prince of the Power of the Air'. Brethren do not own life insurance or purchase any other insurance except third-party liability or have a pet in the house.[39]

As with groups such as the Branch Davidians of Waco, the Exclusive Brethren exercise almost total control over members' daily living. For instance, as has been noted, Taylor ordered all Exclusives to marry. Initially girls were to wed at sixteen or seventeen and boys at eighteen. At present twenty or twenty-one is recommended. Taylor also required that the ceremonies should be conducted by Brethren marriage officers and take place only on Tuesdays at 'Ministry Meetings'. He followed this up with an order that Brethren should have large families. He further ordered that women were not to refuse a proposal of marriage made by any suitable man. Since the Big Jim era Exclusive behaviour has been very tightly controlled right down to domestic minutiae. As already mentioned, this is seen in the order to men not to have beards and also not to wear ties at services.[40] Women are required to wear headscarves at all times. These are to be plain white or blue in colour and are often pinned back behind the ears. Hats are not allowed. They must not cut their hair but let it hang down full length and tied with a bow. It is viewed as a token of their submission to men. Neither are women allowed to wear slacks or jeans. They should instead don clothes that are 'comely'. In some assemblies in India women have been required to have Western-style dresses rather than their customary saris.

It is well known that one of the means by which some New Religious Movements retain total control of their adherents is exclusivity and isolation. In this matter the Exclusive Brethren, as

---

[39] Ibid.

[40] I witnessed this when I visited the Taylorite Exclusive Assembly at South Carlton Street in Cheltenham.

their name suggests, are no exception. They believe that no other body has the 'truth of the Church' or 'walks in the light of the assembly' or 'acts in the power of the Holy Spirit'. Exclusives are isolated from the 'world' and its surrounding culture at every level from the cradle to the grave. In schools, for example, their children are withdrawn from assemblies and RE lessons. They are not allowed to participate in out-of-school activities or socialise with non-Brethren children. In earlier times discipline was often severe in Exclusive homes and there were some reports of brutal punishments including broken limbs. Big Jim put a stop to this, quoting a verse from Timothy, 'Be not a striker.'

A recent development has been home tuition and about one third of all Exclusive children are now educated in this way. Television sets are banned and newspapers not taken. When it comes to funeral services these are kept very quiet. There are no public announcements in the press and the arrangements which are solely in the hands of Exclusives who are appointed as undertakers. Burials usually take place within a day or two before family members in the outside world get to hear the news.

Exclusive Brethren come to have a deep emotional dependence on their movement. They take out mortgages with the Brethren, they only work for Brethren companies and all their socialising which is often enjoyably full is within the context of the Brethren. In short, they know of no other life beyond that of their local fellowship. Not surprisingly, individuals who 'come out' often feel racked with guilt and are emotionally bereft. A recent university thesis indicated high levels of psychological damage on the part of leavers.[41]

Finally, there can be no doubt that, as in other intensive groups, Exclusive Brethren control their following at every level. Women have never been allowed to speak in the meetings and they play a very subservient role in the movement's social life. At the height of his power Taylor ordered that women were not to wear bras or underwear which was nothing more than an excuse to satisfy his predatorial sexual appetites. Notoriously known as 'Breaster' because of his obsession, he 'cuddled and fondled every "sister" who came near him

---

[41] J. Aebi-Mytton, 'An Exploratory Study of the Mental Health of Former Members of the Taylorite Branch of the Exclusive Brethren', 8.

and pulled many of them down on his knee in the intervals between the meetings at Manchester, Preston and Aberdeen in 1970'.[42] The practice was short-lived in England, although there is evidence that it continued for longer in South Africa where the leader was Derek Noakes, who it was thought might succeed Taylor in 1970.[43] Although it was commonly reported that Noakes could have inter-course with any of the women in fellowship, ex-Exclusives with whom I have spoken believe this to be apocryphal.[44] Noakes had attracted many followers by announcing that he was 'Paul the Third', in other words, an apostle. He declared that he had come to carry forward the work of James Taylor Jr who was 'Paul the Second'.

It would be hard to conclude in any other way than to assert categorically that the Exclusive Brethren are a highly intensive movement. Their recent leaders exemplify the old adage that 'power corrupts and absolute power corrupts absolutely'. For the evidence of these two assertions we need look no further than the hundreds of past and present walking wounded in almost every major town and city in the British Isles. Indeed a recent academic study of the psychological damage experienced by Exclusive Brethren indicated 50 per cent still have upsetting memories, 62 per cent still find it hard to trust their own feelings and 47 per cent experience feelings of not belonging to any group.[45]

---

[42] Ibid. 8. See also Adams, *Goodbye Beloved Brethren*. On p. 111 Adams recounts that 'the sect's ban on foundation garments was intended to make sexual fondling easier'. On the same page Adams says that Taylor reported from Brooklyn: 'members are not encouraged to touch every-one's sexual parts. But breasts are for Christ. It's as old as Solomon. The man touches the woman's breast. Of course, they do it in private. You only do it with your wife. It's the best part of the meeting.'

[43] Wyman, South Africa, 'Plymouth Brethren', 1.

[44] For the report see ibid. For a corrective, correspondence with D.S., May 1999.

[45] J. Aebi-Mytton, 'An Exploratory Study of the Mental Health of Former Members of the Taylorite Branch of the Exclusive Brethren', 8.

# Chapter 6

# The Latter-day Saints

In June 1998, when the more traditional denominations of Britain were pondering their dwindling congregations and the government was dithering over how to give the Millennium Dome a suitable Christian theme, the Mormon Church, or 'Church of Jesus Christ of Latter-day Saints' dedicated what is now their largest temple complex in the world. Towering above everything for miles around, its 170 ft spire is considerably taller than the Millennium Dome. Resplendent in white granite imported from Sardinia, it has 147 rooms and boasts a lavish baptismal font supported on the backs of bronze oxen. Mormon sources have been unwilling to disclose the cost of their new edifice but estimates suggest a total bill of around £100 million. Latter-day Saints with whom I have spoken say that in reality it is probably a lot less!

All of this bears testimony to a religious organisation which is both expanding numerically and developing a confident and assertive public image. The Latter-day Saints are not new to England. They first established themselves near Preston in 1837 and grew slowly in Victorian times, reaching 39,000 at the religious census of 1851. In the latter part of the present century, however, progress has been rather more rapid. The Church claims to have grown thirtyfold since the mid-1960s and at the close of 1998 claimed a membership of 180,000. In the 1990s UK membership rose at approximately 5,000 per annum. The Church of Jesus Christ of Latter-day Saints gave its worldwide membership in April 1999 as 10,354,241, organised into 25,551 congregations. At that point in time it had 57,853 active full-time missionaries in the field. Global membership has tripled in the last quarter of a century and is anticipated to reach 11 million in the new millennium. There were

53 temples in operation in 1999 and 45 new ones under construction.[1]

Latter-day Saints have many appealing features. They are frequently outgoing, warm and friendly people. Their missionary endeavours encircle the globe. A high percentage of all members in good standing venture out on a two-year missionary journey at their own expense. For many, this takes place when they are in their early twenties. Mormons set very high stakes on marriage and the family. On 23 September 1995, the First Presidency and Council of the Twelve Apostles of the Church of Jesus Christ of Latter-day Saints issued 'A Proclamation to the World' on 'The Family'. The document which is still distributed from local congregations, solemnly proclaims that 'marriage between a man and a woman is ordained of God and that the family is central to the Creator's plan for the eternal destiny of His children'. The penultimate paragraph issues a stern warning against those 'who abuse spouse or offspring, or who fail to fulfil family responsibilities'. They will one day stand accountable before God and will bring on society 'the calamities foretold by ancient and modern prophets'.[2] Due to their strong emphasis on the home and family most Mormon congregations run courses on parenting. Every Monday evening is a family night. All Latter-day Saints members are expected to be with each other as a family and do something together, either playing games, relaxing or simply enjoying quality family time together. Bishop Ben Lowater explained the reason for this emphasis in the following way: 'We believe we are in the same family units we are in now not "till death us do part" but "for time and eternity." If I'm going to be with my family for eternity I'd better get to like them now.'[3] Along with their emphasis on education, Latter-day Saints in general set a high value on sports, hobbies, dramatics, dancing and home-making courses for prospective brides and marrieds. As Bishop Ben Lowater explained it to me, the Mormon Church encourages what it terms 'fast offerings'. This involves giving up two meals on the first

---

[1] These figures were given at the UK Annual General Conference in April 1999.

[2] *The Family: A Proclamation to the World.*

[3] Written information received from Bishop Ben Lowater of Cheltenham, 25 May 1999.

Sunday of each month, the price of which is turned over to the Church as a voluntary contribution to support and feed the poor. Their money is used both at a local level through the bishop and at an international level through the 'Humanitarian Aid Fund'. This emphasis on caring for the poor has been a marked feature since the years of the movement's inception in Vermont when they loaned capital to poor industrious families to help them improve their holdings.

From being at the margins of society in the early nineteenth century, members of the Church of Jesus Christ of Latter-day Saints have come in the present century to hold high office. In 1953 Ezra Taft Benson, who later became the thirteenth president of the Church, took the oath of office as Secretary for Agriculture in President Eisenhower's administration.[4] Benson served in the cabinet with distinction for eight years.[5] More recently, Governor George Romney of Michigan, was an active member of the Church. In England since the last general election there has been one Mormon MP, Terry Rooney, the Labour Member for Bradford.

## Early Days

The Church of Jesus Christ of Latter-day Saints was formed in the third decade of the nineteenth century in Upper New York State. The movement emerged within a climate of frontier revivalism and a harsh, harrowing and uncertain social environment. Fawn Brodie, one of Smith's biographers, noted: 'These pentecostal years which coincided with Joseph Smith's adolescence and early manhood, were the most fertile in America's history for sprouting prophets.'[6] The religious background against which Smith grew up was unsettled. It was a time of religious freedom for many people, as revivals and declines came and went through the early years of the nineteenth century. In particular, enthusiasm which the great evangelist Charles Finney (1792–1875) incited, reached a peak

---

[4]  M. Thomas and A. Thomas, *Mormonism, A Gold-plated Religion*, 10.
[5]  G.B. Hunckley, *Truth Restored*, 152.
[6]  F.M. Brodie, *No Man Knows My History*, 15.

around 1824. The area inhabited by the Smith family came to be called 'the burned-over district' because there were so many out-breaks of revivalism that it seemed as though it was literally scorched by them.

The origins of the movement are traceable to Joseph Smith Jr (1805–43) who was born at Sharon Vermont on 23 December 1805, the third son of Joseph and Lucy Smith. As a boy he moved with his parents to New York State and settled with them at Palmyra near Rochester. During their first two years, they ran a small shop and saved money. By 1818, they were able to make an initial payment on one hundred acres of heavily wooded land equidistant from the towns of Farmington and Palmyra. In later life, Lucy Smith remembered her son as 'a brave youth' who was prone to deep thought.[7] Fawn Brodie, one of Smith's fairer minded biographers wrote: 'His reputation before he organised his church was . . . of a likeable ne'er do well, who was notorious for . . . tales and necromantic arts (contacting the dead), and who spent his leisure leading a band of idles in digging for buried treasures.'[8] The same writer also described Smith as 'nimble-witted, ambitious, and gifted with an undisciplined imagination', so that for him 'the line between truth and fiction was always blurred'.[9] Rather more hostile was the comment of Isaac Hale, Smith's father-in-law, who denounced Joseph as 'a liar and a cheat'.[10] In reality Smith was probably no worse than many members of the denominational churches who persecuted him. Even Orsamus Turner who knew him and edited several anti-Mormon tracts around 1819 and 1820 later wrote that 'Joseph had . . . some very laudable aspirations; the mother's intellect occasionally shone out . . . especially when he used to help us solve some portentous questions of moral or political ethics, in our juvenile debating club.'[11] Brigham Young who succeeded Smith as the Second President of the Church wrote:

> Who can justly say aught against Joseph Smith? I was as well acquainted with him, as any man. I do not believe that his father and

---

[7]  L.J. Arrington and D. Bitton, *The Mormon Experience*, 5.

[8]  Brodie, *No Man Knows*, 16.

[9]  Ibid. 84.

[10]  Ibid. 418.

[11]  Cited in Arrington and Bitton, *The Mormon Experience*, 5.

mother knew him any better than I did. I do not think that a man lives on earth who knew him better than I did; and I am bold to say that, Jesus Christ excepted, no better man ever lived or does live upon this earth. I am his witness. He was persecuted for the same reason that any other righteous person has been or is persecuted at the present day.[12]

## His Visions and Marriage

Joseph spent his early years at Palmyra, Ontario (now Wayne) County in the State of New York, later moving to Manchester in the same State.[13] In their second year there, a religious revival inspired by a Methodist preacher named Lane, affected the whole State.[14] It created, in Joseph's words, 'no small stir and division amongst the people, some crying, "Lo, here!" and others "Lo there!" Some were contending for the Methodist faith, some for the Presbyterian and some for the Baptist.' Joseph was only fifteen at the time and was somewhat bemused by the array of competing evangelists. His mother Lucy, and brothers Hyrum and Samuel, and sister Sophronia, all joined the Presbyterians while Joseph himself was drawn to the Methodists. He was, however, perplexed in his mind and found it difficult to know how to make an informed decision. He tells us that, while in this uncertain state of mind one day in 1820, he read James 5:1, 'If any of you lack wisdom, let him ask of God, that giveth to all men liberally and upbraideth not; and it shall be given him.'

The verse struck the young Joseph Smith forcibly and he decided to put it to the test and ask God for explicit direction. He therefore retired to some woods not far from his home and asked God to show him which denomination he should join. It was at this point, he related, that he had his first vision. A pillar of light, brighter even than the sun, came over his head and gradually descended till it fell on him. He saw two personages, the Father and the Son standing side by side above him in the light. He asked them 'Which of all the sects were right – and which I should

---

[12] J.A. Widtsoe, *Discourses of Brigham Young*, 9:332, 459–60.

[13] J. Smith, *Pearl of Great Price*, 2:5.

[14] See R.L. Bushman, *Joseph Smith and the Beginnings of Mormonism*, 5.

join.'[15] God told him that he should join none of them 'for they
were all wrong' and 'all their creeds were an abomination in His
sight'.[16] Joseph returned home with a sense of his unworthiness at
having received such a vision. Those to whom he related the
experience were sceptical and caused him to experience considerable persecution. Joseph stated that he felt much like the apostle
Paul when he made his defence before King Agrippa.[17]

For the next three years, Joseph continued to eke out a living.
Not having joined any of the religious groups, his circle of friends
was not altogether wholesome and he related that he mingled
'with all kinds of society' and 'frequently fell into many foolish
errors and displayed the weakness of youth'.[18] Feeling condemned
he adopted the practice of asking God 'for forgiveness of my sins
and follies'.[19] It was at this time, during the night of 21 September
1823, that an angel who announced himself as Moroni
(pronounced 'own eye') appeared in his room. He was clad in a
loose 'exceedingly white' robe and his countenance was 'truly like
lightning'.[20] Moroni informed Joseph of the whereabouts of
certain gold plates containing an abridged history of the former
inhabitants of the American continent together with 'the fulness of
the Everlasting Gospel' as Jesus had delivered it to them. He was
also told that along with the plates he would find a breastplate and
what were termed 'Urim' and 'Thummim'. These were to enable
him to translate the text on the plates. Joseph was instructed that
he was not to show any of these items to anyone except those he
would be directed to.

Smith was directed to a hill known as Cumorah not far from
where he lived near Manchester, where he discovered the box and
the plates together with the instruments which were to assist him in
the translation. Although he tried on this occasion and in the three
subsequent years to remove the objects, he was forbidden to do so
on account of his not 'having kept the commandments of the

---

[15]　Smith, *Pearl of Great Price*, 2:16–19.
[16]　Ibid. 2:19.
[17]　Smith, *Pearl of Great Price*, 2:24.
[18]　Ibid. 2:28.
[19]　Ibid. 2:29.
[20]　Ibid. 2:32.

Lord'.[21] Smith had been ordered by the angel to go to the hill once each year 'until the time should come for obtaining the plates'. It was on the occasion of his fifth visit, at the age of 21 on 2 September 1827, that he was allowed to take possession of the plates.

The Smith family lived on the margins of poverty and owing to the family's straightened circumstances, the Smith brothers often hired themselves out as labourers. At some point in October 1825, Joseph went to work for Josiah Stoal in Chenango County. While in this employment Joseph boarded with Mr Isaac Hale. On 18 January 1827 he married his daughter Emma, much against her father's will.[22] On account of this opposition, Joseph and Emma were forced to elope and were married at the house of Squire Tarbill in South Bainbridge, Chenango County, New York. According to Smith, Isaac Hale's chief objection to the marriage was his detailing his first vision. However, Hale's stated objection was that Smith worked for a set of disreputable 'money diggers', his chief task being to divine the location of treasure by gazing at a stone placed inside his hat.[23] This stone he had apparently discovered while digging a well half a mile from his home. According to his mother, he was able to see things with it which were invisible to the natural eye.

During this period a number of others, in addition to Hale, sought to discredit Joseph and his family circle. The most notable were D.P. Hurlburt, an excommunicated Mormon, and E.D. Howe who published his exposé *Mormonism Unveiled* in 1834. Hurlburt collected seventy-two affidavits from the inhabitants of the Palmyra and Manchester areas. The main concern about them is that they tend to be somewhat standardised in form and are very similar in tone to a community statement by fifty-one residents of Palmyra which asserted that the Smiths were 'destitute of moral character', 'given to visionary projects' and 'addicted to vicious habits'.[24] Howe included the following statement from sixty-two residents of Palmyra in his book:

---

[21] Arrington and Bitton, *The Mormon Experience*, 9.

[22] Smith, *Pearl of Great Price*, 2:58.

[23] Arrington and Bitton, *The Mormon Experience*, 11.

[24] Ibid. 10.

We the undersigned, have been acquainted with the Smith family for a number of years while they resided near this place. We have no hesitation in saying that we consider them destitute of that moral character which ought to entitle them to the confidence of any community. They were particularly famous for visionary projects: spent much of their time digging for money which they pretended was hidden in the earth not far from their residence where they used to spend their time in digging for hidden treasures. Joseph Smith and his son, Joseph, were particularly considered entirely destitute of moral character and addicted to vicious habits.[25]

Care needs to be taken in interpreting this kind of evidence, some of it collected by an excommunicated Mormon, and much of it written up in standardised word forms which could have been dictated to them. It has been pointed out that allegations that the Smith family were malicious and lazy do not altogether convey the ring of truth because between 1823 and 1827, the Smith family cleared large areas of their own farms as well as hiring out as day labourers. In addition other Palmyra residents recalled the Smiths in a positive light and several testified that Joseph was a steady and diligent worker. Money digging was apparently a widespread activity on the part of Palmyran residents and many of those who signed affidavits concerning Smith's money digging were devotees of the same activity.[26]

## The Translation of the Book of Mormon

Joseph took the plates as he was instructed and kept them secretly away from the gaze of everyone, except those he felt God wanted him to show them to. There was little privacy in the Smith household and Joseph was repeatedly pestered by some of his former digging partners who believed they had rights to a share in the plates. Through the help of Martin Harris, a prosperous local farmer, Smith was able to travel and settle in his father-in-law's house which was situated near Harmony in Pennsylvania. Shortly

[25] E.D. Howe, *Mormonism Unveiled*, 264.

[26] Arrington and Bitton, *The Mormon Experience*, 11.

afterwards, he and Emma moved into a two-roomed house owned by Emma's brother Jesse, and there he was able to commence the work of translation with either his wife or Harris acting as scribes.[27] Smith accomplished the translation by means of the Urim and Thummim which he had found together with the plates. These, according to his mother Lucy's description, were like smooth-cornered diamonds set in what looked like 'old-fashioned spectacles'.[28]

Smith had identified the language of the plates as 'Reformed Egyptian', a language unknown to archaeologists and ancient historians alike. Harris who had arrived in Harmony in February 1828, therefore, wanted some assurance that Joseph was interpreting the characters on the plates correctly. Harris appears to have visited several prominent academics, the most distinguished being Charles Anthon of Columbia College in New York. Anthon had added 4,000 entries, many relating to Egypt, to John Lampriere's earlier *Classical Dictionary*.[29] The precise events of this meeting are shrouded by a medley of conflicting accounts. Martin Harris reported that he gave Anthon copies of both the characters and Joseph's translation of them. Anthon then stated that the characters were Egyptian, Chaldaic and Arabic and gave Harris 'a certificate certifying to the people of Palmyra that they were true characters, and that the translation of such of them as had been translated was also correct'.[30] Harris was on the point of departing when Anthon questioned him regarding the origin of the plates. On being informed that an angel had directed Smith to locate them, he asked for the certificate and tore it up. One problem with Harris' version is that the characters on Anthon's transcript are still undecipherable. Either Anthon was making a pretence of knowing or Harris was confused.

Harris' wife, Lucy, was sceptical about the translation and so, in order to quell her doubts, Martin persuaded Smith to allow him to take the first 116 pages to Palmyra. Somehow the manuscript disappeared from Harris' home. Some have theorised that Lucy Harris

27  Smith, *Pearl of Great Price*, 2:61–2.
28  R.L. Bushman, *Joseph Smith and the Beginnings of Mormonism*, 82.
29  Ibid. 87.
30  J. Smith, *History of the Church*, 1:20.

stole them with a view to examining discrepancies between the first and second translation. Whatever the intention, the missing document was never found and a distraught Joseph exclaimed: 'I have lost my soul; I have lost my soul.'[31]

The autumn of 1828 was a dark period for Joseph. His infant son Alvin died just a few days after Emma had given birth and as usual money was in short supply. But somehow in the midst of these disappointments, Joseph resumed the translation work once more. Emma did most of the translation though she stated that sometimes her brother Reuben helped in the matter. Unlike Harris she had little difficulty in accepting the genuineness of her husband's work. When in later years Joseph III asked if his father could have memorised the manuscript which he was dictating, Emma replied that at that time he 'could neither write nor dictate a coherent well worded letter; let alone dictating a book like the *Book of Mormon*'.[32]

Progress on the translation was slow until Joseph and Emma were joined by Oliver Cowdery, a young unmarried school teacher from Vermont. He soon gained their confidence and set to work in earnest to act as scribe. 'Day after day, I continued uninterrupted', Cowdery later recalled in 1834, 'to write from his mouth, as he translated from the Urim and Thummim.'[33] By mid-May 1830, the translators reached 3 Nephi which relates the visit of Jesus Christ to the Nephites, the principal group of people described in the *Book of Mormon* as being the ancient settlers of the American continent. One day, as Joseph and Oliver were out walking and discussing the implications of Jesus' ministry among the Nephites, an angel came to them. He said he was John the Baptist and that he had been sent by Peter, James and John. By the laying on of hands he conferred on them the priesthood of Aaron which held the keys of the ministering of angels, and of the gospel of repentance, and of the baptism by immersion for the remission of sins.[34] The same messenger told Oliver and Joseph that they were also to be given to the higher Melchizedek priesthood which carried with it the power to lay on hands for the gift of the Holy Ghost. They were directed to baptise

[31]  Arrington and Bitton, *The Mormon Experience*, 91.
[32]  Bushman, *Joseph Smith*, 96.
[33]  Smith, *Pearl of Great Price*, 2:69.
[34]  Ibid.

and ordain one another, which they did, and the spirit of prophecy came on each in turn.[35] Joseph stood up and prophesied concerning the rise of the Church and many other related matters as well as predictions regarding his own generation.[36]

In June 1829 Peter Whitmer invited Smith and Cowdery to complete the work of translation at his home in Fayette, some seven miles south-east of Geneva. The Whitmers were German Pennsylvanians and members of the German Reformed Church. David Whitmer, one of Peter's sons, had earlier been acquainted with Cowdery through business connections and had become interested in the plates. As the translation was nearing completion, they came to a passage in 2 Nephi 27:12 where it is stated that 'the book shall be hid from the eyes of the world, that the eyes of none shall behold it save it be that three witnesses shall behold it, by the power of God, besides him to whom the book shall be delivered; and they shall testify to the truth of the book and the things therein'. Cowdery, Whitmer's son David, and Harris, who had joined them all, begged that they might be the privileged ones. Joseph asked for a revelation and when nothing happened Harris offered to leave. The remaining three knelt together and within minutes an angel appeared with the plates in his hands. Whitmer recalled the angel's words: 'David blessed is the Lord, and he that keeps his commandments.'[37] Joseph later found Martin Harris in a woodland nearby, and prayed with him and together they saw the plates. Martin exclaimed: ''Tis enough; 'tis enough; mine eyes have beheld.'[38] The testimony of the three witnesses is printed at the front of every copy of the *Book of Mormon*. Their testimony provided strong support for Joseph for it meant that he no longer had the emotional burden of being the sole witness to the existence of the plates and the authenticity of the translation. As things turned out, Whitmer and Cowdery were charged by their fellow Mormons as thieves and counterfeiters. Additionally, Martin Harris later professed to have seen the plates only 'with the eye of faith'. All three witnesses were later excommunicated from the Church, though Cowdery and Harris were

---

[35] Ibid. 2:72–3.
[36] Ibid. 2:73.
[37] Bushman, *Joseph Smith*, 106.
[38] Ibid.

eventually rebaptised and reinstated.[39] Although none of the trio ever went back on their accounts, the Church later felt it was important to have further witnesses. Accordingly another eight were selected. It has been noted that among the eight were Whitmer and Hiram. Page was married to one of Peter Whitmer's daughters, and three, Joseph Smith Snr, Hyrum Smith and Samuel H. Smith, were all members of the prophet's family. All eight testified that Smith 'has shown unto us the plates of which hath been spoken, which have the appearance of gold'. They went on to assert that they did handle them 'with our hands'.[40]

## Publication

On 26 March 1830 the first printed edition of the *Book of Mormon* was put on sale in a Palmyra bookshop. Its publication made Joseph Smith a minor national figure and soon the Rochester and New York newspapers were causing no small stir by dubbing Joseph as a full-blown religious impostor. The Palmyran *Reflector* called it 'priestcraft' and *The Rochester Daily Advertiser* stated that the book 'partakes largely of Salem witchcraftism'.[41] The Smith family appear to have taken little interest in the press reports and neither Joseph nor Lucy make any reference to them in their histories. Inevitably Joseph worried about the lost 116 pages. The preface of the *Book of Mormon* stated that he had been instructed not to retranslate that part 'for Satan . . . would stir up the hearts of this generation, that they might not receive this work'.

The *Book of Mormon* is named after Moroni's father, an ancient American soldier-historian. It tells the story of various ancient people groups who established themselves in the American continent. In particular it recounts two great waves of emigration from the land of Israel. The first of these is recounted in the book of Ether as the nation of the Jaredites. They left the region around the Tower of Babel about 2,250 BC. Jared's brother who was a prophet, was told by the Lord to build eight barges for the ocean trip. His

---

[39]  Brodie, *No Man Knows*, 78.
[40]  See 'The Testimony of the Eight Witnesses', the *Book Of Mormon*.
[41]  Bushman, *Joseph Smith*, 112.

instructions specified that they were to be as long as a tree, and were to be made exceedingly tight, even that they would hold water like unto a dish (Ether 2:17). When Jared's father informed the Lord that there would not be sufficient air in the barges to allow the occupants to breathe, the Lord gave the following instruction:

> Behold, thou shalt make a hole in the top, and also in the bottom; and when thou shalt suffer for air then shalt unstop the hole and receive the air. And if it shall be that the water come in upon thee, behold ye shall stop up the hole that ye may not perish in the flood (Ether 2:20).

These eight barges were driven by the wind for 344 days and landed simultaneously at a point on the west coast of Central America. Here in a new environment the Jaredites founded a widespread civilisation and built many cities. The text of the book of Ether informed us that 'they also had horses and asses and there were elephants and cureloms and cumoms' (Ether 9:9). The Jaredites did not get along together too well and they engaged in a number of savage battles in one of which two million mighty men, plus their wives and children were slain (Ether 15:2)! The devastating conflict continued to rage with such fury that finally there were only two warriors left alive, Coriantamur and Shiz. The last tragic struggle in which Shiz was killed is charted as follows:

> And it came to pass that after he (Coriantamur) had smitten off the head of Shiz, that Shiz raised upon his hands and fell; and after that he had struggled for breath, he died (Ether 15:31).

The second and more important emigration to America began in 600 BC in the Holy Land as a small band of Israelites made their escape from Jerusalem shortly before the Babylonian invasion. Under divine guidance Lehi and his followers travelled to the Indian Ocean where they constructed a ship somewhat superior to the Jaredite barges (1 Nephi 18). With the aid of a compass (1 Nephi 18:12) they navigated a safe passage to the west coast of South America.

Of the sons of Lehi, the most prominent were Nephi and Lehi. Nephi's descendants (the Nephites) grew strong and migrated to North America. Here they founded a great civilisation and built

large cities. In AD 34 Jesus Christ appeared to them, preached the
Sermon on the Mount in King James English and instituted the
sacraments. In AD 385 another terrible conflict ensued, this time
between the Lamanites and the Nephites. The two groups assembled in final conflict near the hill of Cumorah which is located by
present-day Saints in Upper New York State. In this battle the
Lamanites killed all the Nephites except one, Moroni, whose
father's name was Mormon. Mormon had inscribed the history of
his people on golden plates and hidden them in the hillside shortly
before the battle of Cumorah. It was these, so the Church of Jesus
Christ of Latter-day Saints claims, Joseph Smith discovered 1400
years later in 1823–27.

Clearly the *Book of Mormon* was a history of the Indians. Indeed
Lucy Smith, while journeying to visit her brother Stephen Mack in
Detroit in 1831, informed a fellow traveller that the book was 'a
record of the origin of the Aborigines of America'.[42] The scheme
which the book sets out is very different from that of the Bible. Of
particular significance is its indication that Christianity was practised
among the Israelites before Jesus was born. The Nephites practised
baptism and other Christian ordinances hundreds of years before
the incarnation. There is no clear distinction between the Old and
New Testaments. Joseph Smith's Jews are called 'Christians' while
adhering to the Mosaic Law, keeping the Sabbath holy and
worshipping in temples whose altars are served by their high priests.

Joseph Smith claimed that the *Book of Mormon* was 'the most
correct of any book on earth, and the keystone of our religion', and
'a man would get nearer to God by abiding by its precepts, than by
any other book'.[43] Certainly it was very popular among the converts
of New England. Parley Bratt, one of the early leaders, wrote that
'as I read, the spirit of the Lord was upon me, and I knew and
comprehended that the book was true, as plainly and manifestly as a
man comprehends and knows that he exists'.[44] Samuel Smith
distributed copies of the book in the towns near Palmyra. Among
those who received one were the wife of John P. Greene, a Methodist preacher in Bloomington. Both Mr and Mrs Greene felt the

[42]  Ibid. 133.
[43]  Smith, *History of the Church*, 4:461.
[44]  Bushman, *Joseph Smith*, 141.

book had the testimony of truth and, followed by Mrs Greene's brothers Phineas and Brigham Young, joined the Church.

## Doctrine and Covenants

Although the *Book of Mormon* contains much in the way of new doctrine, it endorses the virgin birth, the divine sonship of Jesus and his baptism by John, Jesus' ministry of teaching and healing, his atoning death on the cross and his triumphant resurrection. The main aspects concerning the new church's structure, leadership and mission were received in a form of direct revelations by Joseph. They were collected together in what was called the *Book of Commandments*. This volume which contained more than sixty revelations was later revised and enlarged with additional material and became the *Doctrine and Covenants*. It was first published in 1835 and accepted as scripture by the Church.[45] The revelations included the calling of the Quorum of the Twelve Apostles and the Quorum of the Seventy, the organisation and duties of priesthood and tithing. It also contains the 'word of wisdom' that members of the Church should abstain from drinking tea or coffee. This includes Coca Cola although some Latter-day Saints do drink decaffeinated Cola and coffee. On 19 January 1841 it was also revealed to Joseph that he should build a temple at Nauvoo along with a House of Entertainment for strangers.[46] It was in this Illinois town that Smith preached a sermon on 1 Corinthians 15:29 in which he introduced the doctrine of baptism for the dead. This ceremony was to take place in the temple when it was completed. Present-day members of the Latter-day Saints now spend considerable time and money in searching out the details of their dead forbears so that they can be baptised on their behalf. In this way ancestors who did not have the opportunity of embracing the Church's ordinances are catered for.

In present-day Mormon organisation there is at least one temple in each region. Three main ordinances in addition to baptism for the dead take place in the temples: washings and anointings, endowments of priesthood and eternal marriage. Some aspects of

---

[45] J. Smith, *Doctrine and Covenants*, 1:37–9.
[46] Ibid. 124:23 and 31.

these ceremonies are based on the Masonic rituals which Joseph first learned when he joined the Freemasons. Latter-day Saints, it should be noted, believe that these sacred rites were received by revelation. A Masonic lodge was established in Nauvoo early in 1842 and Joseph was initiated on 15 March. In his *History of the Church*, Smith relates that he first instructed his apostles about endowments less than two months later.[47] These links and further associations with the occult are explored by William Schnoebelen in his book *The Mormon Temple of Doom* published in 1986.[48] Schnoebelen was for a time both a Master Mason, a Wiccan High Priest and a member of the Mormon Church. When he went with his wife to Salt Lake City to 'take out our endowments' in the temple,[49] his occult background 'made my view of the temple ceremony radically different from that of most other Mormons'.[50] He reports that the Salt Lake Temple alone had an 'All-seeing eye', an eye in a triangle surrounded by rays of light, symbols of the witch goddess Artemis, pentagrams which are the universal symbol of witchcraft, and a hexagram or six-pointed star with a circle, the symbol of antichrist.

Section 132 of *Doctrine and Covenants* contains Smith's revelation that marriage can be extended beyond the grave for eternity. In 'Celestial Marriage', as it is termed, partners are reunited after the resurrection. Schnoebelen describes the ritual as including stripping, washing and anointing after which he was dressed in a one-piece temple garment which extended to just below the knees. It had Masonic markings of sacred significance stitched over the left and right breast, the navel and the knee. In the Celestial Room women's faces were veiled in a way that is similar to Wicca.[51]

The *Pearl of Great Price* which is bound together with *Doctrine and Covenants* is also regarded as part of Mormon scripture. It contains the King James translation of Matthew 24, some further accounts of Joseph's early years and the writings of Abraham while he was in Egypt. This latter document was Smith's translation of papyri which he purchased for more than $2,000 dollars. It became known as the

---

[47]  Smith, *History of the Church*, 4:552.
[48]  W. Schnoebelen, *The Mormon Temple of Doom*.
[49]  Ibid. 7.
[50]  Ibid.
[51]  Ibid. 11–12 and 32–3.

*Book of Abraham*. The originals turned up in New York's Metropolitan Museum in 1967 but their translation differed widely from that produced by Joseph.

## Westward Ho and the Great Trek

The month following the publication of the *Book of Mormon*, Smith and his circle of followers formed themselves into an official Church on 6 April 1830 at Fayette in New York State. Originally called 'The Church of Christ' their name was finalised in 1838 as the 'Church of Jesus Christ of Latter-day Saints'. It was a time when immigrants were pushing westward and early Mormon missionaries to the Indian settlements had stopped at Kirtland, Ohio, which they reported to be a good place. In the spring of 1831 Joseph Smith and other New York Mormons settled in the town forming a church of about a hundred members. By the summer of 1835 they had expanded to nearly 2,000. A new temple was dedicated there on 27 March 1836.[52] The occasion was glorious and Smith and Oliver Cowdery 'saw the Lord standing upon the breastwork of the pulpit'.[53] After this vision 'Moses appeared before us, and committed unto us the keys of gathering Israel from the four parts of the earth',[54] followed by Elias and Elijah.[55] Joseph was deeply struck by the occasion and later wrote in his history:

> A noise was heard like the sound of a rushing mighty wind, which filled the Temple, and all the congregation simultaneously arose, being moved upon by an invisible power; many began to speak in tongues and prophesy; others saw glorious visions; and I beheld the Temple was filled with angels, which fact I declared to the congregation. The people of the neighbourhood came running together (hearing an unusual sound within, and seeing a bright light like a pillar of fire resting upon the Temple), and were astonished at what was taking place. This continued until the meeting closed at eleven.[56]

---

[52] Smith, *Doctrine and Covenants*, 109:2–5.
[53] Ibid. 110:2.
[54] Ibid. 110:11.
[55] Ibid. 110:12–13.
[56] Smith, *History of the Church*, 2:428.

Smith's vision was that Ohio might become a kind of earthly Zion. Sadly, persecution followed his people both here and in other places further west where they sought to establish themselves. Some of it was stirred and provoked by the historic denominational churches who resented the growing expansion of the Saints. A major cause of the opposition in Kirtland, however, was the bank Smith had formed in order to raise money for the new temple. Many investors found that they were unable to redeem the bank-notes which had been issued to them. A $1,000 fine for illegal trading was imposed on Smith who ran up debts of around $150,000. As a result of this, five of the original apostles parted company with Smith, three of their number forming a separate Church. This, together with mob violence against them, including house burnings, caused the Mormons to abandon their foothold in Ohio.

While these events were taking place, Mormonism was extending its influence further west into Missouri. By the summer of 1838, Smith and the bulk of his circle established themselves at Far West City in that state.[57] Once again persecution ensued and in order to protect their interests some of their members formed a paramilitary branch known as the Danites. Their leader urged them to 'waste away the Gentiles by robbing and plundering them of their property, and in this way we will build up the Kingdom of God'.[58] Although Smith was not himself party to the maraudings of the Danites and later denounced them, their skirmishes provoked widespread fear. Smith himself and some of the other leaders were put into Liberty gaol in March 1839.[59] Matters came to a head when, on 27 October 1838, the Missouri State Governor, Liliburn Boggs, pronounced that Mormons must be treated as enemies and must be exterminated or driven from the city. While Smith remained incarcerated, Brigham Young led the Mormon settlers back across the Mississippi and settled them in the Illinois village of Commerce, which they renamed Nauvoo, a Hebrew word which means 'beautiful'.[60] It was here that yet another temple was built and Joseph announced the rite of eternal marriage and more

---

[57]  Smith, *Doctrine and Covenants*, 117:1–5.
[58]  R. Tucker, *Strange Gospels*, 64.
[59]  Smith, *Doctrine and Covenants*, 122.
[60]  Ibid. 124, and Smith, *History of the Church*, 3:175.

controversially received the revelation about plural marriage in July 1843. Set out in *Doctrine and Covenants* 132, it reads as follows:

> And again, as pertaining to the law of the priesthood – if any man espouse a virgin, and desire to espouse another, and the first give her consent, and if he espouse the second, and they are virgins, and have vowed to no other man, then is he justified; he cannot commit adultery for they are given unto him; for he cannot commit adultery with that that belongeth unto him and to no one else. And if he have ten virgins given unto him by this law, he cannot commit adultery, for they belong to him, and they are given unto him; therefore is he justified.[61]

This directive caused some confusion because it ran contrary to the categoric teaching of the *Book of Mormon* that 'there shall not any man among you have save it be one wife'.[62] Additionally it seems clear that Joseph had probably married a number of women prior to 1843. The evidence for this is suggested by earlier sections of the same revelation:

> And let mine handmaid, Emma Smith, receive all that those that have been given unto my servant Joseph, and who are virtuous and poor before me . . . And I command mine handmaid, Emma Smith, to abide and cleave unto my servant Joseph, and to none else. But if she will not abide this commandment she shall be destroyed, saith the Lord; for I am the Lord thy God, and will destroy her if she abide not in my law.[63]

Some writers have suggested that he began this practice as early as 1831.[64] His first plural wife was Fanny Alger, a young woman of nineteen, who had come to live in the Smith household to help Emma with domestic tasks.[65] Estimates of the number of Smith's plural wives vary from Andrew Jensen's figure of twenty-seven to Fawn Brodie's forty-eight.[66] Part of the reasoning behind the

---

[61] Ibid. 132:61–2.
[62] Thomas and Thomas, *Mormonism*, 93.
[63] Smith, *Doctrine and Covenants*, 132:52 and 54.
[64] Tucker, *Strange Gospels*, 65.
[65] Ibid. 65.
[66] Ibid. 67.

practice of polygamy may well have been to increase the number of Latter-day Saints. Certainly there are suggestions of this in Joseph's lengthy revelation. The fact was, however, that proselytising had already increased Nauvoo to a city of 11,000 inhabitants. Arrington and Bitton suggested that by 1844 as many as 35,000 people may well have joined the church.

Smith's revelation and practice of plural marriage was a cause of sharp dissention among Mormon leaders, some of whom pronounced against it in 1835.[67] Equally serious, it provoked strong and bitter hostility from non-believing inhabitants of Illinois.[68] Warrants were issued for Joseph's arrest and appeals were made to the government to take action. The *Nauvoo Expositor*, a newspaper established by dissident Mormons, condemned the prophet's licentiousness. In response, Joseph had the printing offices set on fire and hounded the editor out of town. From this point on Joseph's days were numbered. The State militia were called out and the governor of Illinois persuaded Joseph to give himself up and he was imprisoned in Carthage gaol. He died there together with his brother Hyrum in a gun battle when an angry mob stormed the prison on 27 July 1844.

## First Mission to England

Many of those who joined the Mormon ranks, particularly in Canada, were English and they were naturally anxious to share their new gospel with their relatives in the old country. The first mission arrived by ship at Liverpool on 29 July 1837, led by two of the Twelve Apostles. A second venture followed in 1840 with its leaders including Heber Kimball and Brigham Young. Their endeavours were greeted with widespread enthusiasm. By 1838 when a second conference was held in Preston, English membership counted nearly 1,500 adherents and twenty congregations.[69]

---

[67] Ibid. 65.
[68] R.L. Jensen and M.R. Thorp, *Mormons in Early Victorian Britain*, 69.
[69] Ibid. 77.

The second mission achieved even more spectacular results. By April 1841 it had established churches in almost all the major cities and towns of the kingdom, baptised more than 5,000 souls, printed 5,000 copies of the *Book of Mormon*, 3,000 hymn books and 2,000 volumes of *The Millennial Star*.[70] Much of this success was attributable to the unceasing efforts of charismatic individuals such as Brigham Young and Wilford Woodruff. The latter gave the following summary of his endeavours in southern England in 1840:

> I travelled 4,469 miles, held 230 meetings, established 53 places for preaching, and planted 47 churches and jointly organised them. The baptisms of the year were 336 persons under my own hands, and I assisted at the baptism of 86 others. I baptised 57 preachers mostly connected with the United Brethren, but also two clerks of the Church of England.[71]

Mormon missionaries achieved much of their success because they demonstrated genuine compassion for the working classes and were forthright in their condemnation of the evils of the Industrial Revolution. The call to go up to Zion in Nauvoo offered a prospect of hope and a better way of living. Between 1837 and 1846 there were 17,849 baptisms. Of these more than 4,700 converts journeyed to the United States and joined the Mormon community in Nauvoo.[72] Returning missionaries accompanied some of the early emigrants. Later, in 1849, a plan was established to provide assistance to those who were unable to meet the necessary expenditure. By 1870 more than 38,000 who left the British Isles had been assisted. So widespread was the response to emigrate that Latter-day Saints membership in Britain fell from over 30,000 in 1850 to a mere 2,770 in 1890. M. and A. Thomas noted that if Mormons had not been encouraged to gather in the American Zion, the Church today might have been regarded as European rather than American.[73]

---

[70] Ibid. 88.
[71] Thomas and Thomas, *Mormonism*, 53.
[72] Arrington and Bitton, *The Mormon Experience*, 129.
[73] Thomas and Thomas, *Mormonism*, 54.

## Brigham Young and the Great Trek

After Smith's death, there were rival claims to the leadership between Sidney Rigdon and Brigham Young (1801–77). The latter made his plea on the grounds that he was president of the Twelve and on this basis an assembly of the faithful recognised his rights to power. There were, however, a number of rival Mormon factions. The largest to emerge was The Reorganised Church of Jesus Christ of Latter-day Saints. Led by Smith's first wife Emma, they established the headquarters at Independence, Missouri. Their presidents are descendants of Joseph Smith, starting with his son Joseph Smith III. In 1989 it had a membership of a quarter of a million. It is much more like a Protestant Church and sees the *Book of Mormon* as merely reflecting nineteenth-century thought. The Church's liberal attitude was particularly seen when their chief prophet received a revelation opening the priesthood to women.

Despite the presence of a new man at the helm, the Saints continued to be in conflict with their 'Gentile' neighbours and in 1845 plans were soon in hand to move out to the Great Basin in the Rocky Mountains. Thousands of Latter-day Saints struggled to sell their farms and homes and acquire a solid wagon and supplies to sustain them for the thousand-mile journey. In February 1846 they commenced what proved to be one of the greatest migrations of history, arriving in the Salt Lake Valley in the summer of 1847. In doing so, they had moved themselves so far beyond the American frontier that there would be no significant groups of other settlers for three generations. During this 'exodus' the 80,000 trekkers faced harsh winter weather and a lack of supplies. Several hundred died during the journey.

Young proved himself to be a charismatic leader with immense powers of influence, control, organisational ability and vision. Stanley Hirshon wrote of him as 'a marvel of his age: the husband of seventy wives, the father of fifty-six children, the coloniser of vast areas of the West, the Yankee prophet of God, the Moses of the modern children of Israel, the religious imperialist bent upon conquering the world'.[74] The boundaries of the new settlement embraced some 210,000 square miles covering the whole of

---

[74] S. Hirshon, *The Lion of the Lord*, 3, cited Tucker, *Strange Gospels*, 79.

present-day Nevada, the western half of Utah and large areas of several adjoining States. Young put in place an organisation for the new settlement. There was a High Council of Twelve and a division into nine territorial wards or congregations. Salt Lake City was planned out with 135 blocks of 10 acres and roads 135 ft wide intersecting one another. The Great Temple was erected at a central focal point. When Young died he left behind a highly developed community and Church. After his time, the movement became less dominated by single presidents with a leadership of an overbearing or despotic nature. Young was succeeded by John Taylor (d. 1887) who had been badly wounded when Smith had been murdered. He in turn was followed by Wilford Woodruff (1814–98) who was able in 1890 to persuade the Saints to give up the practice of plural wives in accordance with the Federal Government's requirements. This paved the way for Utah to be granted statehood in 1896. These days plural wives are eschewed by mainline Latter-day Saints.

## Recent Developments and Organisational Structures

Since these nineteenth-century beginnings the Latter-day Saints have expanded their numbers rapidly. Today their churches can be found on every continent in the world and their global membership is growing at 5 per cent a year. This rapid expansion, which easily outrivals that of many evangelical denominations, results from a number of appealing features. Their numerous missionaries are well trained, equipped with literature and supported by the local churches. Usually there are in excess of 1,500 active full-time church workers based in the UK in any one year.

There is no shortage of money as the Church of Jesus Christ of Latter-day Saints requires all of its members to comply with the Old Testament practice of tithing. James Talmage in his pamphlet *The Lord's Tenth* wrote as follows:

The Latter-day Saints profess to be observers of the law of the tithe. The requirement thus made of them is not directly based upon the fact that tithe-paying was part of the Mosaic code, but because the law has been re-established in the Church in this dispensation of restoration and fullness[75]

Apart from executive officers Church leaders are unpaid and so most of this money is invested in new buildings and Church-planting activities.

The Latter-day Saints have a well-organised welfare scheme which enables them to assist in the region of 100,000 needy people a year. Many thousands of dollars are raised for this purpose through the 'Fast Offerings' already mentioned.

Members of the Latter-day Saints are encouraged to adopt a thrifty lifestyle and to keep a year's supply of canned food in case their family should fall on hard times. One of the local Mormon bishop's key responsibilities is that of administering the church's welfare provision. In England this has been a growing emphasis. In 1980 the Presiding Bishopric set up the first Bishop's Storehouse to provide food, clothing and other supplies to members who fall on hard times. Other Bishop's Storehouses were opened in Glasgow, Sheffield, Stevenage, Bristol, Reading and Crawley. The Church has also invested heavily in farmland and in 1995 was one of the top ten owners of British farmland.[76] Latter-day Saints Welfare Service include unemployment centres, counselling and a licensed adoption society.

Another attractive aspect of the Latter-day Saints is their strong emphasis on the family. Every Monday evening all Church buildings are closed and no meetings are permitted. As already mentioned, families are expected to be at home together in an informal context to share recreational and fun activities.

In view of all this it is no surprise that the Church is continuing to grow rapidly. Polls by British newspapers show the Mormon Church to be among the fastest growing in the country. By the 150th anniversary of the Latter-day Saints in the UK, there were 140,000 members.

Although the Latter-day Saints are essentially a sectarian movement, their organisational structure is distinctly churchlike. In short the Church is a hierarchy with international executives at the top

---

[75] J. Talmage, *The Lord's Tenth*, 7.
[76] Thomas and Thomas, *Mormonism*, 64.

and national and local leaders serving below them. The head of the Church is the President and Chief Prophet under whom are twelve apostles. The new Chief Prophet is always the longest serving and therefore the most senior of the apostles. The twelve function primarily as prophets, seers and revelators. The President who is always a man holds office for life. He is expected to continue receiving fresh revelations from God, an aspect many new members find particularly appealing. Below the twelve, there is a Council of Seventy whose responsibility is to oversee the Church's work on a global basis. For administrative purposes the Latter-day Saints have divided the world into about 20 'areas'. Each area is split into regions such as, for example, the East Anglia region in England. Each region is further subdivided into 'stakes' which consist of about ten congregations. Within any given 'stake' there are a number of individual congregations known as 'branches' or 'wards'. One member of the Seventy has particular responsibility for the UK region. Unlike other Mormon leaders, the First Quorum of Seventy serve the Church in a full-time capacity with each major region of the world supervised by three of its members.

At the more local level the 'stake', which is roughly the size of an Anglican diocese, is under the direction of a 'Stake Presidency' which consists of three men. They in turn are assisted by a council of twelve men. In Latter-day Saints' thinking the three correspond to Peter, James and John and the twelve to the council of the twelve apostles. The Stake Patriarch chairs the Stake Presidency and has the additional role of giving patriarchal blessings to members of the Stake. The members of the Stake Presidency are not chosen by election, rather they are 'called' to office. Stakes are further subdivided into 'Wards' which approximate to local parish churches. Each Mormon Ward has its own bishop who is appointed to lead the local congregation for a period of approximately five years. Full-time missionaries are based in the local Ward and congregations support and encourage them in their work.

## Mormon Articles of Faith

The Latter-day Saints clearly offer alternative teachings to those of the Roman Catholic and Protestant denominations. Nevertheless there are also similarities since 27,000 words and many complete verses in the *Book of Mormon* are identical with the King James Bible.

## The Doctrine of Revelation

Mormons believe that further truth for the Latter-day Saints has come through Joseph Smith. They regard his writings the *Book of Mormon, Doctrine and Covenants* and the *Pearl of Great Price* as God's word. Additionally the Presidents may receive further revelation which can be added to *Doctrine and Covenants*. Joseph Smith himself declared:

> We have what we have, and the Bible contains what it does contain: but to say that God never said anything more to man than is there recorded, would be saying at once that we have at last received a revelation: for it must require one to advance thus far, because it is nowhere said in that volume by the mouth of God, that He would not, after giving what is there contained speak again.[77]

Historic Christianity agrees that God still continues to speak to men and women in a 'rich variety of ways' but never in contradiction or addition to the biblical canon. The mainline denominational Churches take the view that the Scriptures of the Old and New Testaments are God's final revelation and no further truths will be added to them.

## The Doctrine of God

Mormons believe in a plurality of Gods but they assert that only one God organised and formed the heavens and the earth.[78] There are many Gods besides God the Father who was himself created; indeed he was once a man. Joseph Smith emphatically stated: 'God himself was once as we are now, and is an exalted man, and sits enthroned in yonder heavens.'[79] Latter-day Saints see God in a strongly human and physical way. *Doctrine and Covenants* is clear that 'the Father has

---

[77] J.F. Smith, *The Teachings of the Prophet Joseph Smith*.
[78] Abraham 4:1.
[79] Smith, *The Teachings*, 345.

a body of flesh and bones as tangible as man's; the son also but the Holy Ghost has not a body of flesh and bones, but is a personage of the Spirit. Were it not so, the Holy Ghost could not dwell in us.'[80] Again Smith was adamant that if we were suddenly to be able to see God today 'you would see him like a man in form'.[81] In most depictions of Joseph Smith's first vision of the Godhead, two personages in human form appear above him in the sky.

For the Mormons, salvation is essentially a process of graduating from manhood to godhood. Joseph Smith wrote in his *Journal of Discourses*: 'Here, then, is eternal life – to know the only wise and true God; and you have got to learn how to be Gods yourselves . . . by going up from one small degree to another, and from a small capacity to a great one.'[82]

In theory this means that the difference between God and men and women is essentially one of degrees. Salvation is a gradual process of climbing up a ladder of perfection assisted by trust in Jesus, baptism and the temple ordinances.

## *Christology*

Some of the early Mormon leaders had very different ideas about Jesus compared with the New Testament teaching. Orson Pratt, for example, maintained that Jesus was married at Cana of Galilee and that Martha and Mary and others were his wives and that he had children.[83] However, *Gospel Principles*, a standard teaching text, affirms that Jesus was born supernaturally of the Virgin Mary and that he came to demonstrate the way to live.[84] He died to redeem us from our sins and save us from death.[85] Mormon sources also stress that Jesus was the creator before his birth and 'created this world and everything in it . . . under the direction of our Heavenly Father'.[86]

---

[80] Smith, *Doctrine and Covenants*, 130:22.
[81] Smith, *The Teachings*, 345.
[82] Smith, *Journal of Discourses*, 6:4.
[83] Ibid. 2:210.
[84] *Gospel Principles*, 59–63.
[85] Ibid. 61.
[86] Ibid. 23. See also Le G. Richards, *A Marvellous Work and a Wonder*, 280–81.

Jesus was appointed to the task of saving mankind before the foundation of the world. Joseph Smith spoke of Jesus as 'the anointed Son of God' and 'the foundation that no man can lay'.[87] Nevertheless neither Smith nor any of his inner circle accepted the Protestant teaching from Martin Luther that a person can 'be saved through faith in Christ alone'. Brigham Young, for example, wrote:

> Joseph Smith holds the keys of this last dispensation, and is now en-
> gaged behind the veil in the great work of the last days. No man or
> woman in this dispensation will ever enter into the celestial Kingdom
> of God without the consent of Joseph Smith . . . every man and woman
> must have the certificate of Joseph Smith junior, as a passport to their
> entrance into the mansion where God and Christ are . . . I cannot go
> there without his consent. He holds the keys of that Kingdom for the
> last dispensation – the Keys to rule in the spirit world.[88]

Smith's view was that mere faith in Jesus was insufficient; it had to go hand in hand with obedience. This obedience included baptism which is essential for entry into the celestial Kingdom.[89] Smith interpreted Jesus' words in John 3 that we need to 'be born of water' to mean that baptism is essential for salvation.[90] Articles 3 and 4 of *The Articles of the Church of Jesus Christ of Latter-day Saints* make these point clearly:

> 3. We believe that through the Atonement of Christ, all mankind may
> be saved, by obedience to the laws and ordinances of the Gospel.

> 4. We believe that the first principles and ordinances of the Gospel are:
> first, Faith in the Lord Jesus Christ; second, Repentance; third, Bap-
> tism by immersion for the remission of sins; fourth, Laying on of hands
> for the gift of the Holy Ghost.

Baptism for Mormons should not take place before the person has reached the age of eight. Prior to that time it is felt that children are not able to take full responsibility for their actions nor are they

---

[87] Smith, *The Teachings*, 265.
[88] B. Young, *Journal of Discourses*, 7:189.
[89] Smith, *The Teachings*, 311.
[90] Ibid. 314.

able to grasp essential teachings. Baptism is by full immersion and in the name of the Father, the Son and the Holy Spirit. Mormons are not only baptised for themselves but, as already mentioned, they may be baptised vicariously on behalf of their deceased relatives in the hope that they may gain entry into the celestial Kingdom. Joseph Smith mentioned this doctrine while preaching at the funeral of Brother Seymour Brunson: 'The Saints have the privilege of being baptised for those of their relatives who are dead, whom they believe would have embraced the Gospel, if they had been privileged with hearing it.'[91]

### Eschatology

The Mormon Church has detailed teaching about the end times and the final destiny of the Saints. Within the limited scope of this chapter, two important aspects need to be noted: the second coming of Jesus and the final states of heaven and hell.

The return of Jesus Christ, according to the Latter-day Saints, will be preceded by a number of signs, some of which have already been fulfilled. These include war, turmoil, wickedness, the return of Elijah, worldwide preaching of the fullness of the gospel and the building of New Jerusalem which will be in the State of Missouri in the US.[92] At the same time Latter-day Saints believe that the Israelites, God's chosen people, will be gathered out of all the countries where they had been driven. This returning will be at two levels: first spiritually and then physically. They are gathered spiritually when they join the Church of Jesus Christ of Latter-day Saints. They will also return physically and settle in the lands of their inheritance; so, for example, the tribe of Judah will be returned to the City of Jerusalem and its environs. The tribes of Ephraim and Manasseh will be gathered in America.[93]

When this gathering is completed, Jesus will return in person to cleanse the earth and to judge his people and the nations, dividing the righteous from the wicked.[94] At this point the righteous will be

---

[91] Smith, *History of the Church*, 4:226f., cited Smith, *The Teachings*, 180.

[92] See Smith, *Doctrine and Covenants*, 84:3–4.

[93] See ibid. 133.

[94] *Gospel Principles*, 266.

caught up to meet him. Jesus will then establish his thousand-year millennial reign on earth. During this period the Saints will assist him in the government of world affairs. Only the righteous will inhabit the continents during the Millennium but it should be noted that Brigham Young taught that non-Mormons will be included among them.[95]

In this thousand-year period of bliss the earth will be restored to its pre-fall original pristine condition, Satan will be bound, there will be complete peace and godly government. There will be no disease or sickness and the animal kingdom will live in harmony with itself.[96] Members of the Church of Jesus Christ of Latter-day Saints will engage in widespread mission activities and temple work in order to solemnise celestial marriage and seal the family unit, as well as helping others to secure their final destiny in the celestial Kingdom.

At the end of the thousand-year period Satan will be set free for a short period. Some of the earth's inhabitants will turn away from God, forming armies of opposition to the people of God. A climactic and final battle will ensue in which Satan and his followers will be cast out for ever. After this, the final judgement will follow and individuals 'will be assigned to the Kingdoms they have earned by the way they have lived'.

### Assignment to States of Glory

Latter-day Saints believe that individuals will be assigned to one of four destinies: the celestial Kingdom, the highest degree of glory; the terrestrial kingdom, the middle degree; the telestial kingdom, the lowest degree of glory; and 'outer darkness', or the kingdom of the devil. This concept of a graded heaven which Smith taught in *Doctrine and Covenants* 76 may possibly have been derived from the apostle Paul's statement that he knew a man who had been caught up in the third heaven.[97] In another place, Joseph stressed:

> bodies who are of the celestial kingdom may possess it forever and ever
> . . . they who are not sanctified . . . must inherit another kingdom, even

---

[95]  Ibid. 271.

[96]  Ibid. 274.

[97]  2 Corinthians 12:2.

that of a terrestrial kingdom, or that of a telestial kingdom . . . And he who cannot abide the law of a telestial kingdom . . . must abide a kingdom which is not a kingdom of glory.[98]

Beyond this there are varying states of glory within each of the three final states. This teaching, 'the doctrine of degrees of glory', Smith drew from 1 Corinthians 15:40–42 where the apostle Paul speaks of the sun, moon and the varying splendours of differing stars. Mainstream Christian Churches and New Testament commentators interpret this rather differently, believing that the point being made is a basic one, namely that resurrection bodies will differ substantially from earthly ones.

## Postscript

The Church of Jesus Christ of Latter-day Saints is clearly an extremely fast-growing religious institution. Worldwide its membership is now 10.2 million. In Britain there are 185,000 members and 430 places of worship. People are attracted by the sincerity of their young smartly dressed missionaries. Mormon care and welfare schemes are impressive for their emphasis on family life and healthy living. Others are intrigued by the Latter-day Saints continuing to receive revelation and the prospect of a bright and wholesome future beyond the grave.

There are, as already observed, a number of differences between the Latter-day Saints' teachings and those of the historic and denominational churches. For the latter, the Bible is held to contain all that is necessary to know for salvation and it is the yardstick by which all doctrine and revelations are measured. For the Latter-day Saints, there are important additional scriptures in the *Book of Mormon, Doctrine and Covenants* and the *Pearl of Great Price*. In orthodox Christianity God comes to his people as Father, Son and Holy Spirit and yet is one being. For the Latter-day Saints, God and Jesus have separate physical bodies. Mormons believe that the Church of Jesus Christ of Latter-day Saints, is the restored Church and, therefore, the only true Church whose priests are the only

---

[98] Smith, *Doctrine and Covenants*, 88:20–21 and 23–4.

legitimate priests. Without becoming a member of this Church and
receiving its ordinances, it is not possible to enter the celestial
Kingdom. Orthodox Christianity takes the view that the true
church consists of all those who acknowledge Jesus as Lord and
Saviour and live in relationship with him abiding by his teaching.
All members are regarded as priests and charged with the responsibility of reaching out to others. Again, members of the Christian
churches believe that when Christ comes again in glory all believers
will enter God's presence and not merely those who have been
'endowed' in temple rites.

In the last analysis, the most significant difference is that
Christian churches take the view that Jesus not only reveals the God
of the Old Testament in all His fullness but that he alone by his
death on the cross and resurrection has accomplished all that is
necessary for salvation. What is, therefore, required of believers is
repentance and trust in his person and his saving death. Mormons,
on the other hand, believe that 'no man or woman will ever enter
into the celestial Kingdom without the consent of Joseph Smith'.[99]
They also believe that 'Joseph Smith, Jr, will again be on this earth
dictating plans and calling forth his brethren to be baptised'.[100] The
matter was put emphatically by Joseph Fielding Smith the Church's
sixth President: 'If Joseph Smith was verily a prophet . . . then this
knowledge is of the most vital importance to the entire world. No
man can reject that testimony without incurring the most dreadful
consequences, for he cannot enter the Kingdom of God.'[101]

---

[99]  Young, *Journal of Discourses*, 7:289.
[100]  Ibid.
[101]  J. Fielding Smith, *Doctrine of Salvation*, I, 189–90.

# Chapter 7

# Christian Science

A religious organisation which does not enjoy the same high profile as do the Jehovah's Witnesses or the Latter-day Saints is Christian Science. Its committed membership is relatively small and has been declining in recent years. Most of its followers are found in the quiet leafy suburbs of middle-class towns such as Bath, Cheltenham or Leamington Spa. Its worship centres are for the most part plain and unadorned, often having the appearance of a community hall or medical centre. Not far away from the main premises, there will be a Christian Science Reading Room where members of the public can go and read the founder's writings or consult the latest issue of the *Christian Science Monitor*. Although Sunday congregations are for the most part small, there is still a steadily growing interest in health and healing. Many people are still drawn to read *Science and Health with Key to the Scriptures* and recognise the value of at least some of its principles such as maintaining that 'true consciousness is true health' and the importance of a positive attitude to life in general. The origins of Christian Science are traceable to a remarkable nineteenth-century New England woman, Mary Baker, who later took the name Mary Baker Eddy, following her third marriage to Asa Gilbert Eddy on New Year's Day, 1877.

## Mary Baker Eddy

Mary Baker Eddy was born at her father's farm on the uplands of Bow, New Hampshire on 16 July 1821. She was the youngest of six children having three brothers and two sisters. Her parents, Mark and Abigail Baker, were devoted members of the Bow Meeting

House on White Rock Hill. Her father, whose views were staunchly Calvinistic, was elected clerk of the Church. Her mother was the summer to her father's winter, the New Testament to his Old. She was later described by a close friend as 'at all times cheerful and hopeful'.[1] This was possibly the one saving grace in the midst of what was a stern religious environment dominated by her father. Sundays were a particularly strict regime and the entire family attended lengthy morning and afternoon services. Between the services no sort of relaxation was allowed, not even a walk to the cemetery. Mary later recalled: 'Father kept the family in the tightest harness I have ever known.'[2] Yet for all this she still retained some positive memories of childhood Sundays, particularly after the family moved to the First Congregational Church in Concord in 1831.

Mary's health was delicate, with the result that she missed a good deal of her schooling. She was, however, possessed of an enquiring mind and was stimulated to read and think by her brother Albert who would bring his books home from Dartmouth College during the vacations. She also had a growing appetite for the things of God. As a twelve year old, she was familiar with the Bible, wrote her own prayers and prayed seven times a day.[3]

In 1836, the Baker family moved to Sanborton, a town now called Tilton. At the age of seventeen Mary was admitted into membership of her parents' Congregational Church in that town, this despite her refusal to accept the doctrine of predestination. She remained in membership with this denomination till well after her discovery of Christian Science.[4] She wrote on one occasion: 'I love the orthodox Church; and in time, that Church will love Christian Science.'[5] In the Congregational Church, Mary Baker became a Sunday school teacher and was given charge of the infant class where she became very popular with her young pupils who were captivated by her brightness and spirited outlook on life.

---

[1] R. Peel, *Mary Baker Eddy*, I, 6.
[2] Ibid. 24.
[3] E.M. Ramsay, *Christian Science and Its Discoverer*, 9.
[4] M.B. Eddy, *Miscellaneous Writings*, 111.
[5] Peel, *Mary Baker Eddy*, I, 68.

In 1843 Mary became engaged to be married. Her fiancé, George Washington Glover, had met her twelve years earlier and said that he would come back and marry her. He had become a successful builder at Charleston, South Carolina, but now returned to New Hampshire to claim the little girl who had become an attractive young woman. They were married on 10 December the same year. Glover's firm was responsible for half the building work in Charleston and he lived in style and comfort. He was also prominent in Masonic affairs, a Royal Arch Mason, and an officer of St Andrew's Lodge. Their marriage though a happy one was short-lived, lasting only six months. Glover contracted yellow fever and died leaving poor Mary with an unborn child in South Carolina.

Mary returned to her native New Hampshire where she gave birth to a son whom she named George. The brief time away from her home state had drained Mary, both physically and emotionally and from that time on, she was never free of pain. It is therefore no surprise that she began to concern herself with issues of healing. To add to her pain, her mother died shortly after her return and a year later her father remarried. It was then arranged that she should live with family friends but they refused to allow her to bring the infant she loved so deeply with the result that he had to be cared for some forty miles away. For much of her life Mary was prevented from being with and caring for her son.

Mary Glover, although a widow and a mother, was still an extremely attractive woman. Sarah Clement recalled in later years that she was at this time 'tall, slender, and exceedingly graceful. She was altogether one of the most beautiful women I have ever seen.'[6] Among her admirers was her dentist, Dr Daniel Patterson. He was a relative of her father's second wife and knew the Bakers socially as well as professionally. Despite family reservations they were engaged on 19 April 1853 and married later the same year. Their union was not a happy one. He reneged on his promise to allow Mary's son to come and live with them on the ground that she was not strong enough to withstand his high spirits. Worse was to follow when a deliberate plot, in which her own family were involved, was formed to separate mother and son permanently. George was taken

---

[6] Sarah Clement Kimball, *Reminiscences*, cited ibid. 91.

away to Minnesota where he was informed that his mother was dead, while Mary was told that he had gone missing. Inevitably her health suffered still further and it was only her strong faith in God's goodness which enabled her to go on searching, only to be rewarded with success many years later.

During the four years which followed, Patterson was frequently away from home treating patients in other towns and villages. Mary often had only her blind maid for company and continued weak in health. The marriage lasted until 1866 when they were permanently separated. The cause of their final parting was Patterson's eloping with the wife of a prominent resident in Lynn, Massachusetts. The woman subsequently went back to her husband but Mary understandably would not consent to Daniel's return and subsequently obtained a divorce on grounds of his adultery.[7]

While her husband was away fighting in the Civil War, Mary's health remained poor and she sought every means possible to obtain a cure for her many ailments which confined her to bed. She had already come to the view that there was a law of God which, if it could be properly comprehended, would be able to release healing of every sort of physical and moral sickness. She believed Jesus had utilised such a law. Not irrationally, therefore, she began to take an interest in the reports spreading across the country of the remarkable healings effected in Maine by a man named Phineas Quimby (d. 1865). Quimby's system was based on creating wholesome moral attitudes in his patients. He believed that any sickness or disease could be dispelled by cultivating healthy attitudes and a positive mindset in place of negative thoughts. His method was to effect this by suggestion rather than the use of hypnotism, which had been earlier advocated by the German doctor Franz Anton Mesmer (1733–1815), and which he utilised for a time. Quimby believed that essentially disease resulted from a disturbed state of mind which in turn affected 'electro-nervous' fluids in the body. Quimby's writings are not always easy to interpret since he changed and modified some of his ideas. Even when he reached the view that all disease was caused by disordered thought patterns and could be treated 'mentally' he still continued to utilise magnetism to change

---

[7] Ibid.

the patient's mind. He often achieved this by rubbing or manipulating his patients with his hands. Many of them recalled experiencing a burning sensation as he did this. For this reason he was frequently known as the 'magnetic doctor'. On some occasions when Quimby administered this kind of treatment he took on the patient's pain.

Mary's husband first made contact with Quimby but the latter seemed unmoved. It was only after Mary begged Quimby to respond that he finally agreed to see her. Her letter was a desperate plea:

> Last Autumn my husband addressed you a letter respecting my case and has always been anxious for me to see you . . . I was getting well this Spring but my dear husband was taken prisoner of war by the Southerns and the shock overcame me and brought on a relapse. I want to see you above all others. I have entire confidence in your philosophy . . . Can you, will you visit me at once? I must die unless you can save me. My disease is 'chronic' and I have been unable to turn myself to be moved by any but my husband for one year at a time . . . Do come and save me.[8]

At last, in the autumn of 1862, her eldest brother Samuel and his second wife took the sickly and weakened Mary Patterson, who was suffering from severe inflammation of the spine, to the International Hotel in Portland, Maine, where Quimby had a suite of rooms in which he received his patients. Mary later recalled him as a 'healthy, dominant' and 'energetic' man with 'shrewd penetrating eyes' and a 'kindly face'. His treatment of her was preceded with little in the way of explanation. He told her 'that she was in bondage to the opinion of her family and physicians and that her animal spirit was reflecting its grief upon her body and calling it a spinal disease'.[9] During the course of these terse remarks Quimby looked her full in the eyes and then proceeded to dip his hands in water and rub her head violently, presumably to impart electricity which was in turn to have a positive influence on the

---

[8] J. Silberger Jnr, *Mary Baker Eddy: An Interpretive Biography of the Founder of Christian Science*, 22, cited R. Tucker, *Strange Gospels*, 154.
[9] Ramsay, *Christian Science and Its Discoverer*, 44.

electro-nervous fluids in her body.[10] Mary's response to this treatment was rapid. Almost at once she felt that the weight of her pain and weakness had been lifted and replaced with a sense of well-being. In the days immediately following, she reported a rapid and continuing improvement. Despite having had severe 'spinal inflammation', in less than a week she was able to climb the 182 steps to the dome of the City Hall. Later, however, she found that her health was not lastingly improved and that some of her previous ailments were recurring.

Mary's initial reaction was one of unbounded enthusiasm and gratitude to Quimby. Shortly after her treatment she wrote a letter to the *Portland Evening Courier* in which she said: 'As he speaks as never man before spake, and heals as never a man healed since Christ, is he not identified with Truth? And is not this the Christ which is in him?'[11] Later when she came to reflect rather more critically on Quimby's methods she saw them in terms of a variation of Mesmer's techniques. Notwithstanding she still regarded him as a person of 'rare humanity and sympathy'.[12]

At the time of this early encounter Mary Patterson found it particularly hard to come to terms with Quimby's method of healing. She had been brought up in a strongly orthodox Congregational background. It was, therefore, difficult for her to reconcile influencing body fluids by suggestion techniques with the healing in Jesus' name about which she read in the New Testament. She was also mindful of the Lord's words that 'It is the spirit that quickeneth; the flesh profiteth nothing: the words that I speak unto you, they are spirit, and they are life.'[13] It was to take her many years to fit the insight she had gained from Quimby adequately into a Christian framework which stressed a transcendent God as well as one who could also be immanent, indeed present within the believer. Nevertheless she soon began to make the attempt. She went to see Dr Quimby in 1863, several times in 1864 and again in 1865. She often spent whole afternoons with him, observing his methods of treatment and discussing his case notes. Silberger suggested that during

---

[10]  Ibid. 43–4.
[11]  Peel, *Mary Baker Eddy*, I, 167.
[12]  Eddy, *Miscellaneous Writings*, 379.
[13]  Peel, *Mary Baker Eddy*, I, 165.

this period Mary developed a psychic dependence on him. Not only did she sense his spiritual presence but she saw his apparition, reporting, for example: 'Last Wed. at 12 M. I saw you in this parlour where I am now writing. You wore a hat and a dress coat.'[14]

During the years immediately following her treatment by Quimby, Mary Patterson supplemented her husband's irregular income by writing short articles for the *Lynn Weekly Reporter* and other local newspapers. She also began what was unheard of at the time, the practice of giving public lectures about her experiences and her understanding of healing. In doing so, she was not, however, making a conscious or deliberate attempt to align herself with the radical feminists of the period. She simply felt compelled to share her experiences. Notwithstanding this, Mary's health continued to have downturns and she visited Quimby in April 1865 and reported temporary relief. The following month he retired from Portland in order to be less active and in the hope of achieving some writing. He died in January 1866.

Only a matter of days after his death, on Saturday 1 February, Mary Patterson slipped on the ice at a street corner in Lynn, Massachusetts. She had been on her way with a group of friends to a meeting of the Good Templars. When they realised how badly she had been injured, she had to be carried to a nearby residence. The doctor who attended her found her 'partially unconscious, semi-hysterical, complaining of severe pain in the back of her head and neck'.[15] Accounts of her physician's diagnosis vary but it is possible that Mary had suffered some kind of spinal dislocation. At all events her friends and a local clergyman who visited her were very despondent as to her making any sort of recovery. In a letter to Julius Dresser, one of Quimby's disciples, Mary wrote: 'The physician attending said I had taken the last step I ever should.'[16] Dr Alvin Cushing, it should be noted, later made an affidavit offering a somewhat different version. His sworn statement ran as follows:

> I did not at any time declare, or believe, that there was no hope of Mrs. Patterson's recovery, or that she was in a critical condition, and did not

[14] Silberger, *Mary Baker Eddy*, 85–7, cited Tucker, *Strange Gospels*, 155.
[15] Peel, *Mary Baker Eddy*, I, 195.
[16] Ibid. 199.

at any time say, or believe that she had but three or any limited number of days to live; and Mrs. Patterson did not suggest, or say, or pretend, or in any way whatever intimate, that on the third day or any other day, of her said illness, she had miraculously recovered or been healed, or that discovering or perceiving the truth or the power employed by Christ to heal the sick, she had, by it, been restored to health.[17]

Doubtless shaken by such a gloomy prognosis, Mary who lay helpless in bed one Sunday afternoon, asked to be given a Bible and to be left on her own. She began to read Jesus' raising the palsied man in Matthew 9.[18] As she did so, the Lord's words began to flood into her mind: 'I am the Way, the Truth, and the Life: no man cometh unto the Father but by me.' Quite suddenly she was filled with the sense that her life was in God – that God was the only Life, the only 'I Am'. At that moment she was instantaneously healed.

Clearly Mary Patterson had experienced a powerful transformation in her life, yet all around her, there seemed to be material turmoil. Her physician, Dr Cushing, was alarmed at her being up and about, and she found it hard to explain to him what had taken place. Some of her friends feared she would suffer a relapse. Her marriage to Daniel Patterson was on the point of collapse and she was overly anxious about the future which lay ahead of her. At this critical moment, in an act of desperation she urged Julius Dresser to take up Quimby's mantle. He replied that 'I would be glad to help you in your trouble, but I am unable to do it.'[19] He also spoke of his demanding work and his commitments to his wife and infant son.

It was now plain to Mary that she was alone and that if she was going to remain healed herself and bring healing to others she would have to trust in the truth she had glimpsed on Sunday afternoon 2 February. 'The divine hand', she wrote, 'had led me into a new world of light and Life, a fresh universe – old to God,

---

[17] Cited A.A. Hoekema, *Christian Science*, 12. A point Hoekema does not emphasise is that Cushing's affidavits were made forty years after the event.

[18] *A Century of Christian Science Healing*, 13. Peel, *Mary Baker Eddy*, I, 197, comments that in later years Mary found it difficult to remember which passage she had read.

[19] Ibid. 199.

but new to his little one.'[20] In essence she had reached the conviction that the all-powerful, all-loving God of truth is ever present, whereas matter and material senses continually contrive to exclude that divine presence. As she put it in *Science and Health with Key to the Scriptures*:

> When apparently near the confines of mortal existence, standing already within the shadow of the death-valley, I learned these truths in divine Science: that all real being is in God, the divine Mind, and that Life, Truth, and Love are all-powerful and ever-present; that the opposite of Truth – called error, sin, sickness, disease, death, – is the false testimony of false material sense, of mind in matter; that this false sense evolves, in belief, a subjective state of mortal mind which this same so-called mind names matter, thereby shutting out the true sense of Spirit.[21]

## Science and Health with Key to the Scriptures

Following her divorce from Daniel Patterson, Mary reverted to the surname of her first husband, Glover. She now gave herself to the task of articulating the truth which had resulted in her healing of February 1866. She had previously begun to absorb the writings of both Phineas Quimby and of Francis Lieber (1800–72), a distinguished American of German origins, who was an authority on the philosophy of Hegel. Although her final system was to differ from both men in certain fundamental respects yet her writings were undeniably influenced by their ideas.

While she was boarding in a Lynn household, Mary Glover became friendly with Hiram Crafts and his wife who were also among the residents. Crafts was a shoemaker who had moved to the town in order to work in one of the factories there. His place at the meal table was next to Mary and he listened enthusiastically to her speak of the possibility of a deeper walk with God. It was what he had longed for all his life. Crafts not only sought physical healing for himself, but wanted to know how to heal others. So for his benefit

---

[20] M.B. Eddy, *Retrospection and Introspection*, 27.
[21] M.B. Eddy, *Science and Health with Key to the Scriptures*, 108.

Mary began to write out some simple principles which drew from her own experiences.

Mary's lessons to the Crafts proved to be so captivating that Hiram abandoned his plan to work in the factories of Lynn and decided instead to devote himself to the practice of Christian Science. He and his wife prevailed on Mary to live with them in their house at East Stoughton (now Avon) so that he could master the key principles. Mary remained with the Crafts for nine months after which time he opened an office in nearby Taunton and for some months supported himself and his wife as a Christian Science Practitioner. Subsequently he returned to his business of shoemaking.

Between 1866 and 1870 Mary Glover went on to reside with a number of other families who were keen to learn and experience her method of healing. These arrangements were mutually beneficial since Mary had only limited financial means at this time and would not otherwise have been able to set her thoughts down in writing. At this point in time Spiritualism was sweeping the American continent and several of those with whom she stayed in various places in Massachusetts were Spiritualists. In July 1867 Mary performed a remarkable healing on her sister Martha's daughter, Ellen Pilsburg. Her niece had lain dying of enteritis. In about ten minutes after entering the room Mary Glover told her 'to rise from her bed and walk'. She got up and walked seven times round the room and then sat down in a chair. The following day she was able to dress and share a meal. Four days later she went on a journey of about a hundred miles.[22]

In 1868 Mary Glover was tired of living with so little money and possibly for that reason decided the time was right to advertise for students. On 4 July she placed the following advertisement in the Spiritualist paper the *Banner of Light*:

Any person desiring to learn how to heal the sick can receive of the undersigned instruction that will enable them to commence healing on a principle of Science with a success far beyond any of the present modes. No medicine, electricity, physiology or hygiene required for unparalleled success in the most difficult cases. No pay required unless

---

[22] Peel, *Mary Baker Eddy*, I, 215. See also Ramsay, *Christian Science and Its Discoverer*, 64.

the skill is obtained. Address Mrs. Mary B. Glover, Amesbury, Mass., Box 61.[23]

With the passing of the months Mary was able to attract several students, some of whom began to practise what they had learned from her. By 1870 she was charging $300 for twelve lessons, though some, including clergymen, were taught for reduced fees. Although this seems a very large sum of money, it perhaps needs to be remembered that on completing the course her students were able to set themselves up as healers and charge fees which were on a level with those of doctors. Occasionally one of their number would turn to Mary when they encountered a difficult case. Her response was always to discourage them from relying on her personality and instead to put their trust in the Divine Principle of her Science. Although what she taught was clearly influenced by things she had learned from Quimby, her system was fundamentally different. Quimby's method of healing had relied on mental energy in conjunction with certain physical therapies such as rubbing the head. Mary Glover's great reliance was on the 'Divine Mind' and allowing the 'Divine Mind' and the presence of God's love to embrace the individual and alter the patient's mental attitude. For this reason Mary remained strongly opposed to the practice of hypnotism as employed by Anton Mesmer and others. On a number of occasions she strongly rebuked some of her students who had engaged in what she regarded as unacceptable manipulation, or to put it in her own words 'animal magnetism'. She parted company with one of her earliest pupils, Richard Kennedy, over this matter.

It was these kind of misconceptions and deviations which eventually led Mary Glover to the conviction that she should produce a definitive textbook on Christian Science. The result was that for the next two and a half years she gave herself wholly to the lonely task of producing such a volume. The first edition of *Science and Health* came out in the autumn of 1875 helped by generous financial support from some of her students.

Fundamental to Christian Science is the supposition that Spirit is 'truth' and 'reality', whereas 'matter' is error and unreality. This did not mean material substances have no objective reality as some

---

[23] Peel, *Mary Baker Eddy*, I, 221.

critics of the movement mistakenly suppose. Rather Mary Glover's conviction that because God is Spirit, Spirit is the ultimate and true reality. By contrast material existence is unreal. As she herself put it in a sermon entitled 'Christian Healing':

> The only correct answer to the question 'Who is the author of evil?' is the scientific statement that 'evil is unreal'; that God made all that was made, but He never made sin or sickness, either an error of mind or of body. Life is Spirit and when we waken from the dream of life in matter, we shall learn this grand truth of being. St. John saw the vision of life in matter; and he saw it pass away, – an illusion.[24]

Furthermore, material substance and physical emotions often mislead us and encompass what human beings perceive to be evil. As Mary saw it the central aspect of personhood is not flesh, blood and bones but spirit. On this understanding physical pain and disease is not the ultimate reality or truth of the situation. If a person's mind and spirit can be positively influenced by allowing the Divine Spirit to embrace it, not only can the mind be changed to take on a positive and wholesome outlook, the body can follow suit. In short, disease can recede as the mind is tuned to the Divine Mind and the Divine Spirit. Mary expressed this point succinctly in a sermon entitled 'Christian Healing' which she preached in Boston in 1888: 'Metaphysical or divine Science reveals the Principle and method of perfection, – how to attain a mind in harmony with God, in sympathy with all that is right and opposed to all that is wrong, and a body governed by this mind.'[25]

In all of this Mary Glover urged that the essential prerequisite is that the patient 'repudiates the evidences of the senses'. When this is achieved the person concerned has fully acknowledged that God is omnipotent. If the divine being is all powerful, it follows, she argued, that no faith should be placed in hygiene or drugs. All faith must be located 'in spiritual power divinely directed'.[26] In summary, Christian Science works on the principle of divine Mind over matter. As Mary herself put it:

---

[24] M.B. Eddy, *Christian Healing: A Sermon Delivered at Boston*, 11–12.
[25] Ibid. 18.
[26] Ibid.

By rightly understanding the power of mind over matter, it enables the mind to govern matter, as it rises to that supreme sense that shall 'take up serpents' unharmed, and 'if they drink any deadly thing it shall not hurt them.' Ah! Why should man deny all right to the divine Mind and claim another mind perpetually at war with this Mind, when at the same time he calls God almighty and admits in statement what he denies in proof? You pray for God to heal you, but should you expect this when you are acting oppositely to your prayer, trying everything else besides God, and believe that sickness is something He cannot reach, but medicine can? as if drugs were superior to Deity.[27]

In looking for divine healing Mary Glover's view was that ideally prayer should be inaudible. Such prayer is less composed of human energy and is therefore more spiritual and more likely to be attuned to the divine Spirit.

Although it was not until 1875 that Mary Glover was able to publish *Science and Health with Key to the Scriptures*, she relates at the beginning of chapter 6 that it was in the year 1866 that she first discovered its divine laws of Life, Truth and Love.

In the same chapter Mary Glover mentions that in her discovery of these principles the Bible was her only textbook. 'No human pen nor tongue taught me the Science contained in this book, Science and Health', she wrote, 'and neither tongue nor pen can overthrow it.'[28] Because of her total belief in the divine origin of what she had written Mary was able to declare later in her *Miscellaneous Writings* that *Science and Health with Key to the Scriptures* 'is a complete text-book of Christian Science' and that 'there is absolutely no additional secret outside its teachings'.[29] In view of her strong convictions on this point it is perhaps not surprising that Mary later asserted that the Scriptures themselves gave 'no direct interpretation of the scientific basis for demonstrating the divine Principle of healing' until God unlocked the mystery to her.[30] In this strong conviction that Mary Glover's writings are absolute and final revealed truth we capture something of the sectarian spirit of this

---

[27] Ibid. 18–19.
[28] Ibid. 110.
[29] Eddy, *Miscellaneous Writings*, 50.
[30] Eddy, *Retrospection and Introspection*, 37.

movement. Indeed the Christian Science Board of Directors publicly expressed their conviction in 1980 that Mary Baker Eddy's teachings are the fulfilment of Jesus' promise that the Spirit of Truth would guide his followers into all truth.[31] It should be noted that in the thirty-five years following the publication of the first edition of *Science and Health*, Mary made extensive revisions to the contents of the book. In this work she was assisted by the Rev J.H. Wiggin who rearranged much of the contents and corrected Mary's grammar.[32] Their purpose in doing so was to make it more effective as the 'textbook' for the study of Christian Science. *Science and Health* was given its final rearrangement in 1904 and Wiggin took no part in the sequence.

The controversial question which has been much debated over the years has been the question of the influence of Quimby and Lieber on Mary's teachings. The debate has inevitably been muddied by the entrenched partisan standpoints of the participants. A balanced assessment of the situation would probably take recognition of the fact that Quimby was an important stimulus to Mary's thinking, but that Mary moved beyond his system. Indeed she rejected many of his methods of healing altogether. Karl Holl, the Lutheran historian. has asserted that 'it was her earnest Puritan faith in God that separated her from Quimby from the beginning'.[33]

One of those who has contended strongly that Mary Glover was heavily dependent on Quimby and Lieber was Walter Martin. He urged that 'as history tells us that Mrs. Eddy was the mother of Christian Science, so Phineas Parkhurst Quimby was undoubtedly its father'.[34] He noted that Quimby had entitled his system in the late 1850s 'The Science of Man', and had also used the terms 'The Science of Christ' and 'Christian Science'. Martin maintained that Mary Glover's *Science and Health* contains numerous plagiarisms from Quimby. He referenced these in chapter 5 of his book *The Christian Science Myth* but noted in passing the Quimby-Eddy

---

[31] *Science and Health, its Pure and Complete Teaching*, 5–6.

[32] D.V. Barrett, *Sects, Cults and Alternative Religions*, 78.

[33] K. Holl, 'Der Szientismus', *Gesammelte Aufsätze Zur Kirchen-geschichte*, III, 463.

[34] W. Martin, *Christian Science: Is This Religious Group Truly Christian or a Science?* 6.

dispute with parallel columns purporting to show her copyings from his book *The Science of Man*. These accusations were all earlier reported in the *New York Times* of 10 July 1904.[35] In his later volume, *Christian Science*, published in 1957, Martin included two pages on which he displayed in parallel columns passages from Francis Lieber's *The Metaphysical Religion of Hegel* and the corresponding passages from Mary Glover's *Science and Health with Key to the Scriptures*. Quite a number of these passages appear to be copied almost word for word. Martin's conclusion on the matter was that it is demonstrably true that 'Mrs. Eddy copied thirty-three pages verbatim and one hundred pages in substance into *Science and Health with Key to the Scriptures*, Edition 1875 from Dr. Lieber's manuscript on the writings of Hegel.'[36] Martin added that it was 'an established historical fact' that Mary Glover had access to Lieber's manuscript while she was residing in the home of Hiram S. Crafts.[37] However, it has to be said that the proposition that Crafts, a simple cobbler and heel finisher, had any acquaintance or correspondence with the eminent Lieber seems unlikely.

For her part Mary simply commented in a chapter in her *Retrospection and Introspection* entitled 'The Great Discovery' that she came to understand 'Christian Science' in February 1866 'after the death of Mr. P.P. Quimby who was in no wise connected with the event'.[38] Christian Science sources take the view that Mary Glover certainly had access to Quimby's work and had 'a very full knowledge of his ideas and beliefs'. However, they point out that Quimby was by no means the first who taught the mental cause of disease and that Mary had herself reached this position well before she met with him. The Christian Scientist writer E.M. Ramsay quoted from a letter written by Phineas Quimby's son, George, in 1901:

> The religion which she teaches certainly is hers, for which I cannot be too thankful; for I should be loath to go down to my grave feeling that my father was in any way connected with 'Christian Science' . . . In curing the sick [conventional] religion played no part. There were no

---

[35] W. Martin, *The Christian Science Myth*.
[36] Martin, *Christian Science: Is This Religious Group Truly Christian?* 9.
[37] Ibid. 10.
[38] Eddy, *Retrospection and Introspection*, 24.

prayers, there was no asking assistance from God or any other divinity.[39]

Shortly after its publication, a review article in the *Boston Investigator* commented that 'Science and Health . . . shows how the body can be cured and how a better state of Christianity can be introduced.' The *Christian Advocate* of Buffalo, New York State, went further and declared, 'This book is a metaphysical treatise showing how disease is caused and cured by mind. The book is certainly original and contains much that will do good.'[40]

When all has been said from both sides in the matter of borrowings from Quimby the fact remains that Mary Glover's system was markedly different from his. The fundamental principle she professed, namely that true healing can only be achieved by the agency of the divine Spirit, could certainly not be traced to Quimby. As Mary herself put it in *No and Yes*: 'Christian Science Mind-healing can only be gained by working from a purely Christian standpoint. Then it heals the sick and exalts the race.'[41]

## The Christian Scientist Association and Mary's Third Marriage

One of the many people who came to Mary Glover for help and healing was Asa Gilbert Eddy who worked as a salesman for the Singer Sewing Machine Company. He had been suffering from heart trouble which caused considerable hindrance to his daily work. An acquaintance urged him to visit Mary which he did in March 1876. He found his subsequent health improved so rapidly that he enrolled and took one of her three-week courses. Eddy who was a bachelor in his middle forties, was totally convinced by what he had learned. He left his bachelor apartment in Boston and his work in an Evangelical Church and set up as a 'Christian Scientist'. He was in fact the first of Mary's students to place these words on his office sign. Mary became increasingly dependent on his calm, clear

---

[39] Ramsay, *Christian Science and Its Discoverer*, 85.
[40] Peel, *Mary Baker Eddy*, I, 291.
[41] M.B. Eddy, *No and Yes*, 12.

and kindly manner and readily accepted his straightforward marriage proposal. They were married on New Year's Day 1877 by the Rev Samuel Stewart, the clergyman of the Unitarian Church Mary had formerly attended. Mary later wrote in *Retrospection and Introspection* that it was 'a blessed and spiritual union'.[42] Eddy proved to be a strong and supportive partner. He was the first organiser of a Christian Science Sunday school which he superintended. He also taught a Bible class and proved to be such an able lecturer that a number of denominational clergy listened to him speak with avid interest. Gilbert Eddy was also a successful mind-healer. According to Mary, he passed away 'with a smile of peace and love resting on his serene countenance'.[43]

Shortly before her marriage, Mary had come to the view that some sort of organisation was necessary to hold her students together and to ensure that there were no deviations from her teaching of Christian Science. As a first step towards achieving this she formed 'The Christian Scientist Association', a small and informal organisation consisting of herself and half a dozen of her students.[44] Nevertheless it was a first step on the road which led to her founding a Church.

## The Move to Boston and the Founding of the Church and College

At a meeting of the Christian Scientist Association on 12 April 1875 it was voted to organise a Church 'to commemorate the words and works of our Master, a Mind-healing Church, without a creed to be called the Church of Christ, Scientist, the first such church ever organised'.[45] Situated in Boston, Mary and Gilbert moved there in February 1880. Initially services were held in private homes and later in halls. The first Christian Science Church was erected in 1894 in the fashionable Back Bay. It is an impressive Romanesque structure built of Concorde granite with

---

[42] Eddy, *Retrospection and Introspection*, 42.
[43] Ibid.
[44] Ibid. 43.
[45] Ibid. 44.

some porticos and turreted corners. Its auditorium seats eleven
hundred people and is capable of holding fifteen hundred. In June
1879 a State Charter was obtained for the church and the
twenty-six members called Mary to become their pastor. She was
later ordained in 1881 although by that time she had been
preaching for five years.

The move to Boston saw Christian Science expand and
prosper. In addition to the Church, Mary founded the
Massachusetts Metaphysical College in Boston in 1881. Its
purpose, in her own words, was 'for teaching the pathology of
spiritual power, alias the Science of Mind-healing'.[46] She obtained
a charter which enabled the College to grant valid degrees to
successful students. The College proved to be a flourishing
institution and applications came in from all over the American
continent and from Europe.[47] In her teaching she was assisted by
her husband, who taught for two terms, and by two other students
of hers. After nine years in operation it became too much for Mary
Eddy to cope with the demands of teaching and revising *Science
and Health with Key to the Scriptures*. Despite appeals from many of
her supporters, she proposed to the College's directors that the
institution be closed. The College's directors by a unanimous vote
decided to follow her advice, the College and Church
Organisation being dissolved between May and December 1889.
One of the more controversial aspects of the College was the high
price of $300 for its course of instruction, which lasted barely three
weeks. Mary herself later wrote: 'The amount greatly troubled
me. I shrank from asking it, but was finally led, by a strange
providence, to accept this fee.'[48] These fees together with sales
from *Science and Health* led Mrs Eddy into considerable prosperity
in her last years and caused some to be strong in their criticisms of
her.

Not long after the move from Lynn to Boston, there was a dete-
rioration in Gilbert Eddy's health. A local physician identified the
problem as organic heart disease. His illness took a rapid hold and he
died in his sleep in the early summer of 1882. Mary's immediate

---

[46] Ibid. 43.
[47] Ibid. 47.
[48] Ibid. 50.

response was that he had been killed by mesmeric poisoning on the part of Edward Arens Jnr. Arens was one of her former students who had drifted away from her and plagiarised some of her ideas. He later acknowledged his bitter hatred of the Eddys but their strained relationship continued. Arens believed implicitly in the power of directed thought to injure and even kill.[49] In short Mrs Eddy believed him to exercise MAM, Malicious Animal Magnetism on her husband.

## Changes in Organisation and Structure

It was not only from her male students that Mary Eddy suffered rivalry, defection and plagiarism of her writings, she also ran into embarrassment and problems with a number of her women associates. This was an age in which there were few opportunities of leadership for women in the denominational churches and for this reason, if for no other, a number of dominant females were attracted into Christian Science. One of the most notable incidents concerned a Mrs Josephine Woodbury, wife of Frank Woodbury, one of the original trustees of the Massachusetts Metaphysical College. Josephine who was a glamorous socialiser, had offered to introduce Mrs Eddy to the best intellectual circles in Boston. Josephine, it appears, soon began to introduce hypnotic techniques into her teaching of Christian Science, and in a personal audience Mrs Eddy sternly rebuked her. Worse was to follow in 1890. On 11 June she gave birth to a baby boy. It was no secret that she had not had marital relations with her husband for a number of years and indeed had advised some of her students to follow her example. No longer able to pass off her growing size as a fungoid formation, she plumped for a dramatic solution and announced it as 'an immaculate conception'.[50] Shortly afterwards in a bold public occasion at Ocean Point in Maine, Josephine Woodbury immersed the child three times 'in a singularly beautiful pool' and christened him 'Prince of Peace'.[51] Mrs Eddy

---

[49]  Peel, *Mary Baker Eddy*, II, 84–7 and 113–15.
[50]  Ibid. 270.
[51]  Ibid.

was willing to be charitable and to pardon this moral lapse but the problem was that Woodbury's declaration bordered on blasphemy and was in danger of portraying Christian Science as a lunatic fringe religious movement.

It was against this kind of background and in an effort to prevent her movement being hijacked by forceful personalities and breakaway groups that Mrs Eddy began to tighten her hold on the movement. She renamed the First Church, the 'Mother Church of Christ Scientist in Boston', so that it could function as the movement's governing body and house the organisational committees. Rules and by-laws for the Church were set out in the *Church Manual* for the Mother Church which was written by her and published in 1895.[52] Among other regulations is the stipulation that none of these ordinances could be adopted, amended or annulled without her written consent. In this way Mrs Eddy came to hold a very dominant position over the movement. Her control was total so long as she lived and since she can now no longer give written agreement it would be difficult to make alterations at the present time. One way in which adaptions of her teachings could still be promulgated was in sermons preached at services in the branch churches. She eventually overcame this difficulty with a regulation which prescribed 'the Bible and Science and Health as pastor on this planet of all the Churches of the Christian Science denomination'.[53] What this has meant is that no sermon is preached in Christian Science worship services. Instead there are set readings of Scripture passages and *Science and Health*. The *Church Manual* also aimed to deal with the threat of personal opposition of the kind Mrs Eddy faced from individuals such as Edward Arens and Josephine Woodbury. Article XI, for example, states, 'If a member of this Church were to treat the author of our textbook disrespectfully and cruelly, upon her complaint that member should be excommunicated.' Part of Article VIII rules that 'A member of the Mother Church shall not haunt Mrs Eddy's drive when she goes out, continually stroll by her house, or make a summer resort near her for such purpose.'[54]

---

[52]  M.B. Eddy, *Church Manual*.
[53]  Eddy, *Miscellaneous Writings*, 352.
[54]  *Church Manual*, 48.

## Closing Years and Death

Despite her teaching which was much sought after and her skill in healing others, Mary herself suffered with bad health particularly in her later years. Much of it was due to the stress of her many responsibilities. Her teeth had to be extracted and she used artificial dentures. She also found it necessary to wear glasses. Much of the time she suffered considerable pain from periodic bouts of renal calculi and when this failed to yield to her own healing methods, she required her doctor to administer morphine. She occupied herself with projects right up to the last. Among the most significant was the founding of the *Christian Science Monitor*, which was to be a high-quality daily newspaper noted for its accurate and careful reporting. The first copy appeared in November 1908. Mary continued active in guiding the affairs of her Church until the end of November 1910 when her constitution began to fail. She passed away peacefully early in December. The last words she wrote were: 'God is my life.'[55]

## Growth and Practice

In 1882 the Church had only one congregation which numbered about fifty people. Two decades later this had increased to some 24,000 and included a few American judges, some businessmen as well as a number of ministers who had been converted from the historic denominational churches. Four years later this number had increased significantly to 65,000 and reached 270,000 by 1926. In July 1888 Mrs Eddy commissioned Mrs Hannah Larminie, a Christian teacher from Chicago, to go to Ireland and then to London where she remained for some six months teaching at least one class. In 1890 Miss Annie Dodge followed and established a Christian Science Society in London, but felt she had accomplished only a little of what she had hoped to do. The first Christian Science Church in the UK was established in London in November 1897. Others followed at Manchester in January 1901 and Leeds in 1906. By the close of 1910 there were seven churches in London and a

---

[55] Ramsay, *Christian Science and Its Discoverer*, 129.

variety of other places including Bexhill, Bracknell, Cheltenham, High Wycombe, Kingston-upon-Thames in the south; and Bolton, Harrogate, Nottingham, Scarborough, Southport, Wakefield and Warrington in the north.

Some of this early growth and popularity may have been due to the opportunities the movement offered to women as leaders and practitioners. Christian Scientists are coy when it comes to speaking of membership statistics but it seems probable that world membership is somewhere between 350,000 and 450,000. Estimates of the current number of British Christian Scientists vary between 50,000 and 9,750.[56] In 1998 Christian Science had 158 places of worship in the UK, one-third of which are situated in the south-east of England. The adherents are largely middle-class people, many of whom have joined as a result of having received a healing through the help of a Christian Science practitioner. Overall the number of committed adherents of Christian Science in England cannot be more than 10,000 and is probably closer to 7,000. An article in the *Christian Science Journal* of July 1972 reported that after the US, the country with the next largest number of churches was the UK. The largest number of Christian Science churches in the US is to be found in California.

As is the case with the majority of historic and denominational churches, Christian Science has seen a decline in its membership in the last quarter of the twentieth century. One reason for this may be the fact that other sections of the Church have begun to take the whole issue of healing more seriously. As sociologists of religion have observed, the lower sections of society are not readily drawn to movements which deny the reality of pain, because they are more prone to poverty, illness and suffering. As it falls within that category, Christian Science is inevitably a largely middle-class religious institution. By the same token manual workers, unskilled labourers and those who have lacked the opportunities of formal education would find it hard to grasp many of the abstract concepts of Christian Science or feel at home in the cerebral atmosphere of one of the branch church's worship services.

---

[56] See M.B. Burrell, The 'Christian' Fringe, 113, and Table 181, 'Non Trinitarian Churches', in P. Brierley and H. Wraight, UK Christian Handbook (Marc Europe, 1996–97), 278.

Local congregations usually meet in buildings which are modest and unecclesiastical in appearance. The interiors are plain and there is little adornment or ornate furnishings. Often the church premises include other accommodation which may be used for Sunday schools and committee meetings. Usually there is a reading room where interested members of the public can either browse through Christian Science literature or take books out on loan for a limited period. The buildings are not used for solemnising Christian Science marriages. Most members follow Mrs Eddy's practice and ask clergy of other denominations to officiate at their weddings.

Mary Eddy had a great dislike of ceremonial and things ecclesiastical. In her own words 'ritualism and dogma lead to self-righteousness and bigotry which freeze out the spiritual element'.[57] For this reason Christian Science has no clergy or full-time officials. The nearest equivalent they have to ordained clergy are 'practitioners' who have received training in the principles of Christian Science and devote all their time to the practice of healing. Their Sunday worship is a quiet and meditative occasion with no dominant leader or president. The central focus is the reading of the Lesson Sermon which consists of readings from the Authorised Version of the Bible together with related passages from *Science and Health*. At the front of each building is a reader's platform from where the Lesson-Sermon is given. It is prefaced by the following announcement: 'The Bible and the Christian Science textbook are our only preachers. We shall now read scriptural texts and their correlative passages from our denominational textbook; these comprise our Sermon.' The Lesson-Sermon is given without any commentary or interpretation by two readers elected from the local membership. The Lesson-Sermons deal with twenty-six topics, each covered twice a year. This means that the same subject arises on the first Sundays in January and July. Titles covered include God, Life, Truth, Soul and Sacrament. One of the readers leads the rest of the Service in which there is a sacred song performed by a male or female soloist. Hymns are sung by the congregation and there is silent prayer and the Lord's Prayer.

There are no sacramental services in Christian Science. Members of the Church take the view that when a person has

---

[57] Eddy, *Retrospection and Introspection*, 65.

become really and intimately conscious of the presence of the healing Christ, he or she can no longer proclaim the death of Jesus because, for them, the risen Christ has come again. Christian Scientists therefore maintain that the Communion commemorates the early morning meal which the risen Jesus prepared for his disciples beside the Sea of Galilee.[58] The focus is not on Jesus' death but on his victory over death. No use of bread or wine is made as Mary Eddy worried that participants might come to depend on out-ward material substance instead of a reformation of the heart. As she put it in *Science and Health*: 'Our Eucharist is spiritual communion with the one God. Our bread, "which cometh down from heaven", is Truth. Our cup is the cross. Our wine the inspiration of Love, the draught our Master drank and commended to his followers.'[59]

Communion is held twice a year on those Sundays when 'Sacrament' is the Lesson-Sermon topic. The order of service includes a period towards the close when the congregation is invited to kneel in silent communion.

Baptism for the Christian Scientist is nothing less than 'a purification from all error'.[60] It includes purification of thoughts and motives. It is not a brief ceremony which takes place on a particular day using water and the Trinitarian name. Rather it is a daily experience as individuals who have been born again appropriate the Life which is Truth and bring forth the fruits of love – 'casting out error and healing the sick'.[61]

Although there is therefore no baptism of infants Christian Scientists consider the teaching of children to be very important. From the earliest days they bring up their offspring to love God and to know that he is an ever present help in times of trouble. They also instruct their children how to overcome evil and to reject suggestions of ill health. Parents are constantly reminded of the vital necessity of keeping the atmosphere in which their children grow up pure and of emphasising obedience to God's laws.

---

[58] Eddy, *Science and Health*, 35.
[59] Ibid.
[60] Ibid.
[61] Ibid.

Sunday schools are regarded as a crucially important part of the branch church's life and work. The emphasis is on the lessons themselves and special treats or entertainment do not feature in the programme. Mary Eddy was insistent that 'we need a clean body and a clean mind, – a body rendered pure by Mind as well as washed by water'.[62] Individuals can stay in Sunday school for a much longer period than is the case in other Churches. It is not uncommon for young adults of twenty years of age to remain in classes.

To become a member of a branch church an individual has to subscribe to the 'Six Tenets of Christian Science' as laid down by Mrs Eddy and they must be sponsored by one or, in some cases, two members of the congregation. As with many sectarian groups, Christian Scientists are strongly opposed to the use of intoxicating liquors and the use of tobacco. Mary spoke of the tobacco user as 'eating or smoking poison'.[63] The use of alcohol and tobacco is a bar to membership. Occasionally individuals can be excommunicated from a branch church. Usually this is because they are living a life which brings the Church into disrepute or the person concerned is teaching something which is incompatible with Christian Science. Weddings and funerals are not held on Christian Science premises. Funerals are usually conducted by a member at a Crematorium. Like many other Churches, Christian Scientists hold regular midweek meetings on a Wednesday. These are known as 'Testimony Meetings' when, as well as hymns and silent prayer, a substantial period of time is given over to hearing members' testimonies. Visitors are welcomed to these occasions with the hope that they will see the relevance of Christian Science as an everyday living faith.

Healing is a very important aspect of Christian Science and many members become recognised healers. To achieve this status a member must apply to take a course with an 'authorised teacher of Christian Science'. Courses last for two weeks and there are up to thirty in a class. Once a person is qualified they are listed in the Directory of Christian Science Practitioners. It is pertinent to note that qualification for listing in the *Christian Science Journal* takes account of the individual's healing ability. There are currently some

---

[62] Ibid.
[63] Ibid. 383.

6,500 practitioners in forty countries. Healing is understood in a wide context and in addition to physical healing includes emotional disturbances such as family problems, confusion, redundancy, anxiety and grief. Although encouragement from the Christian Science teacher is a necessary aid to the healing process, silent prayer is all important. The patient will also be encouraged to take an optimistic attitude and look to the Divine Mind for wholeness.

The Mother Church has established a Board of Lectureship and each branch church is expected to organise at least one public lecture in the course of a year. Lecturers are required to send copies of their lectures to the clerk of the Mother Church before delivering them to the public.

The Headquarters and world administrative centre of the Christian Science Church is in Boston, Massachusetts. The movement is controlled by a five-member Board of Directors. As any vacancies occur the remaining members are responsible for choosing their replacements. The Board's main responsibility is preserving unaltered the teachings of Christian Science as taught by Mrs Eddy. They are also charged with the task of publishing her writings and promoting various Christian Science journals and periodicals. These include the *Christian Science Quarterly*, which contains the Lesson-Sermons, the monthly *Christian Science Journal*, and the daily *Christian Science Monitor*. The Board is also responsible for training experienced Christian Science practitioners to enable them to become authorised teachers who will return to their own countries and impart their knowledge to others.

## Key Beliefs of Christian Science

At the conclusion of *Science and Health* on page 497 there is a six-point summary of the Church's key beliefs:

1. As adherents of Truth, we take the inspired Word of the Bible as our sufficient guide to eternal Life.
2. We acknowledge and adore one supreme and infinite God. We acknowledge His Son, one Christ; the Holy Ghost or divine Comforter; and man in God's image and likeness.

3.  We acknowledge God's forgiveness of sin in the destruction of sin and the spiritual understanding that casts out evil as unreal. But the belief in sin is punished so long as the belief lasts.
4.  We acknowledge Jesus' atonement as the evidence of divine, efficacious Love, unfolding man's unity with God through Christ Jesus the Way-shower; and we acknowledge that man is saved through Christ, through Truth, Life, and Love as demonstrated by the Galilean Prophet in healing the sick and overcoming sin and death.
5.  We acknowledge that the crucifixion of Jesus and his resurrection served to uplift faith to understand eternal Life, even the allness of Soul, Spirit, and the nothingness of matter.
6.  And we solemnly promise to watch, and pray for that Mind to be in us which was also in Christ Jesus; to do unto others as we would have them do unto us; and to be merciful, just, and pure.

The first point in this 'brief exposition' concerns the Bible which is taken as 'the inspired Word' and as 'our sufficient guide to eternal life'. Earlier in *Science and Health*, Mrs Eddy declared that 'The Bible has been my only authority. I have no other guide in "the straight and narrow way" of Truth.'[64] In another place she also stated: 'In following these leadings of scientific revelation the Bible was my only textbook. The Scriptures were illumined; reason and revelation were reconciled, and afterwards the truth of Christian Science was demonstrated.'[65] She continued in the same paragraph: 'No human pen nor tongue taught me the Science contained in this book, Science and Health; and neither tongue nor pen can overthrow it.'[66]

Two things emerge at this point. First, it is clear that Christian Scientists regard Mrs Eddy's *Science and Health with Key to the Scriptures* as their major source of authority alongside the Bible. It is plain that Mrs Eddy regarded the book as 'dictated by the divine power of Truth and Love'. Second, her interpretation of Scripture differs widely at many points from the understandings of the early Church Fathers as well as those of present-day Roman Catholic and Protestant biblical scholars. On occasion she made use of modern

---

[64]  Ibid. 126.
[65]  Ibid. 110.
[66]  Ibid.

historical critical methods and at other times she resorted to a fairly widespread use of allegory. One obvious example is seen in her treatment of the book of Genesis which, taken at face value, clearly recounts God creating the material world and declaring it to be very good. It is basic to her principle that God is Spirit and did not, for that reason, create other than spiritual as opposed to material. Mrs Eddy therefore spiritualised the Genesis account so that, for instance, the creation of the sun is 'a metaphysical representation of the soul outside the body'[67] and the creation of 'fowl which may fly above the earth' 'correspond to aspirations soaring beyond and above corporeality to the understanding of the incorporeal and divine Principle, Love'.[68] In summary, the Genesis 1 account is spiritual and therefore is 'the truth of the divine creation'.[69] What follows in Genesis 2 is 'a statement of the material view of God and the universe and is the false history in contradistinction to the true'.[70] The 'true' is the spiritual; matter, on the other hand, has no mind or sensation and is the source of evil. Our physical senses mislead us to wrong conclusions and to misguided feelings.[71]

### Matter, Evil and Sin

Like the Gnostic teachers of the first and second centuries, Mary Eddy had a low view of matter and the material world in general. In order to experience the spiritual presence of God, both believed it was necessary for individuals to disentangle themselves from its clutches. In her Glossary of terms at the end of *Science and Health*, Mary defines matter as 'mortality', 'illusion', 'life resulting in death', 'the opposite of Truth', 'the opposite of Spirit', 'that which mortal mind sees, feels, hears, tastes, and smells only in belief'.[72] It should be emphasised that the Christian Scientists do not deny the existence of matter or the experience of material things, but simply that in contrast to things spiritual they are unreal and mislead. This is a

---

[67] Ibid. 510.
[68] Ibid. 511–12.
[69] Ibid. 521.
[70] Ibid. 521–2.
[71] Ibid. 489–90.
[72] Ibid. 591.

viewpoint not shared by the historic, mainline and New Churches, who understand the biblical record to affirm the creation as both God-inspired and good. Indeed they take the view that Jesus endorsed and entered fully into the pleasures of the material world. In his resurrection they maintain that Jesus' flesh, body, blood and bones were raised to life so that he could break bread, eat fish and allow his disciples to touch his hands and feet, and feel the scars which had been made by the nails of the crucifixion.

For the Christian Scientist evil is nothing. In Mrs Eddy's own words it has 'no reality' and is 'neither person, place, nor thing, but simply a belief, an illusion of material sense'.[73] In *No and Yes* in a short piece entitled 'Is there any Such Thing as Sin?' she wrote that 'Christian Science gives the lie to sin,' which must be 'small and unreal'.[74] She went on to declare that to reduce evil in this way gives a greater focus and dominance to God.[75]

### Disease and Death

Mrs Eddy's views on disease and death follow naturally on from her convictions about matter and sin. She firmly believed and taught that sickness and disease were an illusory condition of a mind which had become absorbed in matter and material things. She wrote: 'The cause of all so-called disease is mental, a mortal fear, a mistaken belief or conviction of the necessity and power of ill-health; also a fear that Mind is helpless to defend the life of man and incompetent to control it.'[76]

If a person can once shake free of this fear, sickness can, Mrs Eddy asserted, be readily overcome. 'Disease', she urged, 'is less than mind and Mind can control it.'[77] She was adamant that a quickened pulse, a coated tongue, a dry skin, a head pain and bodily aches were all pictures drawn on the body by a mortal mind. What all this means is that for the Christian Scientist to get well he or she simply needs to be aware that they are not really sick and that the perceived

---

[73] Ibid. 71.

[74] Eddy, *No and Yes*, 32.

[75] Ibid. 33.

[76] Eddy, *Science and Health*, 378.

[77] Ibid.

sickness is merely the result of a false belief. She did not, however, mean to deny the individual's experience of illness. In fact she wrote that 'sickness is neither imaginary nor unreal, – that is to the frightened false sense of the patient'.[78] Mrs Eddy wrote: 'Chills and heat are often the form in which fever manifests itself. Change the mental state, and the chills and fever disappear.'[79] It is important to emphasise that Christian Science does not seek to heal by mere human mind-control techniques but by helping the person concerned to focus their thoughts on the Divine Mind. In so doing they are able to draw from the Spirit, as opposed to matter, and find health, peace, and harmony in God, divine love.[80]

Death is regarded by Christian Scientists in much the same way as sin, namely as something that is an illusion which must finally be overcome by eternal life. In *Science and Health* in a section entitled 'No Death' Mrs Eddy speaks of death as 'an illusion'.[81] She writes of the need to master 'the dream of death' by Mind, meaning the divine Spirit Mind. Eventually the material declaration 'I am dead,' she wrote, will be overcome 'by the trumpet word of Truth, "There is no death" '.[82] Christian Scientists of course are very well aware that death is a certainty and happens to their own members, Mrs Eddy included. Nevertheless their view is that this is only people's perception of what has happened.

### Doctrine of God

Mrs Eddy's writings about the Godhead are wide-ranging and her positions not always clear. She begins one section in *Science and Health* by stating that 'God, Spirit' is 'All-in-All' and that God is Love and therefore 'He is divine Principle'.[83] In just this one sentence she refers to God as a 'Principle' but at the same time uses the personal pronoun 'He'. Additionally her assertion that God is 'All-in-All' borders on the edge of pantheism – although it should be noted that she herself thought of pantheism in a more limited

---

[78]   Ibid. 460.
[79]   Ibid. 375.
[80]   Ibid. 416.
[81]   Ibid. 428.
[82]   Ibid. 427–8.
[83]   Ibid. 275.

way where Mind is held to reside within matter. Elsewhere in *No and Yes*, she seems quite clear that God should be thought of in terms of 'Principle' rather than as a 'person'. To speak of God in human terms is to demean his power and presence. Personhood has to do with mortal man, so that even to speak of God as 'limitless personality' is not possible. She refers to the deity mostly in abstract terms of Mind, Truth and Love.[84]

Closely linked with this Mrs Eddy firmly rejected the doctrine of the Trinity. As she saw it three persons suggested polytheism rather than 'one ever-present I AM'. Like many before her and since, she failed to understand that the word 'person' in the creeds derived from the Latin 'persona' which was much closer to meaning a 'role' than a separate being. Mainstream Christianity has never asserted that God is three beings or individuals. Rather He is seen as one being who reveals himself in three ways. Elsewhere Mrs Eddy spoke of God using Trinitarian imagery which was impersonal. She wrote of Life, Truth and Love constituting a 'Trinity in unity'. She also spoke of a Trinitarian office 'the same in essence though multiform in office consisting of God the Father-Mother; Christ the spiritual idea of sonship; divine Science or the Holy Comforter'.[85]

### Christology and the Atonement

In *Science and Health* Mrs Eddy wrote that 'A portion of God could not enter man; neither could God's fullness be reflected by a single man, else God would be manifestly finite, lose the deific character, and become less than God.'[86] The problem for her system of teaching was the impossibility of the 'Divine Mind, Spirit-God' taking upon himself 'unreal' human flesh as a means of revealing himself to the human race. She attempted to solve this issue by making a distinction between 'Jesus' and 'Christ'. Christ is 'the spiritual idea of sonship'[87] and the 'ideal of God now and forever'.[88] The human Jesus merely revealed the 'Spiritual Christ' to the world, indeed he

---

[84]  Eddy, *No and Yes*, 19–20.
[85]  Eddy, *Science and Health*, 331.
[86]  Ibid. 231.
[87]  Ibid. 331.
[88]  Ibid. 361.

was endowed by the divine Spirit without measure and this enabled him to be the mediator or 'Way-Shower', between God and men.[89] In section XV of *Science and Health*, Mary Eddy is clear that whereas the 'material concept' or 'Jesus' disappeared, 'the spiritual self, or Christ, continues to exist in the eternal order of the divine Science'.[90] From this it seems clear that the human Jesus no longer lives and has simply been annihilated.

Clearly, therefore, Christian Scientists envisage Jesus in a rather different way from the understanding of the Protestant and Catholic Churches. For them the central Christian doctrine is that God took human flesh and became a man. He shared human life to the full and died a physical death. He rose again bodily and ascended in his humanity into the heavens and remains 'the Man Christ Jesus' who is the one mediator between God and Men (1 Timothy 2:5). The New Testament test of orthodox Christianity is the full acknowledgement and faith that 'Jesus Christ has come in the flesh' (1 John 4:1–3). Significantly in both these two affirmations there is no distinction or separation between Jesus and Christ.

It follows from this that Christian Science's understanding of the Virgin birth and the atonement are also different from those of the Churches which hold to the teaching of the three great historic Creeds. The mainstream Christian view is that Jesus was born fully man 'at one with the human race in his humanity'. Equally salvation was accomplished by the shedding of his innocent human blood as an atonement for the sins of the entire human race. In contrast Christian Scientists maintain that Mary's conception of Jesus was 'spiritual'[91] and his death also requires 'a spiritual interpretation'. The human Jesus simply achieved an atonement 'for the terrible unreality of a supposed existence apart from God'.[92] Christian Scientists, it should be noted, do hold a deep reverence for Jesus as Lord and Master. They gratefully recognise his human sacrifice which, as Eddy put it, 'stands pre-eminently amidst physical suffering and human woe'.[93]

---

[89]   Ibid. 30.
[90]   Ibid. 334.
[91]   Ibid. 332.
[92]   Eddy, *No and Yes*, 35.
[93]   Ibid. 33.

## *Doctrine of Salvation*

Christian Science regards sin and evil as having no objective reality. They are unreal, illusory and generated by misplaced thought patterns. To overcome sin for the Christian Scientist is to divest it 'of any supposed mind or reality, and never admit that sin can have intelligence or power, pain or pleasure'. In short 'You conquer error by denying its verity.'[94] In *No and Yes* Mary Eddy speaks of sin as a lie promulgated by the devil as the 'Father of lies'. She goes on to state that by diminishing this evil by denying its reality we give 'dominance to God'. This indeed is the core of Christian Science. It is for the human mind spirit to be embraced by the Divine Spirit Mind. Christian Scientists explain prayer as a humble turning to God to learn more of his goodness and love. It is through prayer that immediate and permanent relief from pain and illness is received. There is no sense of sin or guilt and the need for forgiveness achieved through a sacrificial but perfect human death on a cross. Eddy certainly rejected the idea of a substitutionary atonement as a means of individual salvation, yet she fully acknowledged the sacrificial element, writing that Jesus 'purchased the means of mortals' redemption from sin'.[95]

## Postscript

Christian Science has emphasised an important aspect of Jesus' teaching, namely healing. Its stress on positive thinking, healthy living and marital chastity are aspects that all Christians would want to endorse. Nevertheless it is clear that Christian Science differs from the mainline historic and denominational churches on a number of points. At the most fundamental level is Christian Science's denial of the reality of matter. Like the first- and second-century Gnostics they regard the material world as both unreal and misleading. It is something to be eschewed and whose influences must be overcome. Orthodox Christianity, on the other hand, believes that God created a material and physical universe and

---

94  Eddy, *Science and Health*, 339.
95  Eddy, *Miscellaneous Writings*, 164.

that it is fundamentally good and as such is to be valued and stewarded. Mainstream Christians also assert that God affirmed his creation by becoming man in Christ Jesus and involving himself with it to the full. For them sin and evil are objective realities which stand beyond and outside the human mind. They see no distinction or separation between 'Jesus' and 'Christ' and hold Him to be the perfect God–Man who died as the matchless representative and substitute for the sin and evil of the human race. Salvation comes through acceptance of this sacrifice in faith and by entering into a relationship of trust in Jesus Christ, as the one who reveals God in all his fullness. God, for the mainline Christian Churches, is personal rather than an abstract Spirit principle as Christian Scientists maintain. As with some other sectarian groups, Christian Science membership has declined steadily in recent decades. Part of this is due to a general secularising trend in Western society but also to the growing interest and concern to take healing with seriousness on the part of the wider Church.

# Chapter 8

# Spiritualism

Spiritualism in the United Kingdom includes a variety of networks and groups, some holding specifically Christian beliefs and others which are almost totally devoid of any religious dogma at all. They all, however, share one central concept: communication with the dead or spirit realm through gifted or psychic individuals. Strictly speaking Spiritualists do not speak of the 'dead' but rather of the 'departed'. As the title of one of their hymns puts it: 'We cannot think of them as dead'. Early Spiritualism was very largely what today would be understood as 'physical mediumship' in which the 'spirit' operates on a physical level perhaps turning or lifting tables, levitating objects or creating audible rappings. It also includes manifestations of 'ectoplasm', apparently a viscous substance sometimes appearing to exude from the body of the medium during a sitting. Physical mediumship is associated with 'trance mediumship' where the medium passes into an unconscious state and is then 'possessed' by a spirit who communicates with the 'sitters', people attending the seance.

The later nineteenth century witnessed the emergence of clairvoyant mediumship during which the medium remains fully aware and either sees (clairvoyant) in a parapsychological way or hears (clairaudient) or senses (clairsentience) and then passes on the information to the sitters. Modern 'platform mediumship' as practised in most Spiritualist churches is almost exclusively clairvoyant. A popular form of mediumship in Victorian times was table-turning. It reached every part of society from royalty to domestic servants. In 1846 Georgiana Eagle gave a demonstration in front of Queen Victoria at Osborne House. Its appeal to the lower orders of society was satirised in George and Walter Grossmith's novel *Diary of a*

*Nobody* (1894) which highlights the fashionable craze which motivated many such experiments. The practice also drew the attentions of the evangelical incumbent of Cheltenham, Francis Close, who published *Table-turning not Diabolical: A Tract for the Times* in 1853.[1]

In a typical sitting (seance), a group of individuals, sometimes without a known medium, gather in a darkened room around a light table. For table-turning, however, a darkened room is not essential. Darkened rooms are only required for direct voice, materialisation and apports. The participants place their fingers on the table and demand the attention of the spirits. After waiting for a period of some minutes, the table begins to rap, rock or levitate. The sitters call out each letter of the alphabet in sequence and when the table responds they note down the letters. By this somewhat laborious process messages can be conveyed. Various explanations for this occurrence have been put forward including that by Lord Kelvin who attributed the movement of the table to unconscious muscular action being released through the finger tips of those present.

## Origins of Spiritualism

Although modern Spiritualism is generally taken to have originated in North America in the middle years of the nineteenth century, the basic concept and practice of making contact with the departed by means of mediums stretches back into the ancient world of the Middle East. Primitive humans had no doubt that their forebears had survived death and that they had powers to affect the living either for good or ill. For this reason due reverence and respect was

---

[1] F. Close, *Table-turning not Diabolical: A Tract for the Times* (no publisher, 1853). On p. 3 of this document he asserted that 'Holy scripture is as yet the only written communication from the eternal world.' He ends by asserting on p. 15 'that table-turning is not diabolical'. In the same year Close also published *The Testers Tested; or Table-moving, Turning, and Talking, not Diabolical: A Review of the Publications of the Rev Messrs Godfrey, Gillson, Vincent and Dibdin* (no publisher, 1853), 36. On p. 34 of this document he stated: 'I am called to believe that table-moving, turning and talking is effected by supernatural agency good or bad: and I still hold that "table-turning is not diabolical".'

shown to them. Many primitive tribal religions centre their rituals on ancestor worship. The ancient Greeks consulted oracles and the Romans and the Assyrians practised divination. Early Christians, however, followed the Jewish law which forbade contact with the departed (Leviticus 19:26). To engage in such practice they believed from the experience of King Saul was to invite the judgement of God. When the Emperor Constantine was converted to Christianity in AD 312 he passed laws against divination of various kinds. The Council of Nicaea in AD 325 forbade the use of mediums in Christianity and took the view that divine guidance was only possible through the Holy Spirit and the advice of the Christian priesthood. During the Middle Ages the Church adopted a harsh attitude to mediumistic activity. Religious sanction to this persecution was given in a papal bull of 1848 and the publication of *Malleus Maleficarum* (Hammer of the Witches). All this meant that witch trials and burnings were frequent public spectacles. Indeed, right up into the mid-twentieth century, mediums in the UK were the victims of fines and imprisonments.

Spiritualists take the view that the early Christian church did in fact make communication with the spirit world. The appearances of Jesus after his resurrection to the disciples and his followers are seen by them as a classic form of materialisation. His being mistaken by Mary for the gardener meant that the materialisation was not sufficiently complete for her to recognise him immediately. Other instances in which the disciples failed to recognise Jesus on the road to Emmaus and by the sea of Tiberias are regarded as occurrences of the same phenomenon. One Spiritualist minister noted how so often it is recorded that Jesus *appeared*, implying, in his view, a vision or a visitation, but not a physical body. He wrote:

> Physical bodies do not just appear and disappear in front of people's eyes. His [Jesus'] appearance in the upper room, with doors locked says to a Spiritualist that conditions were right for the energy to be contained within the walls of the room, the disciples being psychic, gave the energy to spirit to allow the materialisation of Jesus to appear to those in the room. Physical bodies cannot enter through locked doors or thick walls.[2]

---

[2] C. Lloyd, letter dated 26 May 1999.

In the eighteenth century Emmanuel Swedenborg (1688–1772) sowed the seeds of Spiritualist thought. He had a remarkable gift of clairvoyance. Beginning in 1737 at Mount Lebanon in America, he received communication from the spirit world over a seven-year period. He predicted among other things, that the practice of mediumship and its associated phenomena would spread across the globe. So it was to prove.

Other occurrences in the early decades of the nineteenth century included a number of ghostly visitations in the village of Sullivan, Maine, in 1826. They were carefully recorded by the Rev Abraham Cummings, an itinerant Baptist minister who was keenly interested in psychical research. The events he charted make the happenings at Hydesville (see below) seem almost pale in comparison.[3] In 1846 J.W. Haddock, an English investigator, found his domestic servant, Emma, had a remarkable gift of clairvoyance. In particular she was able to provide accurate and detailed information about both living and deceased persons which Haddock was convinced she couldn't have known by any other means.[4]

Another early significant individual was Andrew Jackson Davis (1826–1910). Born the son of a shoemaker he was brought up in the town of Pough Keepsie. At the age of seventeen he experimented with trance mediumship and began to deliver a series of trance lectures on the origin and nature of the universe and the destiny of the human soul after death. He also went on to give a picture of a kind of living on earth which was most likely to secure happiness both in the present and in the hereafter. These lectures were published in 1847 under the title *The Principles of Nature; Her Divine Revelations; and a Voice to Mankind*. A series of further books followed in which he developed his philosophy. Through his mediumship Davis believed that he was guided in much of his writing by Emmanuel Swedenborg. In the course of his lectures Davis made the following frequently quoted prediction:

> It is a truth that spirits commune with one another while one is in the
> body and the other in the higher spheres . . . and this truth will . . . long

[3] R.I. Anderson, 'Spiritualism Before the Fox Sisters', *Parapsychology Review* 18 (January-February 1987), 9–10.
[4] Ibid. 10.

present itself in the form of a living demonstration. And the world will hail with delight the ushering in of that era when the interiors of men will be opened, and the spiritual communion will be established such as is now being enjoyed by the inhabitants of Mars, Jupiter, and Saturn.[5]

Davis spoke of God in terms similar to those used by Mary Baker Eddy. God is 'positive Mind' and everything else is 'negative'. God is unchangeable and reality is in a constantly changing universe. Davis considered that the universe was designed to produce self-conscious spirit beings. The purpose of human form was to individualise the spirit. Davis identified three major components in a person: the body which is a physical organism, the soul which is an immaterial body which acts as the link with the physical body, and the spirit which is 'the directing power'.[6] Davis did not hold that the soul was pre-existent, rather it emerged with the birth of the physical body. Davis continued to write in the later years of the nineteenth century and his ideas formed the basis of the mainstream of Spiritualist thinking about meaning and ultimate reality.

## Hydesville, New York State

On the morning of 31 March 1848 now known as Hydesville Day, Andrew Jackson Davis recorded a dream. While he was sleeping he heard a voice calling out: 'Brothers . . . the good work has begun – Behold, a living demonstration is born.'[7] He was confused as to what it meant but was reluctant to see it as being fulfilled in the Hydesville rappings which followed.

Katie and Margaret Fox are the first people on record to have held a conversation with a spirit. In December 1847 John Fox, his wife and three daughters, Margaret, Catherine and Katie, moved into a farmhouse near the present township of Arcadia in Wayne County. Two other siblings, Leah and David, were already married

---

[5] A.J. Davis, *The Principles of Nature; Her Divine Revelations, and a Voice to Mankind*, 675–6, cited Anderson, 'Spiritualism Before the Fox Sisters', 11.
[6] G.K. Nelson, 'Ultimate Reality and Meaning', *Modern Spiritualist* 11 (1988), 106.
[7] J. Bassett, *100 Years of National Spiritualism*, 7.

and lived in the locality. In 1848 John left the family who were reduced to poverty. Soon after taking up residence the family began to hear bangs and rapping sounds together with other phenomena which may have been a poltergeist. The two girls seem initially to have treated the whole thing in a light-hearted manner and started to 'play games' with the ghost. They found out that through a series of raps the spirit could give basic 'yes' or 'no' answers to questions which were put to it. Jean Bassett maintained that these were no gentle tappings since the very walls of the house were reported to have been shaken by them.[8] According to Spiritualists, the ghost proved to be that of a murdered peddler, Charles Rosna. He gave information which was later found to be correct when the cellar was subsequently excavated in 1848. A 'Two-Way Link' between the spirit of Charles Rosna and Katie Fox erupted into a widespread publicity exercise. An ordinary man had died but seemingly had retained sufficient intelligent memory of the event to complain about the method of his passing away. News of this strange haunting soon spread and the family who were plagued by sightseers took off to the nearby town of Rochester.

Soon after arriving the sisters discovered that the rappings had followed them, which is what Spiritualists would expect, particularly if one of the daughters was a poltergeist agent. A circle of interested and intelligent citizens began to gather for the first seances or meetings in an effort to make contact with the spirit realm. The possibility of fraud entered the minds of many New Yorkers and their suspicions were later confirmed in 1888 when Katie and Margaret called a public meeting at which they denounced Spiritualism as a fraud and evil characterised by sexual licentiousness. In the following year the two sisters went on a public tour, exposing Spiritualism as fraud. They related that the entire phenomenon had been caused by their simulating the raps by cracking their knee and toe joints. The confession, it later emerged, was given for financial gain under considerable duress and Katie continued to work as a medium! In 1891 Maggie retracted her confession. Whatever the truth of the early events surrounding Hydesville, the matter is probably not as simple as either the critics or adherents of Spiritualism would have us believe.

---

[8]  Ibid. 8.

One thing, however, is sure and that is the resulting publicity stirred hundreds and perhaps thousands of ordinary people to investigate the possibility of communicating with the dead. The whole matter soon spread across the State where others discovered that they had similar powers. By a quirk it was the great American showman P.T. Barnum who brought the Fox sisters to New York City and publicised their abilities. A new 'craze' of Spiritualist sittings developed. These were not always serious, at most half scientific and sometimes religious but to a large extent little more than a party game. Nevertheless interest spread all over the US. By 1853 seances were being conducted in San Francisco and London and by 1860 were reported in Berlin and St Petersburg.

## Spiritualism in England

In 1852 a Mrs Hayden travelled from America to England and was able to share in detail what was taking place in the eastern States of America. Her presence and teaching provoked a good deal of adverse publicity in both pulpit and press. As things turned out however the derogatory reports in many of the newspapers spread interest in Spiritualism throughout the British Isles. It was not long before 'table turning' became socially acceptable. Fashionable women began to serve delicate afternoon teas and then retire to 'communicate' with spirits. For some it was a novel way of passing the time, but for others it was the beginning of a Spiritualist way of life.

Among those who defended Mrs Hayden's mediumship was the Socialist Robert Owen (1771–1858) who was one of the founders of the co-operative movement. He embraced Spiritualism after sittings with her and through his influence and mediumship many were drawn into the cause. In 1853 the first Spiritualist Church was established in England at Keighley in Yorkshire by David Richmond. Two years later, also at Keighley, the *Yorkshire Spiritual Telegraph*, the first Spiritualist newspaper in Britain, was published. By the 1870s there were numerous Spiritualist societies and churches throughout England.[9]

---

[9] *The Spiritualists' National Union Yearbook 1998*, 7.

In 1869 the Dialectical Society appointed a committee to investigate Spiritualism, which subsequently published a more favourable report than any of the previous investigating bodies had done. Two years later Sir William Crookes reported on Spiritualism to the Royal Society and published his findings in the *Quarterly Journal of Science*. The British National Association of Spiritualists was founded in London in 1873. It was renamed The London Spiritual Alliance in 1884. A founding figure in this organisation was a former Anglican clergyman, William Stainton Moses (1839–92), who addressed the inaugural meeting of the renamed body in the Banqueting room of St James's Hall. After studying at Oxford and holding curacies in the Isle of Man and Salisbury he moved to London where he obtained a post as an English teacher at University College School, which he held till ill health caused him to resign in 1889. He became interested in Spiritualism soon after his arrival in the capital and emerged as a prominent medium.[10] The Alliance still exists today as The College of Psychic Science. In 1882, another organisation, The Society for Psychical Research, was set up with a particular brief to investigate spiritist phenomena. In 1887 the Two Worlds, an important new Spiritualist weekly, was founded by Mrs Emma Hardinge Britten. It was known as 'The people's Popular Penny Spiritualist Paper'. Emma served as editor for five years and proved herself to be a talented writer who produced good articles on a whole variety of subjects.

In 1888 *Two Worlds* sponsored a prize essay competition. The winning entry by Phillip Seymour outlined his proposals for a National Organisation of Spiritualist bodies. Following on from this Emma wrote a number of further articles in support of the idea. In the early days of Spiritualism different groups had been left completely free to develop independently but with the passing of the years there was a feeling that some kind of organisation was needed. It started as successful districts emerged and began to share mediums and the distribution of literature. In 1875 the Lancashire District Committee, which represented sixteen to eighteen areas, reported that nearly every town and village in their district had been visited.

---

[10]  W.M. Moses, *More Spirit Teachings*, 7–8.

The first attempt at National Organisation began at Darlington in 1865. Only twenty-five individuals gathered together but they did establish The Association of Progressive Spiritualists of Great Britain. Other area conferences were held at Newcastle, Liverpool and London but no body which embraced the whole of England had yet been established. It needed the drive and determination of a widely respected individual. Through her work, particularly as editor of *Two Worlds*, Emma Hardinge Britten proved to be that person. On Sunday 6 July 1890 a meeting was convened at the Co-operative Hall, Ardwick, Manchester. Sixteen members were appointed as council, among them Dr and Mrs Britten. The president of the day, John Lamont of Liverpool, invited Emma to give the invocation and announced that speeches would be limited to ten minutes each. The first resolution of the assembled company was 'That this assembly considers an annual movable conference of the Spiritualists of Great Britain and Ireland is a necessity of the present position of importance of our movement.'[11] In the course of submission Emma Britten stated that she

> could not then transcend the summary of the religious faith her Spirit friends had given her when she had to lay the foundation stone of the Oldham Spiritual Temple – namely, that religion consisted in the doctrines of the Fatherhood of God, the Brotherhood of Man, the Immortality of the Soul, Personal Responsibility, Compensation and Retribution hereafter for all the good or evil deeds done here and a path of eternal progress open to every human soul that wills to tread it by the path of eternal good.[12]

During the afternoon session when the number of delegates in attendance increased, Mrs Britten tabled a third resolution, 'That the time has come for greater unanimity of opinion concerning the fundamental basis of our philosophy, so that the terms Spiritualism and Spiritualist may be associated with an accepted and definite significance.'[13] The evening of the conference included further impromptu speeches together with singing and

---

[11] Bassett, *100 Years of National Spiritualism*, 17.
[12] Ibid. 18.
[13] Ibid.

dancing. The new national umbrella organisation took the name The Spiritualists' National Federation and was charged with arranging the next year's meeting at Bradford.

In America Andrew Jackson Davis 'saw' clairvoyantly the way in which children were educated in the spirit world and reasoned that 'what is good for angels must surely be good for man' and so established a Lyceum (or school) for the children of the earth.[14] Gradually Lyceums developed in England, most attached to adult Spiritualist Societies and Churches. The British Lyceum movement developed its own character largely as a result of the influence of Alfred Kitson who is often referred to as 'The Father of the British Lyceum Movement'. He became the first Honorary Secretary when the Lyceum Union was formed in 1890.

In the early days the new Federation was not much more than an annual conference at which delegates from Spiritualist societies and individual Spiritualists could come together and debate problems of common concern. As a result of these considerations it became clear that the Federation could only widen the scope of its influence if it obtained corporate status with a legal right to hold property. The result was that in October 1901 The Spiritualist National Union Ltd. was incorporated under the Companies Acts. In July 1902 it took over the property, rights and obligations of the earlier Federation. At the same time The Spiritualists' Lyceum Union which had been formed in 1890 became a branch of the new Union. It was designed particularly to embrace those who could be said to be 'young in Spiritualism'. Although the training which was given was primarily focused for the young the Lyceum movement gradually came to include anyone who wanted to learn more about their spiritual nature.[15]

The newly created Spiritualist National Union (SNU) needed to provide a definition of 'Spiritualism' and 'Spiritualist' for incorporation into the Memorandum of Association. For this purpose those who compiled the new constitution took on the Principles Mrs Britten had received through her mediumship from Robert Owen in 1871 and had put forward to the inaugural meeting of the Spiritualists' National Federation in 1891.

---

[14]   *The Lyceum Today: An Outline*, 1.
[15]   Ibid.

## The Appeal of Early Spiritualism

Early Spiritualism emerged in upper New York State, an area noted for revivalistic enthusiasm. There was a constant stream of immigrants from Britain and Europe, many of whom were free spirits who were ready to try anything new. It was an era of campfire evangelism in which preachers of every denomination and none competed for people's attention. Those who could bring intensive and vivid religious experience to their followers carried a particular appeal. It was this note of seeming reality in the early Spiritualist sittings which appealed to many New Englanders. Alex Owen observed that 'middle-class Spiritualists were often those who had become disillusioned with the aridity of orthodox Christianity and who regarded the Church as a wasteland of dogma and ritual'.[16] Such individuals he suggested 'sought in the Spiritualist seance a direct experience of Divinity and the immortality of the soul'.[17]

Spiritualism offered a particular appeal to women at a point in time when orthodox denominational religion held out little in the way of opportunities for leadership or service. Spiritualists looked and sought for changes in the laws relating to women's rights. It was a sectarian movement in which women in particular were able to excel above their male counterparts. Great stress was laid on what was termed the 'passive' temperament of women. This yielding and receptive quality was believed to be particularly conducive to the harmony of the seance circle.[18] This same quality also made for more skilled mediumship. Women's more natural receptivity, it was believed, gave them a greater openness to messages from the spirit world. As Owen put it, 'Women were considered good trance mediums because of their ability to surrender to Spirit.'[19]

Evangelicalism had set great store on the home as the focus of Christianity. Spiritualism, too, located religion in the home, which was still seen as a woman's rightful sphere. The majority of early seances were held in domestic locations. In a typical seance men and

---

[16] *The Spiritualists' National Union Yearbook 1998*, 9.
[17] A. Owen, 'Women and Nineteenth Century Spiritualism: Strategies in the Subversion of Femininity', in J. Obelkevich, L. Roper and R. Samuel, *Disciplines of Faith*, 131.
[18] Ibid. 132.
[19] Ibid. 134.

women would sit alternately around a table in a darkened drawing room. Time was spent singing and chatting until the sensation of a cool breeze was felt passing over the hands of the participants. This usually marked the arrival of the spirits and the leader would take charge by asking the spirit questions. Contemporary Spiritualists continue to hold the majority of their seances in the home environment.

A number of early women mediums were observed to have a particular gift of healing. Bessie Fitzgerald, for example, could tell the exact disease people had. She could 'see the inside of everybody as perfectly as though they were made of glass'.[20] The procedure for healing usually involved laying on of hands or a process of passing the hands down the sufferer's body.[21] Another constant appeal of Spiritualism was that it held out comfort and reassurance particularly to those who had recently been bereaved. There was always the possibility of getting back into touch with a departed loved one. Early Spiritualists were also noted for their social justice.

An issue of particular concern to Spiritualists was education. There was a strong feeling that it should be wrested from church control. Another matter to which they devoted time and energy was the question of old age pensions. Hanson Hey, secretary of the Spiritualist National Union, worked tirelessly for a number of years for a scheme for old age pensions to be introduced and the Poor Rate done away with. The old must be granted sufficient income to free them from fear of the workhouse and to enable them to live out their days in sufficient comfort. It was also recognised that good diet, fresh air, clean water and exercise were of great importance to the physical body because it is the temple of the spirit. The *Lyceum Manual* states: 'He [humankind] has the right to fresh air and pure water, which by reason of their nature cannot be monopolised.'[22] The same document also declares 'that every human being must be able to obtain the necessities of physical health and happiness. That social irregularities must be removed, and the unjust division of labour and possessions regulated.'[23]

---

[20]  Ibid. 138.
[21]  Ibid.
[22]  *Lyceum Manual*, 143, 'Our Rights'.
[23]  Ibid. 123.

## Twentieth-Century Developments

Despite the fact that the SNU had been constituted in 1901, the newly created organisation still faced difficult times. Many were divided over the issue of war. A minority held strongly to the Spiritualist premise that war is against all that is good and the Lyceumists actively encouraged non-participation. Many Spiritualists, however, responded to Kitchener's call and chose to fight. With large numbers of Spiritualist men conscripted to the battlefronts, numerous societies were forced to close. A further problem was that there were so many anxious families at home waiting for a last comforting message that hundreds of charlatans set themselves up as clairvoyants. Spiritualists bore the brunt of the public outrage and media condemnation for much of what took place.

The major problem confronting Spiritualists was their lack of legal recognition. Their mediumistic activities were regarded as witchcraft and Spiritualist mediums could be prosecuted and convicted in the courts under the Vagrancies and Witchcraft Acts. A medium taking a service at Lonsight, Manchester, at the time of the Great War was charged with fortune-telling. The struggle for recognition was to last almost fifty years. Among the early mediums who suffered were Anne Novack and Helen Duncan. Anne Novack was the first medium to have defence lawyer's expenses paid by the Union's Freedom Fund, set up in 1943. Helen Duncan suffered court sentences on more than one occasion. She was prosecuted and fined at Edinburgh in May 1933 for mediumistic activity, and a decade later was in trouble for holding a seance on board HMS *Barham* in Portsmouth Harbour. Then, on 20 January 1944, she and three others were charged under the 1824 Vagrants Act with organising a further meeting. She was detained for five days in Holloway Prison and subsequently charged with being a witch. She was sentenced to nine months in prison on 4 April but was released in the following September. She returned to her native Scotland tired and weak, vowing never to work as a medium again.[24]

---

[24] Bassett, *100 Years of National Spiritualism*, 40 and 48–50.

The SNU encountered other difficulties as well: their ministers were not recognised in the way that denominational clergy were, their marriage services were not accepted in some quarters, and their burial rights were often denied. In order to fight against these disabilities, a 'Freedom Committee' was started with the specific aim of overturning the laws which stood against Spiritualism. Later a Parliamentary Fund was established to support the introduction of a Bill into Parliament.

## Some Key Figures

In its struggle for the recognition of its ministers and for the protection of its mediums the SNU was aided by several well-known public figures. Perhaps the most prominent among their number was Sir Arthur Conan Doyle (1859–1930) who announced his conversion to Spiritualism in 1916. Conan Doyle, the creator of Sherlock Holmes, became a believer in and a proselytiser for the Spiritualist cause. He was brought up as a Roman Catholic and happily accepted the possibility of apparitions including the Madonna and other saints. Two things caused him to turn away from Roman Catholicism. One was the extreme doctrines of Papal Infallibility and the Immaculate Conception. The other was the church's teaching which he heard from his own priest, Father Murphy 'that there was some damnation for everyone outside the Church'.[25] Conan Doyle remained agnostic from the time he graduated with a degree in medicine in 1881. He was, however, an active participant in Spiritualist activities from that time until he announced his conversion to Spiritualism in 1916. He attended his first seance as early as 1880 and was captivated at another in July 1888 when the medium told him not to read a book by Leigh Hunt. He was convinced because at precisely that moment he was debating whether or not to read the book, something which no one else in the group could possibly have known.[26] Many years later in his *History of Spiritualism*, Conan Doyle wrote that 'spiritualism

---

[25] M. Homer, 'Sir Arthur Conan Doyle: Spiritualism and "New Religions" ', *Dialogue* 23 (1990), 98.
[26] Ibid. 104.

formed our belief in life after death not upon ancient tradition nor upon vague intuitions, but upon proven facts, so that a science of religion may be built up'.[27] Michael Homer viewed Conan Doyle as 'supposedly agnostic' and pointed out that he wrote in August 1906:

> I am a believer in the Christian system in its simplest and least dogmatic form . . . I do not believe that the Divine Message to the human race was delivered once for all 2,000 years ago, but I hold that every piece of prose and verse which has anything which is helpful to the individual soul is, in some sense, a message from beyond – a message which grows and expands as all vital things must do.[28]

From 1916 onwards, Arthur Conan Doyle became a vigorous champion for the Spiritualist cause. Besides his adventures of Sherlock Holmes, which themselves reflect his Spiritualist convictions,[29] he wrote many letters to the newspapers in which he outlined the main tenets of Spiritualism with an apologetic end in view. He addressed the annual conference at Sheffield in 1928 and he and his wife became active Spiritualist missionaries. The war years proved to be a period of rapid growth for Spiritualism and between 1914 and 1919, the number of societies rose from 145 to 309.[30]

Another individual who did a great deal to gain recognition for the Spiritualists was Air Chief Marshall, Lord Dowding (1882–1970). He had been a Spiritualist for a number of years but it was not until 1943 that the Union suddenly became alive to the potential of his public notoriety. He spoke at conferences and at many smaller gatherings across the country. He was also one of a small group who presented a petition to Parliament requesting freedom from persecution. A measure of success was finally achieved in July 1950 with the passing of the Fraudulent Mediums Act. The law now recognised 'genuine mediumship' existed, as

---

[27] A. Conan Doyle, *History of Spiritualism*, 2, 247, cited in Homer, 'Sir Arthur Conan Doyle', 105.
[28] Ibid. 108.
[29] See Ibid. 105.
[30] Bassett, *100 Years of National Spiritualism*, 35.

opposed to 'fraudulent mediums' who could still be prosecuted. The legislation which amended the Witchcraft Act of 1735 and section 4 of the Vagrancy Act of 1824 in effect extended toleration to the Spiritualist movement.

## The Greater World Spiritualist League

In 1927 Sir Arthur Conan Doyle tabled a motion at the SNU's Annual Conference which sparked off what is still an ongoing debate among Spiritualists. His proposal advocated the adoption of a Christian basis. The President in response pointed out that this addition would effectively exclude all those who were opposed to Christianity. The matter was put on hold but defeated when it was put to the vote at the following year's AGM. Although some of the churches in the SNU contained members who came from a Christian background, the Union has consistently resisted incorporating specifically Christian formula into its foundation principles.

Conan Doyle accepted the defeat of his motion and continued to advance the cause of Spiritualism. However, a number of Spiritualist churches which retained elements of Christian belief shared his convictions. From among their number a leader emerged in the person of Winifred Moyes. Winifred had never investigated Spiritualism and felt that it was 'dangerous to meddle with evil spirits'. However, she had begun to hear voices and see visions which, she was convinced, were associated with Christ. In particular she received messages from a spirit guide named Zodiac who claimed to have been a teacher in the temple at Jerusalem at the time of Jesus. Zodiac's purpose was 'to intercede between Christ and the people within our movement, to help us understand and work with the spirit world to spread the truth of Christian Spiritualism'.[31] Winifred, the eldest daughter of a journalist, had health problems from the time she was ten years old. She was 'a natural medium' who from early childhood saw visions. For most of her life she was physically weak and confined to a wheelchair. Strangely, according to Spiritualists, when she was in a trance state, Zodiac would lift her out of the chair and she would walk around the congregation. Then

---

[31]  *The Greater World Christian Spiritualist Association Information Leaflet*, 2.

when the sitting was coming to a close he would pick her up and put her back. After a time Moyes produced a journal *The Great World* which is still published and which serves to promote Christian Spiritualism. This in turn led to the foundation of The Greater World Christian Spiritualist League on 30 May 1931. This name was changed in 1932 to its present title The Greater World Christian Spiritualist Association. The organisation has as its objects 'To spread in all directions the truth of survival after death, of spirit communion, of healing by the power of the Holy Spirit and to disseminate the teachings received from highly evolved Spirit messengers.'[32]

Winifred Moyes devoted her life to acting as the sole instrument for the inspired teaching of 'Zodiac'. He chose this particular name to indicate his purpose which is 'to lift men's thoughts from the earth to the heavens'.[33] Zodiac delivered 1,475 addresses between 1924 and 1957 at meetings which often attracted thousands of people. These teachings have continued to inspire many in the GWCSA (Greater World Christian Spiritualist Association) who seek 'the meaning and purpose of life, the function of the natural gifts of Healing and Spirit Communion, and the reassurance of the immortality of the Spirit'.[34] Zodiac named his great work 'The Christ Mission' and it is on this that Greater World is founded.

The Greater World organisation grew rapidly and by 1935 they had over 500 affiliated churches, almost as many as the SNU, which adopted 'The Greater World Belief and Pledge' worked out by Charles Aischiman in 1931:

1. I believe in one God who is love.
2. I accept the leadership of Jesus Christ.
3. I believe that God manifests through the illimitable power of the Holy Spirit.
4. I believe in the survival of the human soul and its individuality after physical death.
5. I believe in Communion with God, with his angelic ministers, and with the soul functioning in conditions other than the earth life.

---

[32] Ibid. 1.
[33] *The Greater World Newsletter* 30 (autumn 1998), 7.
[34] Ibid.

6. I believe that all forms of life created by God intermingle, are intelligent, are independent, and evolve until perfection is attained.
7. I believe in the perfect justice of the divine laws governing all life.
8. I believe that sins committed can only be rectified by the sinner himself or herself, through the redemptive power of Jesus Christ, by repentance.

### The Pledge

9. I will at all times endeavour to be guided in my thoughts, words and deeds by the teaching and example of Jesus Christ.[35]

Although the GWCSA professed to be a federation of Christian Spiritualist churches, some of its beliefs are clearly different from those set out in three great Catholic Creeds. Perhaps the most obvious is in the area of soteriology. Christian Spiritualists do not accept that the blood shed by Jesus at the crucifixion absolves them from sin. What Christian Spiritualists teach is that 'when through their own efforts they seek to put right any wrongs committed, there is the redemptive power in Christ which helps them to do so'.[36] In Article 2 Christian Spiritualists do express that they 'accept the leadership of Jesus', but this simply means that they take Jesus as their role model and try to live according to the pattern of his life.

Christian Spiritualist churches generally have a President, Secretary and Treasurer. Usually there is a Council consisting of about a dozen or so members and a Medium Secretary whose task it is to obtain a medium for each Sunday's worship service. Such mediums are usually accredited and themselves members of a GWCSA church.

Most Christian Spiritualist churches hold several services a week. Divine service on a Sunday usually includes clairvoyance and sometimes a short service of healing follows. In addition, there are services of healing and clairvoyance on weekdays, usually in the afternoon or evening. Some Christian Spiritualist churches hold services of Holy Communion once a month. These are much the

---

[35]  Ibid. 12.
[36]  A. Clifton, *What is Christian Spiritualism*, 1.

same in appearance as those of the denominational churches with readings from the Bible and the sharing of bread and wine. Greater World Congregations do not hold baptismal services but young children are dedicated to God in a 'Naming' Ceremony. On these occasions the child is given a 'Spirit name' which is entered in a register and a certificate is given to the parents to mark the occasion.

Healing services are an important aspect in the life of Christian Spiritualist churches. They normally take place after the main service is over and people who want to receive healing stay behind in the church building. When the atmosphere is quiet the proceedings begin with a prayer to God that the healers will become pure instruments for healing energy. Usually those who are praying for the sick operate in pairs and those seeking healing come forward to the couple they feel most comfortable with. Strict conditions apply to a healer while giving healing. The patient should be encouraged to seek medical advice if that has not already been sought. There must be no diagnosis given. A patient must give permission before a healer may touch the body. Strict instructions are given that no promise should be made regarding a cure. All forms of massage or manipulation are strictly forbidden at any time.

The healers place their hands on or near the sufferer's head and pray to God, usually in the name of Jesus. If it is appropriate they may ask the person for whom they are praying if they would like them to put their hands on or near the infected or problem area. It often happens that considerable heat is released through the hands of those who are praying and this is seen as a sign that healing energy is beginning to flow. This usually causes the 'patient' to enter a relaxed and sometimes even a comatose state. As prayer continues the healers anticipate that their hands will turn cold or even 'icy cold'. Greater cold usually signals that a greater degree of energy is being released. While this flow of energy is happening some Spiritualists urge that it is important for those who are ministering to locate a 'chakra' or energy point in the sick person's body because here there is often a greater release of power. The main chakra is on the line of the spine to the crown of the head. Early modern Spiritualism did not mention such energy points and merely stated that the healing medium was a channel for healing energies from spirit. When the prayer has ended it is important for the person to be left sitting quietly on their own and to ensure that the energy points are closed down. Christian Spiritualists believe that there are both good and evil spirits hovering in the atmosphere and that the latter are quite capable of invading a person's 'aura' at the end of a healing session if their chakras are not sealed.

Although Zodiac spoke almost exclusively through Winifred Moyes he has come through one or two people in more recent times. In the main, however, his teachings are now communicated through *The Greater World Newsletter*, a quarterly glossy magazine. Each issue includes a message from Zodiac. His words are usually comforting, practical God-centred. The *Greater World Newsletter* for Autumn 1998 carried a four-page excerpt from Zodiac's message given at the Slough Christian Mission on 29 September 1929. It included some advice to those 'forced to do uncongenial work'.

> Then I speak to men who are immersed in business. God can be demonstrated in the humblest most unpleasant task. In all that which raises such swift and fierce rebellion in your mind – the injustices, the hatred of the work at hand and the longing to build that which is your heart's desire. Be as men! Square your shoulders! Look up! What has happened? You are taking the rough road today so that tomorrow you shall see the beauties of the Spirit and the glories prepared for you by the one who loves you best.[37]

At a later point in his message Zodiac urged his hearers to depend on Christ and the Holy Spirit for all the resources of their daily living.

> The blessings of the Holy Spirit, the power of the Cross of Christ be upon you. Raise your hearts and minds and rejoice for to you truth has been given and henceforth you can be disciples of Christ. By the power of the Holy Spirit, under the direction of my Master, I bless you in His name.
>
> Never forget that we who come back in this way are dependent solely upon the Christ for power. Without His gift I must be dumb, indeed the instrument could not be mine.[38]

---

[37] *The Greater World Newsletter* 30 (autumn 1998), 6.
[38] Ibid. 7.

Although the cross is not seen as a substitutionary sacrifice for sin, the cross is a frequent feature in Christian Spiritualist thinking. Zodiac concluded this particular message as follows: 'The Cross is upon you all. Feel its warmth, feel its strength, feel its health, its joy, its peace, its life. The Cross is the gift of Christ to each and everyone.'[39]

While Christian Spiritualists accord a central place to the teachings of Zodiac, they readily receive contact and help from other spirit guides. In more recent years, for example, Ivy Northage has acted as medium for a spirit guide who goes under the name of 'Chan'. Usually when she is in a deep trance 'Chan' comes through. Participants at Ivy's sittings know themselves to be communicating with a completely other or different person. Chan is apparently a very understanding spirit with a 'wicked sense of humour'. He is very down to earth and readily responds in question and answer sessions to people's requests for present guidance or information about the future.[40]

In addition to the help received from these greater luminaries such as Zodiac and Chan, all Christian Spiritualists have their own spirit guides. Such guides can be members of the individual's family who have passed beyond the grave, but this is unusual. A significant number of Christian Spiritualists have spirit guides who were formerly ancient Egyptians or Red Indians. These familiars are believed to be constantly watching over the interests of their earthly charges. Spiritualists are of the view that when a person dies the 'Silver Cord' is broken and the soul is freed from the body. It is then free to embark on an upward spiral in the spirit realms where it can choose to reincarnate or to become a guide. In contrast to this belief, SNU Spiritualism neither accepts nor rejects reincarnation or guide worship. Because reincarnation cannot be proven SNU Spiritualists are encouraged not to mention it in their public addresses.

The GWCSA has 106 affiliated churches, the majority of which are situated in the south and east of the UK. By no means, however, are all Christian Spiritualist churches linked with the association. Some prefer to remain independent. Others have chosen to belong to the SNU.

---

[39] Ibid.
[40] Information received from Joy Smith, Secretary of North Oxford Christian Spiritualist Church, unstructured interview 17 November 1998.

## The Spiritualist National Union

The SNU is an altogether much larger organisation than the GWCSA and has some four hundred affiliated churches with a total membership of over 20,000.[41] At the end of 1996 the Union had 382 fully affiliated churches with a total membership of 20,267. Its registered office is located at Stansted Hall, Stansted in Essex. The hall was gifted to the Union by Arthur Finlay in 1964 and restored and refurbished with the help of grants and loans.

Churches seeking affiliated status must give their assent to the 'Seven Principles' on which the SNU is based. Affiliation provides a number of obvious advantages including charitable status which provides exemption from income tax payments. Additionally, the Union offers an education scheme which includes a wide range of courses, some with examinations and awards. A register of award holders and SNU ministers is kept. This means that churches can check on the credentials of visiting speakers and mediums.

The SNU is organised into fourteen district councils which organise and hold regular meetings during the course of the year. Each church can participate in the business of the district by sending a delegate known as a Class A member. Class A delegates can vote on all business items including district and national elections. The SNU also has what are known as Class B members. These are individual congregational members who have taken out a personal membership with the Union in addition to the membership which they have by virtue of belonging to an affiliated church. Class B members have a number of benefits, including the right to attend meetings and vote in elections. They receive regular published materials and details of courses and activities at Stansted Hall. To become a class B member an applicant must be sponsored by two persons who are themselves class B members. One of the two sponsoring members must have been a class B member for at least three years and be a resident in the same district area as the person seeking membership.

There is an official ministry within the SNU affiliated churches and SNU ministers have governmental recognition as Ministers of Religion in the same way as those of other denominational

---

[41] *The Spiritualists' National Union Yearbook 1998*, 167.

churches. SNU ministers are appointed by the National Executive Committee from candidates who have successfully completed the prescribed training programme. Men or women who wish to embark on a course of ministerial training must at the time of their recommendation have been a class B member and a member of an affiliated church for the previous ten years. They must also have held a 'Speakers Diploma' for at least one year and have successfully completed one of the Union's administration courses. There must be a need for a minister in the area in which the person resides and he or she must be available for duty, particularly funeral services, at all times.

In order to meet the increased need for officiants at marriages and funerals, the SNU has established the position of 'Approved Celebrant' in Scotland and 'Officiant' in England, Wales and Northern Ireland. Those wishing to be considered as candidates must have been a full class B member for at least two years and a full member of an SNU affiliated body for the previous eight years. There must be a need for their ministry within their local area and they must be available during the week to conduct services.[42] If these conditions are all met the person must then be recommended to the National Executive Committee (NEC) to become a minister or officiant.

In many instances there may be little difference in the Sunday worship of a GWCSA- or SNU-affiliated church. In fact until 1987 it was possible for a church to belong to both organisations.[43] The main difference between the two umbrella groupings is that the SNU makes no official commitment to any Christian beliefs. However, some of its churches and their congregational members may well have strongly held biblical convictions. A typical SNU congregation will have a Sunday service followed by healing or clairvoyance. During the week there will probably be further worship which will include meditation, healing and clairvoyance. Many churches advertise private sittings, namings, weddings and funerals. Sunday Services in an SNU church include hymns which may have biblical content and be addressed to God, though not to Christ. There will be prayer to God or the Divine Spirit and

---

[42] Ibid. 13.
[43] Bassett, *100 Years of National Spiritualism*, 85.

readings usually from Philosophy or 'White Eagle' and 'Silver Birch' literature. Healing services, as in the GWCSA, often follow a Divine Service. Healers have to be properly trained at Stansted Hall or be under the supervision of their local church. They operate in pairs, a man and a woman, so that no one is left alone to minister to the opposite sex.

## Other Organisations

In addition to the two main umbrella organisations, SNU and GWCSA, there are a number of smaller Spiritualist Associations. Among these are the SAGB (Spiritualist Association of Great Britain) founded in July 1872 with its headquarters at Belgrave Square in London.[44] The Association which is independent of both the SNU and the GWCSA subscribes to the Seven Principles. In addition to regular Sunday services, the Association organises demonstrations, lectures and development classes.[45] 'Absent' healing (see below) takes place every day.[46] The SAGB has members from all over England and from overseas.

Another organisation, the White Eagle Lodge, dates back to the 1920s and owes its origin to Grace Cooke and Burstow Manor. The building, which was situated in the small hamlet of Burstow about thirty miles south of London on the Brighton Road, was leased from 1932–35.[47] A number of visitors reported seeing visions of monks in brown habits walking in the grounds. Other confirmations of a brotherhood in the spirit world were given and a White Brotherhood was established in 1931 when Grace Cooke (d. 1979) and her husband Ivan (d. 1981) were initiated as the first brothers. Gradually, through the small gatherings of people at Burstow, the spirit guide known as 'White Eagle' made himself known. When the lease expired in the autumn of 1935 the brotherhood hoped to buy Burstow but their hopes were dashed. It was then that White Eagle guided them to Pembroke Hall in Kensington which was

---

[44] *Service Magazine* (December 1998 to March 1999), 1.
[45] Ibid. 10–16.
[46] Ibid. 12.
[47] See *The Story of White Eagle Lodge*, 1–5.

available for lease. Despite bombing during the war the building was refurbished and subsequently extended when the adjoining property was made available.

White Eagle's usual personality is that of an old American Indian chieftain, but he is also familiar to many of his friends as a Tibetan, an Egyptian Priest-king, Pharaoh, a humble brother in an obscure order, and an alchemist in the Middle Ages.[48] According to Grace Cooke, White Eagle has never been known to speak harshly or unkindly or to judge or condemn other people. Always he encourages his hearers in hopeful, loving and gentle ways. This spirit chose to reveal himself as 'White Eagle' because the name signifies one with spiritual vision.

One of the distinctive aspects of White Eagle's revelations was his teaching on healing. He says that if someone has asked us for healing, then 'visualising them perfect within the light of the sun or a six-pointed star can bring healing to them'.[49] An important aspect of all White Eagle Lodges of which there are a number in the UK, as well as Australia, Holland and the US, is healing work.[50] Special colours are prescribed for particular complaints and diseases to bring regeneration, comfort, healing and strength. Members practise absent healing sitting in small circles praying for the restoration of those who are absent. 'Contact' healing is also practised by individual healers who received guidance from White Eagle as to the diagnosis and the manner of treatment. Regular healing services in the context of Communion remain an essential aspect of White Eagle Lodges as does the ideal of service which may involve menial, domestic and practical work in the Lodges and for the brotherhood. White Eagle Lodges are developing in a number of nations and there are now 6,000 members worldwide. The White Eagle Lodge has a set of six key beliefs: God as 'Eternal Spirit' is 'both Father and Mother'. Jesus is seen as the 'Cosmic Christ' and also 'the Light which shines in the human heart'. Life is seen as governed by five cosmic laws: 'Reincarnation; Cause and Effect; Opportunity; Correspondences; Compensation (Equilibrium) and Balance'.[51]

---

[48] G. Cooke, *Who is White Eagle?* 7.
[49] *The White Eagle Lodge*, 6.
[50] See ibid. 64–6.
[51] Ibid. 10.

The ultimate goal of mankind, as White Eagle members see it, is that the 'inner light' should become so strong within a person that 'the cells of their physical body are transmuted into finer substances which can overcome mortality'. This is spoken of as the 'Christing of man'.[52]

## Core Spiritualist Beliefs

All Spiritualists, whether they adhere to a Christian framework or not, are united in the conviction that after death the spirit is set free from the individual's body. It is then free to roam and can either choose to go on to a higher spiritual level, or reincarnate or become a spirit guide to the living. Spiritualists maintain that spirit guides are constantly seeking to make their presence known to people in this world. The major business of Spiritualism is about helping to put congregational members in touch with spirit guides who will then be of assistance to them as they run their earthly course. Spiritualists receive spirit guidance at several levels. First, they will attend sittings where, through the help of trance mediumship, they are able to receive teaching from one of the major spirits such as 'Silver Birch' who communicated through the mediumship of Maurice Barbanell. Second, they will expect to receive more regular guidance and messages of encouragement through clairvoyance at church services. Third, they will seek to find and enter into a relationship with their own personal spirit guide. Christian Spiritualists see Jesus both as assisting in this process and revealing his presence through it. For many Spiritualists all of this is immensely comforting, particularly if they have been recently bereaved and need consolation in the form of a message from their departed loved ones. The messages they receive confirm their conviction that there is life after death and that all human beings survive the transition.

The belief in angelic guardians or guides is widespread within the Christian tradition. Also in some Roman Catholic and High Church circles the practice of interceding to the saints comes close to this Spiritualist concept of receiving help from the departed.

---

[52] Ibid.

Generally, however, it differs in that they do not commune or receive messages back from the saints to whom they pray. In the orthodox creedal and Protestant churches, there is a long-standing tradition which regards the practice of seeking contact with departed spirits as forbidden. Reference would be made to the account of King Saul who needed guidance and sought out a witch who brought up the departed spirit of the prophet Samuel, an action for which he was severely punished (see I Samuel 28). I Chronicles 10:13, which offers a reflection on Saul's kingship, states that 'Saul died because he was unfaithful to the Lord and even consulted a medium for guidance'. Other injunctions such as Leviticus 19:31, 'Do not turn to mediums or seek out spiritists, for you will be defiled by them'; Leviticus 20:6, 'I will set my face against the person who turns to mediums'; Leviticus 20:27, 'A man or woman who is a medium or spiritist among you must be put to death'; are strongly held to be binding in contemporary Christianity. Mediumistic activity is believed to be precluded by the New Testament injunctions against witchcraft in Galatians 5:20 and elsewhere. The outlawing of mediumistic activity became central in Western Christianity in the fourth century following the conversion of the Emperor Constantine, who passed laws against magic practitioners. Later, at the Council of Nicaea in AD 325, all forms of witchcraft and mediumship were condemned. This legislation became more rigidly enforced in the Middle Ages and later by the Puritans of England and America.

Various interpretations of the messages Spiritualists purport to receive from their spirit guides have been given. It is beyond the scope of this chapter to engage with them in any detail. Suffice it to say that some scientific materialists understand the messages as an extension coming from the collective psyche of the sitters or, in other cases, of the trance medium. A few have maintained there is fraud and there have been some evidences of this in the early confessions of the Fox sisters. Others have suggested that messages and voices are in fact those of malignant spirits deluding and leading astray the participants. It is possible, Spiritualists maintain, to counter all these accusations by careful and objective testing.

Other major areas where Spiritualism differs from the teachings of Catholic and Protestant churches is in its doctrine of God and Christology. Scientific Spiritualists have no concept of the divine or

Godhead and speak in terms of the spirit realm or 'Ultimate Reality'. For Christian Spiritualists God is seen as a principle rather than a person. Andrew Jackson Davis wrote that God is 'the Active or Moving Principle, and is different from Nature in this one particular respect, that while God is Active and Moving, Nature is Passive and Moved'.[53] Davis also spoke of God as 'Positive Mind' and all else as 'Negative'.[54] Other Spiritualists such as the followers of Zodiac or White Eagle see God as personal and use terms such as 'father'. Spiritualism lacks a doctrine of substitutionary atonement through the death of Christ, and the cross is infrequently mentioned except occasionally as the exemplar of sacrifice. Perhaps too it is true to assert that much of the focus of Christian Spiritualism is centred on man rather than on God. The worship does not appear to uplift the name of God or to focus on his person.

There is no doubt that Spiritualism is fulfilling a need in many lives. It seems to be more strongly rooted in the south and east of the UK where the majority of churches and lodges are situated. Many members are elderly and therefore possibly looking for comfort as their generation begins to pass away and as they themselves contemplate the prospect of death. Nelson, for example, found in his study of thirty-seven Spiritualist churches in the Birmingham area that 84 per cent of the members were over fifty years of age.[55] Whether Nelson's findings are an indication of the movement as a whole is a matter for further research. Be that as it may the fact remains that Spiritualist churches and lodges embrace about 30,000 active members. Quite probably they also attract significant numbers of inquisitive observers and visitors. Part of the reason for this is that the mainstream churches have lost the dimension of spiritual reality which clearly pervaded Christianity in earlier times.

---

[53] G.K. Nelson, 'Spiritualism in the Midlands: A Research Note', in A. Bryman (ed.), *Religion in the Birmingham Area: Essays in the Sociology of Religion*, 105.
[54] Ibid. 106.
[55] Nelson, 'Spiritualism in the Midlands', 129.

# Chapter 9

# The Jesus Fellowship and the Jesus Army

The Jesus Fellowship Church was born of the charismatic movement in 1969 when Noel Stanton and some of his congregation at Bugbrooke Baptist Church were filled with the Holy Spirit and began speaking in tongues.[1] Bugbrooke was a quiet Northamptonshire village with a small cluster of stone cottages and an ancient parish church. Bugbrooke Baptist Church, founded in 1805, was soon inspired by the proclamation of a young preacher by the name of John Wheeler.

Noel Stanton (b. 1926) was brought up on his parents' farm in Bedfordshire. While serving with the Royal Navy in Sydney, Noel gave his life to Christ. After a course of training at All Nations Bible College and further work experience as an accounts clerk in Bedford, he was accredited by the Baptist Union and inducted as a pastor at Bugbrooke in 1957. After ten years of hard and dedicated work, Noel was concerned about the way forward. There had been no major breakthrough and he sensed a lack of power in his ministry. At the conclusion of the Church's AGM in 1968 he urged everyone to ask for a definite outpouring of the Holy Spirit according to Luke 11:13: 'If you . . . know how to give good gifts to your children, how much more will your Father in heaven give the Holy Spirit to those who ask him!'[2] Within a matter of days the answer was coming. As Noel was praying in the manse he had an experience much like that of the earlier American evangelist Charles Finney. 'It was', he related, 'so intoxicating, so exhilarating,

---

[1] *On the March*, 4. See also S. Cooper and M. Farrant, *Fire in Our Hearts*, 31f.
[2] Cooper and Farrant, *Fire in Our Hearts*, 29.

and so intense that I felt I was just not going to live anymore!'[3]
About the same time as this, numbers of the chapel youngsters were
also baptised in the Holy Spirit and began to speak in tongues.[4]

Noel Stanton was a changed man. According to members of his
congregation 'he looked like a hundred watt light bulb'. Even
Miss Campion, one of the church's long-standing stalwarts was
reported to be 'glowing'. An Anglican lady from the village was
heard to remark, 'I don't know what's going on there, but whatever they've got we haven't!'[5] Whatever had happened, soon
began to have an impact. Young wives were praying in new
languages and choir practice changed from 95 per cent choir and 5
per cent prayer, to 0 per cent choir and 100 per cent prayer, praise
and Bible fellowship.[6]

In the three following years Bugbrooke received input from
some of the early restoration teachers such as Gerald Coates who
'ministered with great freedom' in May 1971. But the fellowship
were apprehensive both about being restricted by denominational
ties or 'covered' by one of the New Churches. As a result the
fellowship gradually came to assert its autonomy as a self-governing
independent Baptist Church. There was a felt need for holiness of
life and radical social action. Things began to take a further step in
this direction in July 1973 when Noel read Michael Harper's book
*A New Way of Living*, which favourably described the community
lifestyle of the Church of the Redeemer in Texas.[7] At the time
members of the church were holidaying in the Yorkshire Dales and
Noel frequently read extracts to the group. The example of the
Redeemer church was a 'massive inspiration' and they were
challenged by the fact that members there stopped buying new cars
and televisions and began to value their possessions only in so far as
they were useful to the community.[8] Before the fellowship returned
home from Malhamdale they had already begun to work out a
vision for a new community. People who lived away from

---

[3] Ibid. 30.
[4] Ibid.
[5] Ibid. 37.
[6] Ibid.
[7] M. Harper, *A New Way of Living*.
[8] Cooper and Farrant, *Fire in Our Hearts*, 80.

Bugbrooke seriously began to consider moving into the village to be where the action was. Ideas were put forward for bulk buying, for a second-hand clothes store and for sharing needs and gifts. Three types of community homes were projected. There would be Jesus Family Homes which would be extended families, Jesus Welcome Homes which would serve as bases for evangelism, and Jesus Central Homes which would train Christians within a community context.

The Jesus Fellowship emerged against a background of the American-based Jesus Movement of the 1960s. By the 1970s this influence had spread to England and Jesus tents were being set up at pop festivals with the aim of capturing teenagers. A number of Jesus People involved themselves in the controversial 'Festival of Light' held in London in 1971. A parallel but equally significant religious influence which impacted the NCCC (New Creation Christian Community) was the Restoration House Church movement with its emphasis on a charismatic apocalyptic message coupled with a stress on shepherding and tithing. This found reflections in the system of 'fathering' and 'mothering' adopted by the NCCC in its early days.[9]

The 1960s witnessed a reaction to the growing materialism which had its roots in the 'never had it so good' days of Harold Macmillan. People were rapidly losing confidence in the wealth and respectability of those who attended the established churches. Families, too, began to crumble with easier divorce arrangements. This in turn led to youngsters from fragmented families being attracted into tight-knit loving, caring and upright communities such as the Jesus Fellowship were offering.

In June 1974 the vision for community began to materialise with purchase at an auction of Bugbrooke Hall for £67,000. It had been empty for two years and renovation proved to be an uphill task. Nevertheless a start had been made. A grant was obtained to convert the house into flats which enabled families to have a degree of privacy. About thirty people eventually squashed into 'New Creation Hall'. Others took up residence at one of the Welcome Homes in Northampton or in extended families. Further houses

---

[9] It should be noted that the Jesus Fellowship never adopted the apocalyptic theology of the Restoration movement.

were established in Leicester in 1980, Coventry in 1981 and Milton Keynes in 1984.

In 1974 shepherding was emerging in a widespread way in the new charismatic churches. At its best this system of pastoral care was seen as a means of strengthening and bonding fellowships together. The new group felt strongly that they needed mature men who could exercise leadership and pastoral care. During a time away at Ashburnham in Sussex, a number of small groups were formed and new leaders were commissioned by laying on of hands.[10] A 'senior brother' was to be supported by two others who were given pastoral responsibility. Groups of about ten 'sheep' were placed in the care of one 'shepherd'. This all-male leadership was publicly recognised and on occasion proved to be quite authoritarian.

Michael Harper had written in *A New Way of Living* that 'Individualism has been the bane of the churches.'[11] This prompted an immediate concern to share resources within the community houses. Guitars, tape recorders and even cars were placed at the disposal of all the members. There was a general aim to try to live more simply. Community houses took a newspaper but they decided against either television or radios. In the early days single 'sisters' lived mainly in the cottages at Great Lane, at the house in Harlestone Road in Northampton or in various extended family houses in Bugbrooke area.

Describing these early experiences of community life, Cooper and Farrant wrote: 'New Creation was the theme and a distinctive "Kingdom Culture" began to take shape.'[12] 'New Creation' was seen as important because they regarded themselves as Christians who had been born again. Additionally they wanted to follow what they understood to be the communal lifestyle of the early Christians at Jerusalem in Acts 2. The New Creation Christian Community, according to Campbell and Bird, was to be 'a largely residential church-community which fully practises the teachings of Jesus, and shows a clear alternative lifestyle in the midst of an increasingly hedonistic society.'[13] It is for this reason that there are no sports,

---

[10]  Cooper and Farrant, *Fire in Our Hearts*, 96.
[11]  Ibid. 83.
[12]  Ibid. 103.
[13]  J. Campbell and J. Bird, *Christian Community in Central England*, 5.

holidays, televisions, videos or fashion clothes. These things, it is felt, do not figure in the simple lifestyle of Jesus which they seek to follow, but are believed to be against the teaching of Scripture. 2 Timothy 3:2–4 is often quoted: 'Men will be lovers of self, lovers of money . . . lovers of pleasure, rather than lovers of God.' There is a library in the New Creation Hall formed when members pooled their own books, but it contains only books with a Christian perspective and which do not stand in opposition to the views of the Jesus Fellowship.[14]

## Community Lifestyle

Community living is not mandatory for membership of the Jesus Fellowship. In the 1980s approximately half of the members lived in their own accommodation, keeping personal charge of their own finances but supporting the community vision and practice of the Church. By the later 1990s the proportion of those living in the New Creation Christian Community was closer to one quarter.[15] In May 1999 John Campbell, the Jesus Army/Jesus Fellowship Communications Officer, wrote: 'There is relatively free movement between styles of membership, so a common pattern will include a stay in community before moving on to a more independent lifestyle. We see this as a constructive option for many and an answer to some of the [fair] criticism.'[16]

Within the Church there are a range of different styles of membership. These are as follows:

Style 1:   This membership is similar to 'normal' church membership in many churches.

Style 2:   Voluntary accountability over income and expenditure, surplus committed to the community or Church.

Style 3:   Full common-purse community, with all income, wealth and possessions shared.

---

[14]   Cooper and Farrant, *Fire in Our Hearts*, 102.

[15]   Letter from John Campbell, 11 May 1999.

[16]   Ibid.

Style 4:    Includes members at a distance in the UK or overseas who
            are unable to fully practice their commitments to the
            Fellowship.[17]

It should be noted that Style 2 was changed in 1999 to 1. Regular
meeting attendance. 2. Regular giving to the church. 3. Holy and
godly lifestyle.[18] Those joining the Jesus Fellowship must accept
their statement of faith and be baptised as a believer if they are new
converts. They must also take a Covenant Pledge of loyalty to
Christ and the members of the Church. This is reaffirmed at the
weekly Agape, a lengthy mealtime accompanied by worship,
ministry, heart-sharing and confession of faults which centres on
Holy Communion. Their statement of membership of the Church
includes the following paragraph:

> Covenant Membership is open to those who have been born of God
> through repentance of sin and faith in the Lord Jesus Christ, been
> baptised in water and in the Holy Spirit, and who wish to become
> committed to the Fellowship. Both residential and non-residential
> Styles of Membership of the Church enter into this Covenant pledge.[19]

An integral part of this Covenant is Section 4, entitled 'The
Community Life of God's People', in which all new members are
invited to pledge themselves as they are able 'to respond to the
command of Jesus to love one another as He loves us, by sharing as I
am able, any possessions, property, money and income within the
brotherhood, according to the pattern inspired by the Holy Spirit in
the first Church'.[20] It should be noted that not all members in fact
take the pledge.

---

[17] *Jesus: The Name Jesus: The Foundation*, 2.

[18] Written information received from John Campbell, Communications
Officer, Jesus Army / Jesus Fellowship, 3 June 1999. The JA/JF also have
baptised members who have not taken the pledge. In addition they have
congregational members and cell-group members who wish to express
their varying degrees of adherence to the movement.

[19] *Jesus: The Name Jesus*, 4.

[20] Ibid.

In seeking to follow the pattern of the earliest New Testament Christians in the book of Acts 2:44–5 and Acts 4:32–5, the NCCC has come to the view that they should share all things in common. Indeed their view is that 'nowhere in scripture are the principles of renunciation and sharing material possessions contradicted and there is nothing to say that Jesus' teaching on the subject is not for believers now'.[21] Integral to this is the concept of a common purse which Jesus Fellowship members understand Jesus and his disciples to have had, kept by Judas.[22] Each community house therefore operates a common purse. Members are not permitted to spend money from the shared fund on luxury items and bills must be presented for all purchased items. Those who join the community share their income in the household 'common purse', but do not contribute any capital wealth until after a twelve-month probationary period which cannot begin until they reach the age of twenty-one. This procedure is adopted in an attempt to ensure individuals do not make rash, spur-of-the-moment decisions. In 1999 the probationary period was extended to twenty-four months.

As a means of preventing themselves from getting caught in the consumerist trap, members of the community are required to order their food, clothing and other household goods through the Food Distribution Centre. This is an attempt to follow the pattern of distribution set by the deacons of the Jerusalem Church in Acts 6:1–7 who were appointed 'to ensure fair distribution among the saints'.[23] The Food Distribution Centre also fulfils another of the Community's principles, namely equality. Campbell and Bird emphasise the point as follows: 'There are no rich or poor within the community and those who used to be on the breadline now live equally with those who were once among the privileged, so producing a society of equality.'[24] Members in community express their relief at escaping from the consumerist indulgence of the empty world around them. Typical of many was Jill who commented: 'I graduated recently. Many of my friends already have

---

[21] *Newness* 2, p. 6. The JF are clear that Acts 2 and 4 are not the only pattern in the first church.

[22] See John 12:6 and 13:29.

[23] *Newness* 3, p. 4.

[24] Campbell and Bird, *Christian Community in Central England*, 6.

high-flying jobs and are really making it in the world. But I'm grateful to God for calling me out of the destructive rat race. I see my future as helping to love the lost and the poor and taking a radical stance for Jesus at all costs.'[25]

The Jesus Fellowship owns seventy-six communal houses in the British Isles. Some are small, 'single family' houses, others have between twelve and thirty adult residents.[26] The members are bonded together by a covenant pledge. This involves joining with others in the community in 'the mutual confession of faults, recognising that there must be a full openness in the brotherhood and all must be accountable to one another'.[27] The Covenant also includes a lifetime commitment to the Church which is expressed in the following declaration: 'My desire is that for all my earthly life I shall be a Covenant Member of this church and a soldier in the modern JESUS army.'[28]

One of the distinctive features of the NCCC is the large number of celibates and the strong emphasis placed on celibacy. According to Katz in 1991 'around half the single members have taken vows of celibacy'.[29] Writing in 1995 MacDonald-Smith suggested that 'about a quarter of the members, including Noel Stanton, have made a lifelong vow'.[30] The Jesus Fellowship themselves attach value to both marriage and celibacy. Both are seen as callings from God. Families are needed 'to provide the essential base of homeliness and security'. Celibates, on the other hand, are free to engage in pioneering and evangelistic work. On the matter of the single lifestyle the Fellowship states: 'The call to celibacy has been embraced by many within the Church. Because they are free from the demands of family life, celibate brothers and sisters are often more available for vital evangelistic and church-building ministries.'[31]

---

[25] *Jesus Lifestyle* 27 (First Quarter, 1994), 18.

[26] The number of seventy-six was given by John Campbell, Communications Officer, JA/JF, in writing, 3 June 1999.

[27] *Jesus: The Name Jesus*, 5.

[28] Ibid.

[29] I. Katz, 'The Theocrats', Weekend Guardian, 6 July 1991, 20–21.

[30] F. MacDonald-Smith, 'The Jesus Army Wants You', *The Independent Magazine*, 29 April 1995.

[31] *On the March*, 14.

During the course of a brief stay with the Jesus Fellowship, MacDonald-Smith encountered one of the sisters who was 'anxious' because she was told at a prayer meeting 'that God has sent a word for her – that word was celibacy'. Noel Stanton stopped her after the meeting was over to check that she had heard the message. She replied that she had heard it but she wasn't receiving it. She meant no disrespect but, in her own words, 'I don't think I am ready yet.'[32]

Families are fully incorporated into the life of the Community household of which they are a part and care is taken to preserve their identity and privacy. The Jesus People pledge themselves to maintain 'holy, biblical standards, emphasising the sanctity of Christian marriage'.[33] Children take part in the life of their community house but they are not insulated from the outside world. They attend local schools and some go on to university.

Single men and women are strictly segregated in the community houses and even on minibus journeys men and women sit separately. Dress codes are conservative. Sisters wear long flowing skirts, sensible shoes and no make-up. There is a principle that women should not dress as men though it is up to each sister to make up her own mind as to what is appropriate. Their Flame Leaflet 10, 'Women in the Church', written by a 'sister', gives the following guideline on dress:

> So, what about dress and fashions? Well we recognise that men and women differ in role, appearance and dress. So we avoid short hair cuts and wearing trousers! We try to dress simply and modestly. We don't go in for fashions which provoke sensuality. In the Bible we're encouraged to give more importance to the 'inner man'. Better to spend time in prayer, or serving, than in front of the mirror making up our faces.[34]

The female writer of this leaflet underscored the fact that 'there is neither male nor female, but all are one in Christ Jesus'. The result of this, she emphasised, is that 'as women we don't need to prove

---

[32] MacDonald-Smith, 'The Jesus Army Wants You', 22.
[33] *On the March*, 13.
[34] 'Women in the Church', *Flame Leaflet* 10.

our equality. God has done it!'[35] Notwithstanding this principle, women are seen as having a subservient role because 'man was not made from woman, but woman from man' and 'the head of every man is Christ, and the head of every woman is man'. The implication of all this is that 'women accept the leadership of strong godly men'. This is not seen by the Jesus Fellowship as inequality but rather as a difference of function which works effectively because it has the divine sanction behind it. 'When Eve did her own thing instead of consulting Adam, things went wrong. It's just the same to-day! When women try to lead men in the Church, things go wrong! It's not God's way for us. This is not a burdensome thing. It's the way of blessing, freedom and fulfilment.'[36]

In earlier times the whole Church gathered once every two or three weeks in the morning for a large 'celebration' meeting which is centred on Bible teaching and Holy Communion. By the late 1990s 'whole church events' were held about six times a year. On other weeks several regional meetings are held in different areas. On Sunday afternoons members can go back to their own homes or to their community houses. On Sunday evenings gospel meetings are held in various towns and community members participate in these.

Weekdays sometimes begin around 7 a.m. with a brief period for household worship. Then for most there is a full day's work with members returning home in time for the evening meal about 6.15 p.m. This forms the focus of the day for the community. Following supper, the pattern of each evening of the week varies. On Tuesdays there is a house Agape which is a kind of extended informal Communion service. On Wednesday there are Jesus Groups which are ideal for welcoming new friends and prospective visiting members. On Thursday there are informal friendship meetings and non-residents can come for a meal. Fridays are less structured though small groups may meet to provide members with instruction in the basics of the Christian faith. Saturday is the day when members of the community spend their time working around the house and garden and carrying out maintenance and DIY tasks. It is also the time when guests may be welcomed and community members can visit their families. There are no television sets in the

---

[35]  Ibid.
[36]  Ibid.

community houses and members do not engage in sporting activities. Leisure time is for the most part spent on musical, artistic and administrative pursuits which have a practical outcome.

## Jesus Fellowship Businesses

One of the most important aspects of the New Creation Christian Community is the businesses it owns. These have expanded considerably during recent years and provided employment for some 250 members in an atmosphere of Christian brotherhood, many of whom were formerly unemployed.[37] 'House of Goodness Ltd.' operates Goodness Foods, a health-food wholesale and distribution service, which employed about 250 members and had a turnover of about £15 million in 1995 and £18 million in 1997. The company has a chain of nine stores and the Jeans Plus Shop in Northampton. The Community is also responsible for the farming operations which encompass some 280 acres of land at New Creation Farm and Plough Farm near Stockton in Warwickshire. In addition to this, Skaino Services Ltd. ran a building, haulage and vehicle operation. This business maintained a garage, vehicle repair centre and body shop where Jesus Army vehicles could be sprayed in distinctive Army colours. Jeans Plus and the haulage business had been closed down by the later 1990s. According to their representative Ali 'ablaze', 'We have about 150 cars, 50 minibuses, 5 double-deckers and a single-decker coach.'[38] There is a further subsidiary business, Towcester Building Supplies Ltd. which runs builders merchant supplies in Towcester and Daventry. Another business, White and Bishop deals in outdoor clothing.

Businesses which are owned and run by the community generally only give employment to community members who are paid wages in the normal way. All workers are given the same wage but community members pay it back into the common purse. Observers report a strong sense of purpose in the way in which work is carried out and there is a sense of rhythm to their daily pattern of life. Just as the apostle Paul supported his evangelistic

---

[37] *On the March*, 17. See also *Church Alive*, 5.
[38] *Fair News* (summer 1996), 16; *Church Alive*, 5.

work by tent-making so these businesses are seen as providing a solid financial base to the community's evangelistic outreach activities. The aim has always been that the businesses should function as the servant of God's work and not control it.

## The Appeal of Community

One of the significant features of postmodern culture is what sociologists have termed 'anomie' or normlessness. Generations of young people have grown up with little or no values or moral framework. Fifty per cent or more of their number have grown up in dysfunctional home situations where there has been abuse or brokenness. The close-knit family unit of former generations has now largely been disintegrated because of what D. Clark termed 'spatial, social and cognitive mobility'.[39] Andrew Lockley drew a similar conclusion and wrote: 'Our relationships can no longer be developed to the depth of yesterday when an individual could be almost certain of spending most of his life with the same people in the same place. Indeed, we have suddenly noticed the poverty of our relationships because we no longer take them for granted.'[40]

In view of this context it is not difficult to understand the appeal which the NCCC and other similar groups can exercise for young people in particular, but also to others on the margins of society who have fallen victim to unemployment or fractured relationships. The NCCC is able to offer a stable alternative to the nuclear family in which there is a strong moral framework together with love, care and affirmation. There is no doubt that for some, living in community can make a very positive impact on their lives. A 1998 issue of *Jesus Life* featured Mary Callard, a married woman with five children whose life was totally changed through living in community: 'God has worked a miracle in me through community living. I was a narrow-hearted loner and over these years have become a great-hearted one who flows with others and loves to be with them.' She went on to say that 'Community living is the only way I know to break out of my tightly-held Christian "niceness" and find

---

[39] D. Clark, *Basic Communities: Towards an Alternative Society*, 39.
[40] A. Lockley, *Christian Communes*, 85.

reality, openness and flow together.'[41] The lifetime covenant which members enter into also helps to reinforce the feeling of security on the part of the more vulnerable and recently joined members. John Campbell, the Fellowship's Communications Officer, wrote that 'the pledge is carefully phrased to represent a present desire or intention for a lifelong commitment not a binding vow'.[42]

The aspect of belonging and feeling affirmed is further reinforced by the community's use of 'virtue names'. People are generally known by their Christian names but surnames are avoided since they do not generate a sense of being one family. In order to distinguish individuals, and at the same time create strong feelings of unity, the use of virtue names in place of surnames has become standard practice. A 'virtue name' conveys a favourable description of the person concerned while at the same time reflecting something of their character. Examples might be Philip Perceptive or John Gentle. Men tend to have names like 'Rockfast' or 'Able' whereas women are termed 'Pureheart' or 'Glowing'.

The constant use of 'virtue names' and the reference to each other as brothers and sisters further enhances the bond between new members. Typical is Prisca whose parents were divorced when she was only a year old, and she went on to live with her grandparents. As a result of this she grew up struggling with her identity. Living in community, however, changed both her life and her outlook. She testified: 'I have come to value brotherhood friendships, covenant, openness and I've been freed from many fears of others.' She continued:

> Over several months I've really begun to find my true identity in Jesus. One thing that really touched me was the way people accepted me as I was – I didn't have to prove myself or have to achieve anything in their eyes. I've seen that everyone in the Church has a place and is important. This has brought freedom for me to be myself and to be practical in my service to God.[43]

Eileen Barker suggests that this quest for belonging, which the NCCC appears to be meeting, is one of several factors promoting

---

[41] *Jesus Life* 46 (Fourth Quarter, 1998), 31.

[42] Written information from John Campbell dated 3 June 1999.

[43] *Jesus Lifestyle* 27 (1994), 30.

the growth of sects. She wrote that many religious movements, 'including those whose members or clients do not live with other members, offer instant friendship and understanding within a community of like-minded believers'.[44]

There is no doubt that the community life inside the Jesus Fellowship houses is strong, affirming and supportive. New members who have come from a background of prison, drugs and homelessness are often able to make surprisingly positive steps forward. *Jesus Lifestyle* magazine provides regular stories of those who have been able to overcome past hurts or conquer alcohol problems and smoking addictions. On the other side of the coin there are those who appear to have found the atmosphere claustrophobic or at the very least too confining. Clearly some are going to flourish in a highly structured environment, but the latter will represent to others a loss of freedom to make their own decisions on many of the issues of daily living. It is undoubtedly the case that the fewer decisions people are able to make for themselves, the less likely they are able to become mature adults capable of self-determined responsible behaviour. Just as counsellees can become dependent on their counsellor, so community members can become overly dependent on their leaders. Indeed in any close relationship the reverse is also a danger, namely a leader can become dependent on his or her following for affirmation and identity.

Those who have expressed their concern about the Jesus Army have done so largely on the basis of their perception that community members are too tightly controlled and could be kept in the movement against their will. The latter issue receives some credence from the fact that community members are urged to covenant themselves for life and promise never to leave the army. This, as has been noted, is seen by the Jesus Fellowship as an intention rather than a binding commitment. The difficulty here is that it is not possible to make generalisations. One individual may by nature be passive and therefore naturally more ready to submit to the collective will. Others of a more extrovert temperament are possibly more able to stand their ground. I have known several people of adult age who have disengaged themselves from the Jesus Fellowship without too much pressure being applied to them and

---

[44] E. Barker, *New Religious Movements*, 27.

without any major repercussions. Although in each of these instances none had committed any of their capital resources if indeed they had had any. According to Jesus Fellowship sources such capital is always returned on application to the trustees. It needs of course to be restated that the majority of Jesus Fellowship members do not live in community and that a fair proportion of the communities are transient.

Inevitably there are reports of abuse in the community's houses. In the summer of 1997, for example, *Fair News* reported on the case of twenty-nine-year-old Edwin Jindu, a Jesus Fellowship adult member, who was found guilty at Isleworth Crown Court of indecently assaulting a young woman who was born into the movement at the Army's farmhouse in Nether Heyford.[45] The abuse took place in London. It has to be said, however, that the number of such cases reaching the media are relatively few and seem proportionately less than the incidence of abuse on the part of clergy in the established mainline churches.[46]

Much of the concern about the Jesus Fellowship seems to revolve around their strong control over their members' sexuality and domestic freedoms. *Fair News* gave details of a five-and-a-half page Guideline document which dealt with 'the complicated process of strictly supervised and restrained courtship'. It included the following: 'the importance of Godly covering; the brother's heart and condition; the sister's heart and condition; leadership sharing procedures and beginning relating'.[47] If a brother is attracted to a sister he has to ask his elder to contact her elder and at the same time to promise not to make 'furtive advances by telephone calls, letters or messages relayed to a third party'. Once this has been agreed and the woman has reciprocated his advances, stage one can commence. They will be allowed to 'see one another at either of the households concerned'.[48]

---

[45] *Fair News* (summer 1997), 7. See also *News of the World*, 20 April, 15, which recounts the same story. Edwin Jindu, according to the JF was not an elder as the *News of the World* reported. This information was received in writing from John Campbell 3 June 1999.

[46] A careful reading of *Fair News* reveals the above instance to be the only reported case of sexual abuse.

[47] *Fair News* (summer 1993), 7.

[48] Ibid.

They must 'refuse to engage in physical contact of any sort, or to flirt either in the nature of their conversation or any physical action'. This stage will last for four to six months depending on how 'the covering brother feels about things'. Stage 2 is an agreed break during which the couple have no contact for anything up to six months. The purpose of this is to test out whether or not they should give preference to celibacy. After this Stage 3 begins and the couple can see each other once more for a period of four to six months. Their meetings will be twice a week but with the same constraints that operated in Stage 1. The fourth stage includes 'fixing the date of marriage; visiting parents and intensive counselling by the covering brother and his wife'. This instruction includes their roles: headship for the husband and 'submissiveness' for the wife.[49] Physical contact is restricted right up to the time of the wedding.

John Campbell was adamant in an interview with *The Independent Magazine* that 'sexual relations should take place within the context of marriage. That obviously is heterosexual, so, within the context of Christian morality, we would see homosexual activity as being no part of the Christian moral code.'[50] In this, he would doubtless have the support of most mainstream Christian churches, but many would also see potential dangers in the excessively tight procedures for entering into a relationship. Repressive restrictions can, on occasion, lead to a reverse reaction as happened, for example, more recently with the Children of God, known as The Family. David Berg, the movement's founder, began by exercising a very strict Puritanical regime over his following in the late 1960s but by the early 1980s he had substituted this with a libertine arrangement which included free love and the use of 'flirty fishing' as a means of evangelism. A number of modern sectarian movements reveal a similar pattern of repression followed by varying degrees of licence. Examples include the Oneida Community, Love Family, and Rajneeshism. In summary, on this issue concern revolves around the high degree of control exercised over young people's relationships with the opposite sex to a point where they have limited opportunity to get to know their partner in an unrestricted environment. For some this may work well. For others it may prove oppressive or provoke libertinism.

---

[49]  Ibid.
[50]  *The Independent Magazine*, 29 April 1995, 22.

## The Jesus Army

In the mid–1980s those in the leadership of the Jesus Fellowship, together with large sections of the membership, were becoming disappointed by their lack of success in evangelistic endeavours. About a quarter of those who had been baptised in 1986 were found to have left the movement by the end of the same year. In the Midlands, four campaigns had left the people drained and the eldership felt exhausted and overstretched.[51] Against this background the servant groups overseer in Birmingham began to develop a keen interest in William Booth and the Salvation Army. Books on the 'General', his wife Catherine and their early endeavours, were exchanged and read avidly. Noel Stanton, the movement's leader, reread the accounts of the early campaigns in Whitechapel among the poor of London's East End. Together they recognised that here were people who knew the power of God, who were persecuted, who loved holiness and, significantly, made inroads for God among the working classes.

Thus it was that the Jesus Army began to take shape. Booth's motto 'Blood and Fire', the blood standing for the 'cross' and the 'Fire' for the Holy Spirit, was seen to have the right focus. Additionally, the Fellowship felt it vital to add covenant with God and the brethren. So the battle-cry became 'Blood! Fire! and Covenant!'[52] They recognised that while Booth's earlier Salvation Army had been very effective in soul-winning it had overlooked the importance of baptism, the Lord's Supper and charismatic gifts which were all essential aspects in the life of the New Testament Church.[53]

Some of the Fellowship hoped that the military aspect would not be carried too far and they all considered that the Salvation Army's peaked caps and dressy uniforms failed to convey an image appropriate for the late twentieth century. However, Stanton was of the opinion that combat jackets conveyed a manly image and these were chosen as basic battledress. Cooper and Farrant state: 'A "War Fund" was set aside, community houses were seen as battle

---

[51] Cooper and Farrant, *Fire in Our Hearts*, 238.
[52] Ibid. 241.
[53] Ibid. 240.

stations, the Marquee as a battlefield and inner city houses as Battlefronts.'[54]

The Jesus Army was born on 18 April 1987 at a ceremony in Northampton. A long procession of people clad in combat jackets and carrying coloured flags pursued their way past the bustle of shoppers to the town's guildhall. Here prayers of dedication were led by the Rev Ken Thomason.[55] They included the following pledge:

> Do you promise to be faithful in prayer, in the reading and study of the Holy Scriptures, to cooperate in love and loyalty with all your fellow workers, to build up the Church in truth and peace, to witness by word and deed to your faith and to live a life worthy of the calling as members of the Jesus Army.[56]

Later the newly commissioned soldiers were taken to Hyde Park from where there was a 'march for Jesus' to Trafalgar Square. Here a national rally was held and the Jesus Army Manifesto was read. Among other aspects the manifesto commits to uphold 'the Biblical, evangelical faith, set out in the faith and practice of Jesus Fellowship Church (Baptist)' and 'to minister to the needs of the body, soul and spirit'.[57] The importance of Covenant is strongly emphasised in the Manifesto:

9. The JESUS ARMY consists of men and women who have repented of their sin, believed in the Lord Jesus Christ, been regenerated and baptised, and who have made a covenant commitment to the Jesus Fellowship Church (Baptist).
11. JESUS ARMY soldiers declare their full lifelong loyalty to the cause and thus to the purposes of God in seeking the lost and building the Church of Jesus Christ. They pledge themselves always to be available.[58]

---

[54] Ibid.
[55] *Jesus Army Introduction*, 7.
[56] Ibid.
[57] Ibid. 'A Manifesto of the Faith and Aims of the Jesus Army.'
[58] Ibid. 7, paragraphs 9 and 11.

These paragraphs were conflated in the 1992/1993 version of the Jesus Manifesto which removed 'the covenant commitment' in an effort to reflect the movement's varied styles of membership.

Following the events in Trafalgar Square Mick 'Temperate' led a small section which carried the flag to 10 Downing Street. The following letter was handed in to the Prime Minister and a copy later went to the Queen. An edited version was printed in the Fellowship's social action magazine *Heartcry*:

> Dear Mrs. Thatcher,
> We urge you to call the nation back to faith in God. Christians are praying for a revival that will change society. The members of this Church have become a Jesus Army to fight the evils in society and bring the gospel to the victims of vice. We pray that God will give you wisdom, compassion and strength for your responsibilities.
> Yours respectfully, The Jesus Fellowship.[59]

## Parallels with the Salvation Army

There are a number of similarities between the Jesus Army and the earlier Salvation Army. In 1891 William Booth adopted a scheme of Social Salvation which was recounted in detail in his celebrated book of that year *In Darkest England and the Way Out*. It took Booth almost two decades of army warfare to recognise fully the importance of addressing the needs of the body as well as those of the soul. In contrast, the Jesus Army with its slogan 'We fight for You' grappled with key areas of deprivation and injustice from its inception. Among its particular concerns were the issues of poverty, homelessness, unemployment and drugs, including the dangers of alcohol and cigarette smoking. The *Jesus Army Introduction Magazine* of 1987, for example, vigorously underlined the fact that in 1985 £26 million was spent by London boroughs on bed and breakfast accommodation for homeless families and that 80,000 young people were homeless at some point during the same year. Jesus Army members visit many prisons and correspond with inmates who write to them.

---

[59] Cooper and Farrant, *Fire in Our Hearts*, 246.

William Booth aimed in his campaigns to reach the 'submerged tenth', by which he meant those who lived below the poverty line and lacked the basic necessities of food, clothing and shelter. Similarly the Jesus Army declares itself to be on the march against 'derelict British Society', which it identifies as 'the poor, the homeless, the unemployed, victims of abuse and addiction'.[60] Booth's temperance activities in the 1870s and 1880s caused a number of publicans to become worried on account of the decline in their number of customers who were pledging themselves to total abstinence. Similar accusations were made against the Jesus Army in Soho. Two brothers were arrested. The pimps had apparently got annoyed that the gospel was reducing the number of their customers. A court case followed and the Army was awarded costs.[61]

One other parallel between William Booth's Salvation Army and the Jesus Army is in the matter of worship. Booth was accused of promoting worship like 'musical hall entertainment' and which was too simplistic. On one occasion Booth exclaimed 'Why should the devil have all the best tunes?' He later set up a music department which set Christian songs to the music of the day. Commenting on the worship at one of the Wembley Jesus Army 'Praise-Days' one participant declared: 'It's raw, it's real, it's getting a reaction!' Farrant and Cooper made the comment that the Jesus Army's 'upbeat style of praise' speaks powerfully to the present generation.[62] Critics were particularly harsh on Booth's use of the penitent form, usually a rough wooden bench placed at the front of the meeting rooms. Those who were brought under conviction about their past and their need of Christ's forgiveness were invited to come and sit there to receive prayer. At some of William and Catherine's early holiness meetings new converts screamed out or fell to the ground and rolled around on the floor. Similar occurrences have been observed at Jesus Army celebrations and street meetings. The Salvation Army, concerned to take the message of the Christian faith out on to the streets of the industrial towns and cities, accomplished this by their use of bands and marching. These days the Jesus Army have adopted modern 'marches for Jesus' and street walks.

---

[60] *Jesus Army Introduction*, 4.
[61] Cooper and Farrant, *Fire in Our Hearts*, 246.
[62] Ibid. 247.

Additionally they have made use of multi-media, singing, dancing and drama. Inevitably criticisms have come from a variety of individuals, mainly from the establishment. Northampton's Archdeacon compared the Jesus Army to 'paramilitary rebels' and one local MP described them as a 'Rambo Cult'. A major setback occurred in 1986 when the Jesus Fellowship Church was forced to resign from the Evangelical Alliance and their membership of the Baptist Union was brought to an end. The Jesus Fellowship is now linked to the EA through Multiply Christian Network of which they were a founding member.

Eventually William Booth's Salvation Army moved from being a persecuted minority to becoming a fully accepted part of British society. The high point of this change of heart was perhaps reached in June 1904 when Booth was invited to a reception at Buckingham Palace. There are growing signs that the Jesus Army is beginning to adopt a less isolationist policy and to work with other Christian groups. For example, they have worked alongside other groups such as British Youth for Christ in evangelism at events such as the Glastonbury Festival. In the 1990s they have held a number of Praise-Days at the Wembley Conference Centre with speakers from other churches. For example in 1994 *Jesus Lifestyle* reported on a 'Wembley Praise-Day' at which the speakers included Gerald Coates and John Noble of Pioneer, Tony Morton of Cornerstone Ministries and Peter Brierley of Christian Research Association.[63] At another Wembley Praise-Day, messages of support from Dr Carey, Cardinal Hume and the Bishop of London were read out.[64] In fact, part of the Army's vision for the nineties was 'Jesus "platoons" from different Churches and networks standing together for God'.[65]

## Denouement

The Jesus Fellowship and Jesus Army is an evangelical Christian body with a strongly charismatic emphasis. In its doctrines it is

---

[63] *Jesus Lifestyle* 27 (1994), 11.
[64] R. Waterhouse, 'Hungry for Souls', *Independent on Sunday: The Sunday Review*, 13 January 1981.
[65] Cooper and Farrant, *Fire in Our Hearts*, 267.

thoroughly orthodox, upholding the historic Christian Creeds. Although quite strongly independent it is linked to a number of churches through the Multiply Christian Network. Unlike many modern sectarian movements there is a strong emphasis on both the sacraments of Baptism and Communion. Baptism is seen as a particularly powerful means by which new converts, many of whom come from harsh and dysfunctional backgrounds, are able to sever themselves from their past. Communion is shared weekly in the Community houses and there are frequent opportunities to share in the breaking of bread at celebrations and Sunday worship services. Part of the reason for the emphasis on Communion is the way in which it fits well with the Fellowship's strong focus on community living.

The Church has grown rapidly during the past twenty-five years. From being a small congregation of around 60 members based in Bugbrooke Baptist Church it grew to 431 in 1980 and reached 1,260 in 1990. By the close of 1998 it had extended still further to 2,500.[66] The core units are household churches of which there are more than 60 situated around the UK. Each house consists of between 6 and 60 people. They are led by teams of two or three elders, all of whom are men. There were some 150 elders or church leaders at the close of 1998.[67]

There is no doubt that as a movement the Jesus Fellowship and the Jesus Army have changed in character with the passing of the years. Now that they are a more widely recognised part of the Christian landscape there has been a mellowing. This is seen particularly in its willingness to work alongside other church groups and to learn from speakers and teachers of other denominations. There is an openness about the community houses and visitors are always welcome to stay for shorter or longer periods of time. There is an increasing emphasis on local congregations, not just on church households. The Fellowships have made a bold attempt to develop a radical expression of Christianity which encompasses the twin New Testament ideals of evangelism and personal salvation, on the one hand, with corporate community, on the other. The community-house model with a

---

[66] See 'Welcome to the Jesus Army' (http://www.jesus.org.uk/figures.html). See also *Church Alive*, 2.
[67] *Church Alive*, 3.

common purse has certainly demonstrated a way of overcoming the class barrier which bedevils so many of the mainstream Christian churches. The organisation has provided a secure base with friendship and a caring and supportive atmosphere for many who might otherwise be roaming the streets, engaged in crime or returning to the prisons from which they had been released.

One of the aspects of the Jesus Fellowship and Army which classifies it as a sectarian movement[68] is its charismatic leader and hierarchical leadership structure. Noel Stanton is the movement's 'senior pastor'. Alongside him there is a hierarchical structure which consists of an all-male eldership. Stanton has frequently been described as authoritarian. In 1989 the Archdeacon of Northampton referred to him as 'a dominant leader with an exclusive hotline to God'.[69] The then Archdeacon was probably not in a position to know whether his statement was true since he never met with Noel Stanton nor did he visit their community or worship meetings which were open to him. It is the case that some ex-members say they were told that if they disobeyed Noel they were disobeying Christ but many other New Church leaders have given similar teaching. To his credit Stanton lives in a Community house with those just off the streets and enjoys no special benefit or luxuries. W. Dalrymple found him 'a far cry from the terrifying autocrat portrayed on the tabloids'. He recalled that he looked 'over-worked and tired; he was balding and badly dressed'.[70] The Jesus Fellowship stress that their strong stand on the 'Reformed' teaching of the 'Priesthood of all believers' makes it unlikely that Noel Stanton or any other of their leaders would come to be regarded by them as Messiah-like authoritarian figureheads.

A reason behind some of the expressions of concern about the Jesus Fellowship is the way in which they appear to target those who are young and vulnerable. Numbers of those who join come from a previous background of drugs, crime and prison. Unstable individuals are inevitably going to be more vulnerable. On the other hand it can be argued that significant numbers of these people

---

[68] See Chapter 1.

[69] *Fair News* (1989), 14.

[70] W. Dalrymple, 'The Jesus People', *The Independent Magazine*, 8 April 1989.

are given a framework and a life of stability. Both the tabloids and the broadsheets have given occasional instances of psychological pressures and invasive counselling sessions, but the level and extent of these reports do not seem any greater than parallel stories on the part of other groups.

Perhaps, however, it is the psychological pressures which can often be exerted by communities that have caused some concern about the Jesus Fellowship. In particular there is strong compulsion on community members not to leave the community. This is reinforced by the fact that many have declared a lifelong commitment to the work. In the words of their manifesto, 'JESUS ARMY soldiers declare their full lifelong loyalty to the cause.'[71] There is also the difficulty that leaders and members of communities can become overly possessive of certain individuals. This becomes visible in the occasional expressions of deep hurt when membership is renounced and someone leaves the community. Some however take the view that when this degree of attachment has been reached it is healthier that such people be allowed to leave. Having made this point there is strong shepherding within the movement. According to the summer edition of *Fair News* 1996 one recent arrival observed: 'Wherever you go there are leaders.'[72] Another aspect of this pressure is the strong encouragement to become celibate and to follow the movement's leader. Although many members are married, including about half of the leaders, there is a strong feeling that celibacy is a higher calling.

While it may be true that considerable pressures are put on those who have joined to remain faithful to their pledge to stay for life, the fact is many do leave. Some are even commended to other churches for membership. Visitors who have stayed in the Jesus Fellowship observed photographs of ex-members covering the walls as a reminder to keep praying for their return. They stand as proof against the more extreme accusations of brainwashing. It needs of course to be remembered that not all members of the Jesus Fellowship live in community. There are various styles of membership, only one of which requires members to live in community.

---

[71] *Introducing the Jesus Army*, 7.
[72] *Fair News* (summer 1996), 14.

Life in community can prove for some to be overly controlling. It is not possible to opt out of the intense round of evening meetings and evangelistic activities to put your feet up and read a book. There are no televisions, radios, stereos or CD players in the Jesus Fellowship Houses.[73] Those in community do not go swimming for exercise or pleasure or engage in competitive sports or games.[74] They do not purchase sweets, drinks or snack refreshments from shops.[75] Nor do they keep pets or any animals on the community premises.[76] All this amounts to the fact that the Jesus Fellowship is essentially what Roy Wallis termed 'a world denying sect'. His term serves to indicate that this is a community which insulates or cuts off its members from the prevailing surrounding culture. This is well-reflected in one of their own earlier songs, the final verse making it clear that these things are renounced for the sake of the community:

> World begone! I hate your spirit
> All these years my life you ruled.
> 'Til the cross of Jesus triumphed
> 'Crucified unto the world!'
>
> I don't need your fancy fashions
> Nor your cold, expensive goods.
> All your sports and entertainment
> I renounce for brotherhood.

Many mainstream Protestant Christian churches see potential danger in such a stance as that expressed in these verses and are of the opinion that it is an unbalanced attitude to the world which God made and for which Christ died. The verse 'World begone!', quoted above, does not sit comfortably with a Jesus who turned water into wine, was accused of being a glutton and a wine-drinker and who ate with sinners and tax collectors. Nor does it resonate with the stories he told about new wine and new wine-skins, killing

---

[73] *Zion's Aims and Precepts*, 9.
[74] Ibid. 8 and 2.
[75] Ibid. 1.
[76] Ibid. 2.

fatted calves and music and dancing. New Testament metaphors include reference to competitive games, running races and even boxing. Paul himself stated that bodily exercise does profit a little (1 Timothy 4:8). Members of the denominational churches take the view that some, if not all, of these pleasures of life are given by God to be enjoyed not abstained from.

Perhaps when all is said and done it needs to be recognised that a shared-purse community is only one expression of church. There are those who take the view that the total sharing principle adopted by the Jerusalem Church in Acts 2:44 was in the nature of a failed experiment. It was for this reason that they maintain that Paul had to collect money on their behalf from the gentile churches of Asia Minor. Jesus by his attitude and teaching clearly endorsed both the right and the value of having personal possessions, while at the same time urging against overpossessiveness. It is clear that some possessions are part of 'selfhood' and personal identity. Equally they can provide outlets for developing God-given creativity.

There is no doubt that the Jesus Fellowship and the Jesus Army are a radical Christian organisation which will remain controversial on account of their intensive community lifestyle. It is probably the case that they have suffered beyond their deserving on account of scare stories in the tabloid press and denominational church periodicals.

# Chapter 10

# The International Church of Christ

One of the religious movements which seems to have been most in the news in recent years is the CLCOC (Central London Church of Christ) and their subsequent church plants in Birmingham, Manchester, Oxford, Cambridge, Edinburgh, Cardiff, Dublin, Belfast and elsewhere. Together their membership totalled 2,559 in May 1999. The CLCOC hit the headlines particularly in the earlier years of its existence in the 1980s on account of its high profile evangelistic campaigns on university campuses and its 'in your face' witnessing on the London Underground. There were complaints about the use of mind-control techniques and excessive monopolising of members' time.

The London Church of Christ was formed in 1982 and owes its origin to the earlier Boston Church of Christ which came into existence in 1979. The Churches of Christ emerged from American Restorationism in the later nineteenth century and finally became a denomination in their own right in 1906. Beginning with a membership total of 160,000 in that year they reached 1.2 million in the 1990s.[1]

In 1967 one of the Churches of Christ at Gainesville, Florida, embarked on an evangelistic campaign at the University of Florida. Directed by Chuck Lucas under the name 'Campus Advance', the programme had a number of controversial aspects. Particular questions were raised about 'Soul Talk Bible Studies' and a system of 'prayer partnerships' which ran in parallel. The leaders of the 'Soul Talk' groups were given authority over their

---

[1]  R. Paden, 'The Boston Church of Christ', in T. Miller (ed.), *America's Alternative Religions*, 133.

members who were expected to share at a deep personal level. In the 'prayer partnership' scheme those who were new to the faith were paired with older Christians who were charged with giving them personal guidance and direction. Both procedures were felt to be unnecessarily intrusive and opponents accused the Church of abuse.

One of those who was converted through Campus Advance at the University of Florida in 1972 was Kip McKean who was later to be the leader of the Boston church. He was powerfully impacted by what had taken place and later wrote:

> The innovations of 'one another Christianity', evangelistic small group Bible Studies, and the vision of dynamic campus ministries were put on my heart through the powerful preaching of Chuck Lucas and his associate, Sam Laing. The seeds of discipling were placed in my life as I saw personally how one man could affect another's daily lifestyle and eternal destiny for God.[2]

Following the completion of his degree McKean held several posts as campus minister with mainline Church of Christ congregations. Then in 1979 he was invited to take the leadership of a declining congregation in the Boston suburb of Lexington. The name 'Lexington Church of Christ' was changed to 'Boston Church of Christ' and inspired by McKean's leadership the membership grew to 300 by the close of 1981. As a result of this, Kip McKean's horizon expanded rapidly and he felt that the Lord had called him to set up 'pillar churches' in key world cities. These would in their turn become bases which would establish congregations in other localities in their areas.

In 1982 planters had gone out from Boston and established congregations in London and Chicago and the following year in New York City. By 1993 the movement had 130 congregations in different parts of the world and had expanded to 42,855 members. Forty-eight of those congregations were in the US with a membership of 27,055. The Sunday morning attendances at New York and

---

[2] K. McKean, 'Revolution Through Resolution', *Upside Down* (April 1992), 6, cited in Paden, 'The Boston Church of Christ', 134.

Boston were both over the 5,000 mark in 1993 and the Los Angeles congregation stood at about 4,000.[3]

Russell Paden suggested that much of this rapid growth was attributable to the fact that the mainline denominational Churches, and the 'Church of Christ' in particular, were in a state of institutional decline and general apathy. Charismatic individuals like McKean were therefore provoked into evangelistic action. McKean stated that he had visited many mainstream churches between 1976 and 1979 and found their spiritual condition 'ranged from lukewarm to disgusting'.[4] There was also a strong conviction both on the part of McKean and his new membership that ongoing churches were also growing churches.

## The Central London Church of Christ

In 1982 the Boston Church sent a small team to London consisting of Douglas and Joyce Arthur, Douglas Jacoby and James and Tanya Lloyd. As a result of their endeavours the 'London Church of Christ' which at that time was called the 'South London Church of Christ' was established. The first service was held on 4 July 1982 with eight disciples and seventeen people attending. The London church was the first planting outside the US; its early meetings were held in Lambeth Methodist Mission. The first year proved one of considerable encouragement. An invitation service was held on the 24 October with sixty-six people being present. By the end of the first year fifty-two people had been baptised including Mike de Souza, a young teenager who was to become a prominent leader in the 1990s.[5]

McKean had been won for God as a result of a university campaign and he was acutely aware of the strategic importance of winning college students to his cause. They were tomorrow's leadership. They were also young and in many cases well motivated and

---

[3]  Paden, 'The Boston Church of Christ', 134. See also 'Love and Sects on the Streets', *The Times*, 30 December 1992.

[4]  McKean, 'Revolution Through Resolution', 6.

[5]  History and Information about the UK Churches of Christ, at Web site www.icoc.org.uk/London, 26 November 1998, 1.

with high ideals. For this reason 1983 witnessed an increasing focus on university halls of residence. The church reported that 'the campus ministry at London University takes off as dozens of students are baptised'.[6] By the close of 1984 over a third of the regular London congregation of 150 were students at London University. In 1983 the first anniversary service attracted an attendance of 176 and the October 'Bring Your Neighbour Day' saw over 350 people crowded into the Lambeth Methodist Mission.[7] It became clear as a result of this that larger premises were needed and the congregation moved to St John the Divine, Kensington.

The Church of Christ takes the view that there should be one church for one city. This is based on a literal reading of the second and third chapters of the book of Revelation. This means that once a church begins to expand they develop the idea of zones. The London Church formed North, South and West zones during the course of 1984. This year proved to be one of growth and distinction with Noel Loban, one of the leadership team winning a bronze medal at the Seoul Olympics and Jaime McGrath, a model and church member, appearing on the cover of *Good Housekeeping*.

1985 was a year focused on evangelism for the CLCOC. Douglas Jacoby was sent out with a team to establish a church in Sydney, Australia. An India night was also held and the London disciples contributed £3,000 in order to fund a 'scouting out the land' trip to the continent with Bangalore chosen as a target city. In the following year the London Church grew to 300 members with an attendance of 400 by the end of December. There were nearly a hundred student disciples. In 1986 also, John Partington, a future elder and his wife, Rose, moved to London to join the congregation. In 1987 the church membership swelled from 300 to 550, a growth which continued into 1988 with twenty-five baptisms in January alone. In April the Birmingham Church of Christ was planted by seventeen disciples and succeeded in baptising a hundred disciples in the first twelve months.

In 1989 the London Church not only continued to send out leaders to other parts of the world, but began to focus on the needs

---

[6]  Ibid.
[7]  Ibid.

of the poor and homeless on its own doorstep. Walter Evans and John Partington spent weeks away from their families roughing it on the streets of London in preparation for what became known as Two Step. This pioneering work promoted by the CLCOC eventually led in 1991 to the establishment of the charity HOPE World-wide.

The years 1992–97 were marked in the Church's own words by 'significant media opposition'.[8] Part of the reason for this was the visit to London by Douglas Arthur. In some straight and radical talking he warned members that they 'must shape up or shake out'. His conviction was that because the Church wasn't growing fast enough the fault lay with the congregation. Those who wanted to remain had to meet with their leaders and respond to certain basic questions, one of which was, 'Do you believe that this is the only Church?' This was a traumatic time for the Church and 'many disciples left'. Estimates put the figure at the 350 mark. Those who left were for the most part considered to be 'dead wood'. The leaders made it clear to those who remained that no friend, parent or job can be more important than the CLCOC.[9] Some, it was admitted, did leave the church 'due to a lack of compassion shown to them'.[10] In 1997 the entire Church came together at Alexandra Palace in North London 'to hear a convicting and inspirational message from Mike de Souza on the theme of heaven, and how to get there'. In July a 'Victory' Service was held at Hammersmith in celebration of fifteen years in the UK with Douglas Arthur coming all the way from Washington to preach.[11] The high point of 1998 was the 'International Women's Day' on 1 March at Alexandra Palace with over 4,300 women in attendance. Thirty-nine women were baptised that day.[12] The ICOC (International Church of Christ) has a deliberate policy of meeting in hired premises. It is felt to be much more effective to invest in people rather than buildings. For this reason they tend to hire community halls and school

---

[8]  History and Information about the UK Churches of Christ 1997, UK Churches of Christ Web site.
[9]  Ibid. 7.
[10] Information about the London Church of Christ, INFORM, 1995, 2.
[11] History of the Church, Web site www.icoc.org.uk/London, 2.
[12] Ibid, 1.

buildings. For larger whole-group meetings the Church often uses major venues such as Alexandra Palace, the Odeon, Leicester Square or the Royal Albert Hall.

The worship of the CLCOC and other ICOC congregations is not dissimilar from that of many of the so-called New Churches. Services last about an hour and a half and there is a good deal of very lively singing which includes harmonisation. On some weeks the singing is a cappella as they have discovered this produces a better volume of sound and praise than when there is a band. When the singing is unaccompanied there are still several vocalists with microphones on the stage. The ICOC have their own ring-bound song books which contain a large number of songs including traditional hymns and choruses. Communion is a regular feature of the worship, and the bread, in the form of broken water biscuit, is passed along the rows with each individual who wishes to take part serving themselves. The wine is administered in a similar manner with trays of small egg-cup size glasses. Each person helps themselves, drinks and replaces their cup before passing it to the person next to them. Sermons can be a lively affair lasting half an hour or more with a good deal of audience participation. During the sermon members of the congregation shout out words of encouragement to the preacher such as 'Come on, Iggy!' 'More, Iggy!' I later discovered that Iggy was an abbreviation for Ignatius, the person who had preached the sermon I heard. These outbursts from the congregation is a fairly standard procedure known in the ICOC as 'firing up'.

Members of the ICOC are expected to make a time commitment to their congregation which is considerably greater than is the case with other denominational churches. There is a gathering for teaching on a Wednesday night and a family group night on a Friday evening. In addition there are other evening commitments including ministry to the poor, evangelism of various kinds, and time spent with one's disciples.

The ICOC follows the New Testament custom of having only one designated church for each town or city. When numbers expand the congregation is divided into zones. At the close of 1998 the CLCOC had seven zone churches, each with their own full-time leaders who are sometimes styled 'evangelists'. In addition there are women's leaders and elders who are chosen from suitably trained persons as they become available. By the close of 1998 the CLCOC were supporting eighty full-time leaders, fifty of whom were working in London itself. Such a large leadership demands a high level of sacrificial giving on the part of the membership. Published figures for giving are not readily attainable but INFORM has published an account for 1990 which reveals the Church's income for 1990 as £1,028,328.[13]

Many members of the congregations are students or are fairly young and live together in communal flats and houses. Church leaders keep a strong hand on these arrangements and single men and women are strictly segregated. Disciples also ensure that those in their care are exercising proper discretion in their behaviour towards the opposite sex.

With this level of input, financial support and commitment it is no surprise that worldwide the International Churches of Christ are growing rapidly. In April 1991 there were 340 churches worldwide with an average Sunday attendance of 179,732.[14]

## Baptism in the International Churches of Christ

One of the more distinctive features of the ICOC are their doctrine of baptism. They assert that for a baptism to be valid the candidate must be 'someone who has already become a disciple'. This is derived from a particular understanding of Matthew 28:19–20 where Jesus gave the great commission to 'go and make disciples, baptising them in the name of the Father, the Son and the Holy Spirit'. This is understood to mean a person should first be a disciple. 'Make disciples' is thus seen as the main verb and 'baptising them' and 'teaching them' as participles which modify the main verb. Bare faith or mere trust in Jesus for forgiveness is not sufficient for salvation. It is not counted for righteousness until the candidate obeys God by being baptised with the conscious knowledge that at the moment of baptism one is being saved. Douglas Arthur, Douglas

---

[13] J. Jensen and C. Armstrong, 'London Church of Christ Memorandum on The Roger Cook Report', 2.

[14] 'The LA Story', Bulletin of the Los Angeles Church of Christ, April 1999, 2.

Jacoby and James Lloyd make the matter explicit in their joint ICOC publication *Shining Like Stars*: 'Baptism is simply redeeming a coupon, collecting that which God has freely promised anyway. The fact that salvation is conditional on our response in no sense detracts from God's generosity, or from his grace . . . To get into Christ – into a right relationship with God – you must be baptised.'[15]

In a subsequent paragraph based on Romans 6:4 Arthur, Jacoby and Lloyd are emphatic that 'the new life begins in baptism'.[16] In conformity with this interpretation is their understanding of John 3:5 where Jesus says 'except a man be born of water he cannot see the kingdom of God'. This is taken to mean that unless one is baptised, one cannot enter into God's promised salvation. They suggest that to claim in accordance with most denominational teaching that the new birth begins 'before' baptism would mean that the new creation is put to death in the act of baptism.[17] They suggest this view from the writings of the early Church Fathers whom they maintain are unanimous that 'baptism was for the forgiveness of sins' and was 'the only way to become a Christian'.[18] They give quotations from Justin Martyr's *Apology* and Hermas' *Shepherd*. Justin writes that 'as many as are taught by us . . . are brought by us where there is water, and are born again'.[19] Similarly Hermas wrote of a time 'when we went down into the water and received remission of our former sins'.[20]

Kip McKean and a number of earlier leaders came to the view that they had not been in the position of a disciple as understood in this way at the time of their baptism. They therefore had themselves rebaptised and others followed their example. For example, Gloria Baird was rebaptised in Boston in October 1986 and her husband Al in April the following year.[21] Summer McKean was rebaptised at the

---

[15]   D. Arthur, D. Jacoby and J. Lloyd, *Shining Like Stars*, 288.

[16]   Ibid.

[17]   Ibid.

[18]   Ibid. 291.

[19]   Ibid.

[20]   Ibid.

[21]   R. Bauer and S. Bauer, *The Boston Movement: Analysis, Commentary and Media Reports*, 41.

Boston Seminar in 1991.[22] Kip McKean has been unequivocal in his teaching on this issue. Speaking at a World Mission Seminar at Boston under the title 'Go Make Disciples' he said:

> And let me just flat lay it out. If people have not had faith in Jesus Christ, if they have not been moved to the point of conviction to repent and to place Jesus Christ as the Lord of their life . . . And if they have not been immersed for the forgiveness of sins to receive the gift of the Holy Spirit, my Bible teaches me they are outside of Jesus Christ.[23]

This teaching on baptism by McKean has been a pronounced ongoing emphasis. In a subsequent Boston speech he was once again emphatic: 'We can never compromise the issue of salvation what it takes to be saved. You have to have faith, repent, confess and be baptised.'[24]

## Evangelism

Kip McKean was himself converted to Christ during an intensive evangelistic campaign. It is therefore no surprise that from its inception the ICOC has placed high emphasis on evangelism. Each new disciple is charged with the responsibility of actively sharing their faith in Christ with as many people as they can whenever they have the opportunity. Immediately following baptism the new disciple will be invited by his disciples to work through a study course such as *Your First Forty Days*. This course is designed to help the new Christian to listen to the voice of God and 'to help you have some direction each day for the next forty days'.[25] Several of the daily lessons urge the importance of sharing one's faith. Day 18 for example, which is based on Colossians 4:2–6, makes the following suggestion: 'List all the things you find here that relate to sharing your faith with someone.' Subsequent questions ask: 'What does it

---

[22]  Ibid. 41–2.

[23]  Ibid. 40.

[24]  Ibid. 40–41.

[25]  *Your First Forty Days* (London Church of Christ), INFORM MS 1624, 1.

mean to 'make the most of every opportunity'? 'How have you used the opportunities of this week? What can you do to use them more for the Lord?'[26] Day 19 covers sharing the gospel in difficult situations and Day 20 is about the boldness and courage necessary to go and make disciples. At the end of Day 21 a short paragraph suggests that the new convert should seek out help if he or she is not making an impact on other people's lives. 'You have now been a disciple for three weeks. You should be having an impact on others for Jesus Christ by now. If this is not happening, or if you see that it could be happening more, spend time with an older brother or sister and share what is going on. Let them encourage and help you.'[27]

With this kind of stress on evangelism the ICOC grew rapidly. When the first ten-year report was produced it noted that the Boston Congregation was almost 5,000 on a Sunday and that disciples had been sent out to all six populated continents of the world. Notwithstanding this rapid progress the leadership were not satisfied. In late 1986 they issued a call to repentance to all 'mainline' and 'campus' churches who were willing to pay the price to multiply disciples. Interested churches were asked to send their lead ministers to Boston to be discipled. Boston-trained evangelists were then put in their place. During the first few weeks of this change-over period, each member of the churches was called either to renew their commitment at baptism to be a disciple of Jesus, to be baptised as a disciple or leave the Church.

1986 also saw the operation of HOPE which stands for 'Heaven's Opportunities Proclaimed Everywhere'. This proved particularly effective in London where, despite a considerable exodus, there was an impressive influx of new converts. It was in 1987 that Arthur, Jacoby and Lloyd co-authored their handbook *Shining Like Stars*, which contains a number of radical and innovative ideas on how to evangelise more effectively. They begin with some general principles such as 'speak always with as much conviction as you can' and 'don't let audience reaction affect you'.[28] They underline the fact that 'the gospel needs to be taken to the places where the people are'. In London this means 'street markets,

---

26  Ibid. 8.
27  Ibid. 9.
28  Arthur et al., *Shining Like Stars*, 190.

shopping malls, High Streets (Main Streets), Covent Garden and Hyde Park's Speaker's Corner'.[29] In such locations the authors commend the practice of 'blitzing' which is basically inviting as many people to church as possible. For the sake of encouragement, it is recommended that disciples go out 'blitzing' in groups. Blitzing is described as an 'intensive' and 'exciting' activity glorifying God. Mohan Nanjundan, an Indian ICOC leader, said: 'When I'm out blitzing, my attitude is "If it moves, invite it!" '[30]

In a section entitled 'Going the Extra Mile' the reader is introduced to a variety of more novel, not to say in some cases, extreme forms of sharing one's faith. These include 'Halling', 'Restauranting' and 'Boating'. 'Halling', which involves 'standing up at the end of a classical concert to invite a hall of 2,000 middle-class concert-goers to your Church', is said to be 'the most nerve-racking experience a Christian can face'.[31] Most regular flying disciples would probably prefer to engage in what the authors call '747 evangelism'.[32]

The CLCOC also encouraged their members in the practice of 'tubing' and 'busing'. Basing this strategy on the New Testament account of Philip's witness to a man travelling by chariot along the Gaza Road (Acts 8:29), groups of disciples take journeys on the London Underground or public buses with the specific aim of evangelising fellow travellers. In the words of the authors, 'What could be more interesting than to enter into a conversation with a pleasant Christian or to receive a friendly invitation to a Church service.'[33] Although 'busing' and 'tubing' were strongly promoted in the early 1990s, they became a less favoured means of evangelism by the end of the decade. In fact by the close of 1998 inviting neighbours and work colleagues and street evangelism were proving much more effective.[34]

The goal or objective of these invitations is to try and interest non-Christian people in an informal Bible study. The aim is that

---

[29] Ibid.
[30] Ibid. 192.
[31] Ibid. 195.
[32] Ibid.
[33] Ibid. 196.
[34] Personal interview with Adrian Hill, one of the London ICOC leaders, based at the Riverside Zone Church, 6 December 1998.

these occasions should take place as soon as possible. For a few individuals this might be 'after your first meeting', but for most, it will be after two or three visits to the church. In setting up the study ICOC members are advised that everything must be on a friendly basis. The 'Oh, no, she's trying to convert me!' reaction should be avoided at all costs. For this reason three participants, including the non-Christian, are felt to be ideal.[35] Additionally it is strongly recommended that the study be kept somewhere between thirty and ninety minutes in length. Their suggested working maxim is that 'the mind can absorb only as much as the seat can endure'.[36] If the person is seriously interested these studies may take place every four or five days. The level of the person's interest can be gauged by their willingness to 'deal with sin in their lives', 'initiate phone calls', 'attend church services' and 'change their opinions when confronted with scripture'.[37]

In the earlier days of the movement at least there were some controversial aspects attaching to these Bible studies on what are termed 'First Principles'. For example, before commencing the study on the cross the person is told to read Galatians 5:19–21 and then 'make a list'. They are urged, 'be specific – it's for yourself so you can see the sin and have the heart of a sinful woman'.[38] Such lists may well hurt, but the seeker is cheered by the prospect that 'you will heal and feel better'.[39] For 'the Cross' study the ICOC member reads the account of the crucifixion of Jesus from Matthew 26:14 – 27:54. As this is read the inquirer may be invited to reflect as to where he or she is in the narrative by being invited to say, 'I am Judas' or 'I am Peter.'[40] They are then asked whether Jesus wanted to die on the cross. After reading the account of Jesus praying in the garden of Gethsemane, the disciple emphasises that he begs God not to let him go through with it and that he was under such stress and anxiety that he sweated blood. Nevertheless he did die and he did it for you.[41] When the crucifixion is described, according to one

---

[35] Arthur et al., *Shining Like Stars*, 223.
[36] Ibid. 225.
[37] Ibid. 227.
[38] D. Zimmerman, 'Controversy in the Boston Church of Christ', 2.
[39] Ibid.
[40] Ibid.
[41] Ibid.

former member, theatrics were used in an effort to personalise the story. The ICOC Bible study leader punched the air at the same time saying with strong emphasis, 'You punched his face. You taunted him. You whipped him.' At the point where the nails were hammered into Jesus' hands and feet, disciples have been known to say such things as 'This is for you, Cynthia. This is for your sexual immorality; this is for your pride.'[42] Inevitably the emotional impact of this kind of procedure will affect different people with varying degrees of intensity. However, it is not difficult to appreciate the ways in which some individuals might become distressed or even traumatised by such procedures.

## Authority and Control

Associated with these highly intensive methods of evangelism, the ICOC has rigorous teaching on submission. There are five general areas of authority which God gives to his creation: government over citizens; masters over slaves; husbands over wives; parents over children and spiritual leaders over Christians.[43] Submission to each of these authorities, according to Al Baird, one of the Boston leaders, is required by Romans 13:1–2 which emphasises that 'there is no authority except that which God has established'.[44] Baird went on to ask how this could be, considering all the Hitlers and Neros who have governed through the ages? His answer was that at the very time and in the very place that Paul wrote Romans the government was persecuting Christians. 'Our call', he emphasised, 'is to submit to those authorities since they are God's; to do otherwise is to rebel against God.'[45] Baird went on to raise the question of abusive or hostile authorities: 'But what if the government is abusive? Submit! What if the laws restrict my freedoms? Submit! What if the government persecutes and kills Christians? Submit.'[46]

---

[42] R.C. Hornish, 'Group's Intense Methods Confusing', *University Daily Kansas*, 4 March 1991, 9, cited Zimmerman, 'Controversy', 3.
[43] J. Jones, *What Does the Boston Movement Teach?* 57.
[44] A. Baird, *Boston Bulletin*, 6 September 1987, cited Jones, *What Does the Boston Movement Teach?* 57.
[45] Jones, *What Does the Boston Movement Teach?* 57.
[46] Ibid.

Are there any exceptions to this? In Baird's view there are only two. God must be obeyed above government authority and no Christian must violate his or her conscience.[47]

In considering the authority of spiritual leaders over Christians, Baird focused on Hebrews 13:17, 'Obey your leaders and submit to their authority. They keep watch over you as men who must give an account.' He went on to state that 'perhaps more has been done in modern times to explain away this passage among the members of the Church of Christ than any other Scripture'.[48] In his view, however, this text requires submission since the word translated as 'obey' means 'be persuaded'. 'There is', according to Baird, 'no scriptural basis for thinking that Church policies are to be determined democratically.'[49] It is perhaps worth pointing out at this stage that Baptist and Congregational Churches argue for a democratic system of church government on the basis of Paul's teaching about the Church as a body in which every member has an important role to play. Other precedents are also found in the drawing of lots in Acts 1 when choosing a successor to Judas.

Joe Garmon who was discipled by Al Baird inevitably reflected his views. Writing in the *Boston Bulletin* in September 1988 he stated: 'If we are to imitate Jesus we must learn not to fear authority over our lives. Our trust is based not on the righteousness of the person in authority but on the power of God to take care of godly, submissive people' (2 Peter 2:9).[50]

The key to understanding the ICOC's view on authority is the fact that Jesus submitted to sinful man. This means that even if leaders are sinful and un-Christlike, submission is still a requirement. Garmon reiterated the point in a further article the following month.

Often we are afraid to submit to authority because it might be abusive. Jesus was not afraid of abusive authority; he was even willing to submit and obey authority that was abusive . . . When we trust God, we do not

---

[47] Ibid.
[48] Ibid. 59.
[49] Ibid.
[50] J. Garmon, *Boston Bulletin*, 25 September 1988, in Jones, *What Does the Boston Movement Teach?* 7.

have to be afraid to submit to abusive authority. After all, when Jesus submitted, it looked like Satan had won; but God raised Him from the dead. God knows how to take care of the righteous (2 Peter 2:10).[51]

Later when Joe became the Zone leader of the Brockton House Church in Boston, he extended this teaching on submission still further. He maintained that members should obey their House Church leaders even if it contravened rational common sense for the reason that 'every single person is a disciple and has given up themselves'. In practice this might mean that if he insisted everyone wear a red shirt, 'then everybody has to wear a red shirt'.[52]

The result of this kind of teaching is that the various Church plantings including London came to have what many considered to be an overcontrolling influence over their membership, with Kip McKean functioning as the undisputed overall leader. His dominance over the movement has been seen in the ways in which he changes the leadership of individual Churches and moves people from place to place. During the reconstruction of the Denver Church of Christ in 1988, for example, McKean put the matter in stark terms as he announced a new leader:

> You know, if there'd been a democracy at the Red Sea, it'd been a disaster. It is God's wisdom to have a kingdom. Amen? And the man that will lead this work, though not perfect, but he is of God, is Preston. And you need to obey in the Lord ... I think we got to understand that Preston may say, 'I want you over here;' 'I want you in Boulder' ... And, you know, when he assigns you a zone, when he assigns you a Bible talk, you will go, because that's part of the plan. Amen? Even if it's the Dung Gate. Now it's okay to want to be at the Fountain Gate. But you've got to obey. Amen?[53]

It is clear from all of this that the ICOC is a highly authoritarian organisation with a top-down management structure. The

---

[51] J. Garmon, *Boston Bulletin*, 9 October 1998, in Jones, *What Does the Boston Movement Teach?* 7.

[52] J. Garmon, 'Reconstruction of the Brockton House Church', autumn 1988, in Jones, *What Does the Boston Movement Teach?* 8.

[53] K. McKean, *Reconstruction of the Denver Church of Christ*, May 1988, in Jones, *What Does the Boston Movement Teach?* 9.

principle which underlies this is that a congregational member learns to trust his Zone leader. The Zone leader in turn trusts his congregational leader. This means in effect that a congregational member can then trust his overall leader through his zone leader and so on right up to the top of the movement. Submissive trust is in fact required at every level from Bible Talk leader and disciples to senior management level.

Kip McKean, although discipled in his marriage by the elders at Boston, nevertheless disciples them in spiritual matters. He makes the major decisions about leadership of the individual International Churches of Christ. McKean is held in very high esteem by the inner circle of Congregational leaders. Whether this veneration is on account of his natural charisma, a holiness of life or merely the fact that job security is ultimately in his hands is not altogether clear. Probably the reason varies from one individual leader to another. Within each congregation it is the evangelist 'without the elders' who is the authority of God. McKean established this polity in 1987 in a seminar address entitled 'Why Do you Resist the Spirit?'[54] It is often the case that new churches are planted by evangelists with small groups of disciples. Elders are then brought in at a later point in time when the Church life has become established. In the CLCOC full-time elders were not introduced until 1995.

ICOC makes no distinction between clergy and laity. Everyone is seen as a disciple. It isn't felt necessary to be a minister to baptise someone or preside at Communion. The various positions within the Church are seen as 'categories of service'. Some disciples have been trained to be full-time evangelists and women's ministry leaders. There are people who lead new plantings. There are also deacons, deaconesses, teachers, administrators and counsellors.

My brief encounters with members of the International Churches of Christ in 1998 suggested that they were generally happy with their leaders and not intimidated by them. As with all religious movements, there is constant change and most learn from their mistakes and correct aspects of their life and worship in response to constructive criticisms. Leaders with whom I spoke readily admitted that some of their number had been overly author-itarian particularly in the early 1990s and later 1980s. Ayman and

---

[54] Jones, *What Does the Boston Movement Teach?* 9.

Jane Akshar left the London Church of Christ in 1993 after seven years in membership and founded TOLC (Triumphing over London Cults) which is largely focused on helping individuals exit from the ICOC. They have set up a Web site on the Internet and published a good deal of their story. They recount late-night meetings starting at nine and sometimes ten o'clock after evening evangelism. Jane related how when she offered to take other members of the Church into her house, the leadership decided who and how many should share rooms and the level of the rent. At one point a female leader who disliked her cat Rahotep stayed in her house. It was made quite clear to her that the cat must be got out of the house, with the result that Jane took the cat to the vet and had it put down. She writes: 'I feel so ashamed that I let them make me do this but I really thought it was what God wanted.'[55] She also reported: 'The late hours and constant pressure had a huge impact on my health.' The year before she joined the Church she had six days sick leave. Afterwards she had between twenty-one and twenty-four days every year she was a member.[56]

## Discipleship

One of the most distinctive features of the ICOC is its system of discipling. This is based on Jesus' great commission 'to go and make disciples'. Discipling is not an optional extra for class-one membership or for the especially spiritually mature, it is a requirement for everyone. In 1987 Al Baird wrote a series of articles in the *Boston Bulletin* on the whole area of authority and submission. In one of them he wrote as follows: 'Similarly we expect every member to be discipled by a more spiritually mature Christian who is given the authority to teach him to obey everything that Jesus commanded (Matthew 28:20).'[57]

In this expectation Baird was in reality merely reflecting the views of his leader. During a leadership conference McKean made it

---

[55] Jane's Story, TOLC Web site, 1.
[56] Ibid.
[57] A. Baird, *Boston Bulletin*, 4 October 1987, in Jones, *What Does the Boston Movement Teach?* 10.

abundantly clear that everyone in the congregation needs to have a discipleship partner: 'To not have a discipleship partner', he declared, 'is to be rebellious to God and to the leadership of this congregation.'[58] Anyone who joins the ICOC will therefore be discipled by a more spiritually mature Christian who is given authority to teach and instruct them. As in the matter of leadership so in the issue of discipleship everything is based on trust. The disciple has to trust his discipler's motives and is urged not to have hidden reservations about him or her.

Members of the congregation who are discipling others are urged to establish a friendship trust so that the one being discipled will fully believe they are totally out for God and their best interests. The aim is to ensure that the disciple believes that the discipler's judgement is better than his or hers. As McKean put it in an address entitled 'Discipleship Partners', 'They must believe that your judgement is better than theirs.'[59] In order to increase the level of trust on the part of those being discipled the leadership have, on occasion, suggested various trust games which can be played in small groups. These include a bag containing various objects with just sufficient room for an arm to fit in. Each person in turn can put their hand in and feel what is in the bag. Another recommended trust game is to blindfold a person and then guide them around the room.

Discipling is felt to have a number of benefits. The study manual *Your First Forty Days* suggests three in particular. It facilitates the wise use of money, it promotes freedom from immoral relationships and it eliminates wasted time.[60] In these processes the disciples are made aware of the importance of 'opening up your struggles to others who can help and encourage you'.[61] The most important reason behind the discipling process is to help each member 'grow in his or her Christian walk'. The discipling practice, it is felt, 'increases the likelihood that members will remain faithful to God'.[62] ICOC research has shown that the percentage of their

---

[58]  Ibid.
[59]  Bauer and Bauer, *The Boston Movement*, 31.
[60]  *Your First Forty Days*, 7.
[61]  Ibid.
[62]  London Church of Christ, undated MS in INFORM archives, 7.

members who remain faithful is more than five times higher than that of the traditional church of Christ.[63]

One of the criticisms frequently levelled against ICOC's system of discipling is that it is too intrusive in that individuals are required to come clean and hold nothing back. The disciplers, some of whom are young and inexperienced, are reported to be too prying or overly controlling. An article in the *Boston Bulletin* gave the following guidelines for dating:

1. In general, we encourage all single adults to go on a date once a week.
2. If a single is not dating steady, but is interested to get to know a brother or a sister, we suggest dating that person every week.
3. If a single is interested in going steady, we recommend doing so after at least six dates or about three months. Steady dating is not a lifetime commitment, but a testing to see if the relationship is going to go anywhere!
4. How long should a couple go steady before engagement? We suggest a period of nine months so that each person can really get to know the other's strengths and weaknesses, likes and dislikes, etc.
5. How long should the engagement period last before the marriage? We recommend three months.[64]

Some members of the ICOC find this kind of guideline and the restrictions which go with it too confining. Others with whom I spoke in December 1998 at the Riverside Zone Church, which meets in Southfields Community College in South-West London, said they were grateful for the wisdom and oversight they had received. Ayman and Jane Akshar, on the other hand, found the level of control during their dating claustrophobic. Jane wrote: 'we were allowed very little time together, a phone call once a week and a Saturday night date'.[65] She also resented the fact that 'an enormous amount of pressure was put on Ayman to finish with me'. She continued: 'He was told he would never go on a mission, would

---

[63] Ibid.
[64] J. Jones, *What Does the Boston Movement Teach?* I, 9.
[65] Jane's Story, TOLC Web site, 1.

never rise in the leadership if he married me'.[66] The procedures in force at the time of Jane's courtship required that when a brother liked a sister he would go to his discipler. The discipler would in turn make contact with the girl's discipler to discuss their feelings. The matter would then go to the leadership and if they approved, the couple would commence dating every four weeks. While the couple were going out together they were investigated all the time and 'only if you did what you were told were you allowed to continue'.[67] Perhaps rather strangely once couples were married puritanical strictness and secrecy appeared to be thrown out of the window. Jane recalled: 'The first thing you were asked when you came back off honeymoon was what night did she have an orgasm? How often did you do it, where etc.?' She further remembered that 'couples were given weekly goals of sexual frequency and it was discussed in groups if you did not make the goal'.[68]

## High Commitment Level

As with many modern sectarian movements the International Churches of Christ demand a high level of commitment. In preparation for the BBC documentary about the CLCOC entitled 'Living with the Enemy' shown in October 1998, Damien Thompson spent a week living in a communal flat in Muswell Hill. He found that several of his hosts, along with others in the Church, had to endure a gruelling round of Bible study, three services a week, and street evangelising. Jane Akshar's experience resonated with Thompson's. 'For seven years', she wrote, 'this was all my life.' She continued: 'Nearly all our friends were members, everything we did revolved around Church meetings and activities. There was no part of my life that it did not impinge upon.'[69] Although she wanted to leave, she was reluctant to do so because 'we had been taught . . . that to leave the church was leaving God.' If I did make the break, she recalled, 'I would go to hell and so would my

---

[66] Ibid. 2.
[67] Ibid. 3.
[68] Ibid.
[69] Ibid. 1.

husband and child.'[70] On the other hand, a young couple with whom I spoke at the south-west London Zone Church always had one night together on their own and said they attended services and church commitments on the other evenings because they wanted to. The wife in particular, who spent on average one-and-a-half hours a week with her discipler, said she valued this input and was glad to be a part of the Church because she wanted to be account-able. It was clear too that students were able to participate fairly fully in CLCOC activities and still had time for their work.[71]

Another facet of the high level of commitment required by the Church is seen in tithing. Members are expected to contribute a tenth of their income on a weekly basis. This figure is regarded as a basic minimum. In addition collections are held from time to time during Sunday worship services for urgent and needy causes. For example, offerings were taken for 'HOPE', the Church's social out-reach arm, for the people of Honduras following the Hurricane Mitch disaster. Perhaps most challenging is the fact that once a year disciples are required to give eighteen to twenty times their normal weekly tithe. This is seen by many as a major challenge. Adrian Hill told me that he and his wife save during the course of the year so that they are able to meet this requirement without putting their normal household budget in jeopardy. Probably many others do the same. Some of those who have not set aside a regular sum to meet this requirement find themselves in a real dilemma. Sidney Juachon who left the London Church in 1994 related how he 'came within millimeters of cashing my bonds'.[72] 'They think it's a challenge,' he wrote, 'but I think it's one of those mind control tactics.'[73]

Disciples are also expected to keep high standards of conduct. Discos, drugs and gambling are eschewed and they are particularly against smoking, which is seen as a bad example that hurts one's influence, violates others' rights, dishonours God and takes years off your life, causing lung cancer, emphysema and heart disease. In short, God's call, as the 1998 *Leaders' Resource Handbook* puts it, is as follows: 'Each of us must seriously reflect on the depths and

---

[70]  Ibid.
[71]  Interview with M. and I., 6 December 1998.
[72]  S.J. Juachon, 'This is My Open Letter to You about the ICOC', 2.
[73]  Ibid.

importance of biblical righteousness in our lives. We must begin to live out this concept with the passion of Jesus, never compromising its purity for our own selfish ambitions or pride.'[74]

Keeping high standards in family life are seen as an important aspect of a person's commitment. Fred Partington, one of the London Church leaders, wrote a hard-hitting article in *The Edge*, the Church's magazine, 'What Really Breaks Up Families?' He laid particular store on the role of the father and the importance of discipline. 'Next to God', he wrote, 'a man's first priority should be his wife and his family.'[75] The generation gap, in his view, was often used as a feeble excuse for neglect and selfishness. A father and a child should be best friends. Partington urged his readers to 'dare to discipline' since children cry out for 'tough love'.[76] He continued: 'It is my belief that society's lack of "tough love" is the single most destructive force contributing to the break up of the family to-day; the consequent effect upon our society is all too apparent.'[77]

The accusation is sometimes made that new religious movements cause their adherents to pull away and cut themselves off from parents. Such does not seem to be the case with the CLCOC. Partington urges his ICOC younger readers 'to be more thoughtful and to prioritise staying in touch with their families'.[78] Again he reminds them that 'many conflicts are caused because young people learn something, think they know everything and promptly go home to "sort out" their parents who in their opinion know nothing'.[79] Partington concluded his piece by stating: 'I can confidently say that the London Church of Christ stands for principles that will unify families and help them to work through conflicts.'

The ICOC's new *Leader's Resource Book* published in 1998 has extensive instruction on such topics as 'Relationships with the Family', 'Parents who Make a Difference', and 'Family Discipling.' There are even some practical ideas such as 'Have a Deuteronomy 6 Day with Your Children' and a 'Personal Marriage Retreat', which

---

[74] *The Leaders' Resource Handbook*, I, 147.
[75] *The Edge*, December 1993, 1
[76] Ibid. 2.
[77] Ibid.
[78] Ibid. 3.
[79] Ibid.

involves going away with your spouse for a three-day, two-night retreat taking with you a copy of Sam and Gery Lang's *Friends and Lovers*.[80]

## Summary

The ICOC has many orthodox aspects in keeping with the mainline denominational churches. For example, it accepts the Bible as the inspired Word of God, it is Trinitarian and holds to the two sacraments of Baptism and the Lord's Supper. Along with most Protestant churches ICOC also affirms the Virgin Birth, the deity of Jesus and the Resurrection. It is, however, despite its lively worship strongly anti-charismatic. One of their published papers entitled 'The Holy Spirit' presents a strongly secessionist view of the spiritual gifts. Point IVb. states: 'When the generation after the apostles died, so did the gifts of the Holy Spirit'; equally the miracles were only there to 'confirm the spoken word of God'; 'Once the New Testament was completed, therefore, there was no need for them any longer.' In another section it is stated that Paul prophesied the passing away of the gifts (I Corinthians 13:8).[81] Additionally Derek Jacoby who was one of the London leaders produced a substantial book entitled *The Powerful Delusion: How to Study with Charismatics*. Part of the weakness of this volume is that it judges charismatics largely by reference to Kenneth Hagin's volume *You Can Be Led by the Spirit of God*.[82] Charismatics, according to Jacoby, dwell too much on their feelings and 'need pointing to the word of God'.[83]

The London Church of Christ has a published basic outline of belief which has ten bullet points. Interestingly there is no reference to their distinctive teachings on baptism and discipling. Salvation is also stated to be 'through faith and not works'.[84]

A basic outline of our belief is as follows:

---

[80] *The Leaders' Resource Handbook*. See 61, 165 and 167.
[81] Paper entitled 'The Holy Spirit', INFORM archives.
[82] D. Jacoby, *The Powerful Delusion: How to Study with Charismatics*. See 20–21.
[83] Ibid. 28.
[84] London Church of Christ, INFORM MS 9/94, 1.

- We believe the Bible to be in its entirety the divinely inspired Word of God (2 Timothy 3:16).
- We believe that God the father sent his son Jesus to earth (John 3:16) to die for our sin (1 Peter 2:24).
- We believe that Jesus Christ was both man and God in the flesh (Philippians 2:6–8, Hebrews 1:3).
- We believe that the Holy Spirit also, is God (Acts 5:3,4) and that there is only one God (I Timothy 2:5).
- We believe in the death and resurrection of Jesus Christ (I Corinthians 15:3,4) and that salvation is through him alone (John 14:6, Acts 4:12).
- We believe in salvation by grace, through faith and not works (Ephesians 2:8–9).
- We believe in the great commission (Matthew 28:19–20) and as such our goal is to spread the gospel and to help others come to know God.
- We believe that the church also needs to continue the work of Jesus in helping the poor and needy (Galatians 2:10).
- We welcome all people regardless of colour, race, background, culture or religion as the message of the gospel is for all people. This is reflected in our membership.
- Churches of Christ have been meeting in Britain since the 1800s. They have no connection with groups such as Mormons, Jehovah's Witnesses, Scientologists, Children of God, Christian Scientists.

Yet despite this orthodoxy ICOC's teaching on baptism is distinctive when compared to that of the historic and creedal churches. The idea that one must be a disciple as understood by the International Church of Christ as a precondition of baptism, others have argued it is really only sustainable on the basis of one interpretation of Matthew 28:19. Other churches, particularly those of Baptist denominations, emphasise that the sole precondition for baptism was faith in Jesus as Lord and Saviour. This, they maintain, comes out clearly in the case of those baptised on the day of Pentecost (Acts 2:41), those at Samaria who when 'they believed . . . were baptised' (Acts 8:12), Simon (Acts 8:13), Paul (Acts 9:18), those in the house of Cornelius (Acts 10:48), the Philippian jailer (Acts 16:31), and those who heard Paul at Corinth (Acts 18:8). One obvious case in point is the Ethiopian official who was converted while riding in a chariot along the road to Gaza (Acts 8:38). Clearly there was no time for any discipling! He simply called his vehicle to a halt and was baptised in a pool by the roadside. The ICOC notion that baptism is the means of our being incorporated into Christ and claiming our salvation, comes close to the Catholic notion of 'baptismal regeneration', that is, that baptism is, as Thomas Aquinas taught, 'the instrument of our regeneration'.

The ICOC's teaching on discipleship typifies the intensive aspect common to all sectarian religious movements. It is justified on the ground that salvation produces 'fruit' and this fruit shows itself in evangelism in winning others into God's Kingdom. Many members, particularly the young singles, are pushed to the limits of their capacity in a constant weekly round of Bible studies, services, discipling meetings and evangelism in shopping malls, local neigh-bourhoods and college halls of residence. All of this comes close, in the view of some, to a form of salvation by works.[85] If you do not engage at this level and produce the fruit of new Christians your salvation has to be questioned.

One person with whom I spoke who had been in membership with the Manchester ICOC related how they encouraged many talented individuals to lay aside their careers and career prospects to train for full-time leadership and ministry. She felt the Church lacked a really positive biblical attitude to work as a creation ordinance of God.[86]

As with all sectarian movements, the ICOC believe themselves to be 'the sole possessors of the truth'. In the words of M., a former Manchester member: 'The thing that really saddened me is that they just don't acknowledge any other denomination or any other ceremony. If you're not in the Church of Christ, you're not a Christian.'[87] Or, to put it in Kip McKean's words, 'if you don't love the church you don't love God'.

Sectarian movements, as noted in Chapter 1, are led and controlled by a dominant and charismatic leader. Clearly Kip

---

[85] See, for example, Zimmerman, 'Controversy', 4.

[86] Personal interview with M.H., a former baptised disciple at Manchester ICOC, 13 December 1998.

[87] Ibid.

McKean is such a person. Not only is he an able speaker, gifted organiser and a strong leader, he is widely venerated by those in the movement. This becomes apparent in public addresses and writing. In a speech in Chicago Marty Fuqua said: 'I want to be just like him [Kip] . . . I can tell you honestly, there are a few times that I bucked Kip. And I can tell you honestly that I did wrong every time. It was not right to be arrogant, to be proud, to be rebellious.'[88]

Similarly at the Boston leaders conference the following year Scott Green taught a class on 'Imitation' in which he said: 'I want to be able to imitate Kip McKean. I want to preach like him, I want to think like him, I want to talk like him'. He continued 'You see what I am saying? Are you an imitator or are you an information gatherer?'[89] This kind of veneration always has the potential to legitimate some form of cultic dictatorship, but so far McKean seems to have remained merely a highly authoritarian leader. For these reasons the media assertions that the ICOC is a sinister cult cannot be regarded as a correct assessment of the situation. It does, however, have most of the ingredients of a highly sectarian movement whose members live under constant scrutiny and engage in a demanding schedule of intensive meetings and evangelistic outreach campaigns which, in a number of cases, have led to emotional exhaustion, physical burnout and defections.

---

[88]  Bauer and Bauer, *The Boston Movement*, 30.
[89]  Ibid.

# Chapter 11

# Rastafarianism

There are few people in the UK who will not at some time have seen a Rastafarian. Readily identifiable by the symbol of the Lion, red, black and green berets and 'dreadlocks' (see below), they are most in evidence in London, Birmingham and Manchester. Rastafarianism which emerged in Kingston, Jamaica, in the 1930s first began to make its appearance in England in the 1960s as West Indians started to arrive in large numbers to take up jobs in the transport industries and the public services in the post-war years. At their high point in the 1970s,[1] Rastafarians numbered between 70,000 and 100,000 in Jamaica and perhaps as many as 20,000 in the British Isles.[2] Following rising unemployment and the Brixton riots in South-East London, many young blacks who felt oppressed and disadvantaged became active in Rastafarianism as a way of expressing their alienation and dissatisfaction with white-dominated society. In the late 1990s there are probably in the order of 5,000 Rastafarians in England, but it is not easy to be precise.[3] The reason for this is that Rastafarianism is both a culture and a religion and not all those who have a religious commitment express it in terms of active participation in a weekly meeting. Like most other sectarian groups which have emerged from the Christian tradition, Rastafarianism has changed in character and emphasis particularly in recent

---

[1] I. Morrish, *Obeah, Christ and Rastaman*, 89.

[2] Present Rastafarians reckon that most Afro-Caribbean youngsters in the UK in the 1970s aged between 15 to 25 identified with the Rastafarian movement.

[3] 15,000 is probably a generous estimate of those Rastafarians who are active members of a Nyabingi.

decades. There have been significant developments in its messianism both before and after the death of Haile Selassie, Emperor of Ethiopia in 1975.


## Out of Africa

In order to appreciate fully the central tenets of Rastafarianism, it is necessary to understand the place of Africa, and Ethiopia in particular, in West Indian thinking. Leonard Barrett wrote: 'The emergence of the Rastafarians will remain a puzzle unless seen as the continuation of the concept of Ethiopianism which began in Jamaica in as early as the eighteenth century.' When told by their white slave masters in the eighteenth century that the black peoples were the subservient peoples of Ham depicted in the book of Genesis they turned to the Bible but began to uncover a rather different story. They read, for example, in Psalm 68:31, 'Princes shall come out of Egypt; Ethiopia shall soon stretch out her hands to God.' Later they learned from historians that Egypt, and Ethiopia in particular, was the earliest and most creative civilisation in the ancient world and remained so until crushed by a Roman victory at Carthage in 814 BC. Diodorus of Sicily noted that 'the Ethiopians call themselves the first of all men and cite proofs they consider evident'.[4] Although Egyptologists have attempted to put forward Egypt as the pinnacle of African culture, Ethiopia came to stand for all of Africa including Egypt. Significant also was the fact that Ethiopia of all the African nations remained most free from European domination and colonisation. It therefore came to be the symbol of freedom from white oppression. This image of Ethiopia as the great civilisation of Africa's past and as the nation which had been kept from European control began to permeate black consciousness in both the Caribbean and America. It formed the basis of a new dream of an emancipated Black Christianity. For these Blacks Ethiopia was like Zion or Jerusalem to the Jews – it had millenarian end-time significance.

From the beginning all American Blacks knew themselves as Africans. In fact the earliest Baptist Church to be established in the

---

[4] L.E. Barrett, *The Rastafarians*, 68–74.

South by the Blacks in 1775 was called 'The First African Baptist Church in Savannah, Georgia'. The first ordained Negro minister of this church, George Leile, went out to Jamaica in 1783 to engage in missionary work. In Kingston he founded the first non-Anglican chapel on the island, naming it 'The Ethiopian Baptist Church'. By 1814 when the first English Baptist missionary arrived in response to his invitation there were about 8,000 members of his newly formed Baptist Church. The missionaries worked alongside Leile and became fearless in their defence of the slaves.

In the British Caribbean all slaves were pronounced free in 1834, although it was several years before the full impact of the legislation was felt at the grassroots level. One result of the abolition of slavery was the rapid growth of many of the black churches. This in turn gave a new impetus to missionary work, with West Indian Christians in particular beginning to feel a missionary concern for the people of Africa. The new mood was endorsed in the planning of English organisations such as the Baptist Missionary Society. They put forward the theory that people from the West Indies, who were used to a tropical climate and possessed racial and cultural affinity with the peoples of Africa, would be the most effective missionaries. This concern to reach out to the African continent further stimulated interest in Ethiopian culture and promoted a desire for deeper links with black people groups.

In his *Rastafari Roots and Ideology*, Barry Chevannes demonstrated that the indigenous Caribbean Myal religion was also influential in the emergence of Rastafarianism.[5] In the 1770s Myal, which was growing rapidly, began to absorb and reinterpret Christian doctrines. In particular it asserted that an individual's relationship with God is to be sought not through the person of Jesus but through the Holy Spirit. Myal also emphasised the Spirit as possessor and urged people to seek his direction in dreams. Chevannes observed that 'possession by the Spirit thus became the quintessential experience of Myal ritualised Christianity replacing prayer and hymn singing'.[6] In some of the Myal gatherings, which took place away from the plantations, worshippers danced and groaned until they fell down under the power of the Spirit. Myal

---

[5] B. Chevannes, *Rastafari Roots and Ideology*, 19.
[6] Ibid.

was brought closer to orthodox Christianity by the 1860 revival which impacted many parts of the world including the Caribbean. Chevannes became convinced as a result of his researches that these currents of revivalism have remained an integral aspect of Rastafarianism.

## Marcus Garvey

Marcus Garvey (1887–1940) was born in the parish of St Ann at a time when Jamaican society was at a low ebb and the mood was one of general apathy and lethargy. Every aspect of Jamaican life was under European control and there was very little opportunity for the Blacks to improve their position. People were ready to respond to a charismatic leader who could generate political and religious change and inspire hope for the future. As a young man Garvey was an apprentice printer who got involved in union affairs. As a result of his part in a printers' strike he achieved a reputation as a trouble-maker and found it hard to get work. In consequence he decided to travel and see how Blacks were coping in the Caribbean and on the American continent. Later in 1912 Garvey came to England and enrolled in a college course. During this time he met with Druse Mohammed Ali, an Afro-Egyptian scholar, who stimulated his interest in Africa and its culture.

Garvey's middle name, Moses, was a sign of what he was to become for the Blacks of Jamaica and America. Leonard Barrett wrote of him: 'No other Black man in history was able to understand so clearly the world-wide oppressions of Black people, and no other was in turn perceived by so many Blacks as the one person with the solution to their problems.'[7]

Garvey returned to Jamaica in 1914 and with four friends founded The Universal Negro Improvement Association in Kingston with the aim of improving the lot of black people in Africa, America and elsewhere. He desired most of all to give his fellow Africans complete independence from white society and to provide them with the opportunity to establish their own culture and institutions.

---

[7] Barrett, *The Rastafarians*, 66.

Marcus recognised the truth of Jesus' words that 'a prophet is not without honour, but in his own country' and he therefore returned to America in 1916 to seek further backing for his movement. Just before he departed he is alleged to have said in his farewell address: 'Look to Africa for the crowning of a Black king, he shall be the Redeemer.' To Rastafarians this King was Haile Selassie. Garvey wanted above all to see Africa as a powerful, developed continent to which all Blacks could look for inspiration and to which they could return. He also urged the teaching of black culture and the setting up of black educational institutions. As a result of Garvey's efforts a programme was established to encourage emigration to Liberia. On arrival in America, Garvey travelled around thirty-eight States before he finally established himself in New York in 1917. During the next year he started a newspaper called *The Negro World* which at one point reached a circulation of 200,000. In 1920 he was a major inspiration in the setting up of 'The First International Convention of the Negro Peoples of the World' held in New York. The convention attracted 25,000 delegates from more than twenty nations. Garvey was interviewed by the *New York Times* and quoted as saying: 'We shall organise the 400 million Negroes of the world into a vast organisation to plant the banner of freedom on the great continent of Africa . . . If Europe is for the Europeans then Africa is for the black peoples of the World.'[8]

In order to try and meet these goals Garvey set up the African Orthodox Church in New York in 1921 and established the 'Black Star Line', a shipping company, which would be ready at the right time to take his followers back to Africa. As a result of his mishandling of this venture Garvey and three of his co-organisers were arrested on charges of fraud and subsequently tried and sentenced to five years in Atlanta Penitentiary.[9] However, he was deported back to Jamaica in 1927 and soon recommenced his former campaigns on behalf of the downtrodden sections of his fellow countrymen.

The 1930s were a period of economic depression made worse by a series of hurricanes which caused considerable destruction. In this context Garvey's preaching that the glory of Ethiopia and of Africa was the glory of things to come, was readily received. Indeed it

---

[8] *New York Times*, 3 August 1920, cited in R. Dix, *The Rastafarians*, 10.
[9] Ibid. 10–11.

powerfully resonated with a significant event which took place in 1930. In that year Haile Selassie was crowned Emperor of Ethiopia. His full title was 'Ras Tafari, son of Ras Makonen of Harar, King of Ethiopia, Haile Selassie, King of Kings. Lord of Lords, Conquering Lion of the Tribe of Judah.' The word 'Ras' means prince and 'Tafari' is simply the name of the Royal house in the same way that 'Windsor' is the designation of Queen Elizabeth II and her family.'Haile Selassie' means 'Power of the Trinity'. For the people who followed Garvey this crowning of a young Ethiopian king with a biblical title was a revelation direct from God himself. To Rastafarians, Haile Selassie is 'the Living God', 225th in a direct line of Ethiopian kings stretching back to the Queen of Sheba. Reflecting on the image of God Garvey declared:

> We, as Negroes, have found a new ideal. Whilst our God has no colour, yet it is human to see everything through one's own spectacles, and since white people have seen their God through white spectacles, we have only now started out (late though it be) to see our God through our own spectacles . . . We Negroes believe in the God of Isaac and the God of Jacob. We Negroes believe in the God of Ethiopia, the everlasting God – God the Son, God the Holy Ghost, the One God of all ages. That is the God in whom we believe, but we shall worship Him through the spectacles of Ethiopia.[10]

Garvey was always strong in his assertion of the superiority of the ancient black race. In one of his speeches he addressed his hearers in strident tones: 'When we come to consider the history of man, was not the Negro a power, was he not great once?' He went on to assert that 'students of history can recall the day when Egypt, Ethiopia and Timbuktu towered in their civilisation, towered above Europe, towered above Asia'.[11] In another utterance Garvey quoted from the psalmist: 'Princes shall come out of Egypt and Ethiopia shall stretch forth his hands unto God.' This verse from Psalm 68 became a central theme of Garvey's following and it has since become the most quoted text in Rastafarianism. Garvey returned to it again and again. In his address 'Who and What is a Negro?' for example, he urged:

---

[10]  Barrett, *The Rastafarians*, 77.
[11]  Ibid. 78.

The power and sway we once held passed away, but now in the twentieth century we are about to see the return of it in the rebuilding of Africa; yes a new civilisation, a new culture shall spring up from among our people, and the Nile shall once more flow through the land of science, of art, and of literature, wherein will live black men of the highest learning and the highest accomplishments.[12]

In Garvey's speeches and writings Ethiopianism reached its highest development. Many Jamaicans saw the crowning of Haile Selassie as the fulfilment of Bible prophecy and they began to read the Scriptures seriously. Among them were individuals such as Archibald Dunkley, Leonard Howell, Joseph Hibbert (d. 1985) and Robert Hinds. All of them were probably original Garveyites and after their leader's death in England in 1940 they carried Rastafarianism forward. A sizeable number of the new followers of this second generation of leaders were former Garveyites.

Archibald Dunkley was a seaman employed by the United Fruit Company. He established a small group at Kingston in 1933 basing all his teaching on the Authorised Version of the Bible. As a result of his studies in 1 Timothy 6:6–13 and Revelation 17 and 19, which speak of Jesus as 'Lord of lords' and 'King of Kings', he became convinced Haile Selassie was the Messiah. Dunkley also possessed a copy of the book of Maccabees, an apocryphal document not included in the King James Version. He claimed that it contained truths for the black man which the white man had tried to hide from them. Dunkley was a somewhat dictatorial individual who often conducted meetings with a sword in his hand. He was fined for disorderly conduct and committed to Bellevue Asylum in 1933 along with other leaders. He was also noted for his prophetic utterances and had announced the burning down of the Roman Catholic convent on Duke Street which subsequently took place in October 1937.[13]

## Leonard Howell

Born in 1898 Leonard Howell claimed to have served as a soldier before joining the US Army Transport Service as a cook. It was in

---

[12] Ibid. 79.

[13] Chevannes, *Rastafari Roots and Ideology*, 143.

that occupation that he arrived in New York in 1918 where he was apparently the victim of racial discrimination. He returned to Jamaica some time before 1930 and began ministering to the down-trodden and poor in the slums of West Kingston. He soon attracted a large following. Howell was to become the most significant influence in the early development of Rastafarianism. In fact all branches of the movement regard him as one of the first, if not the first, preacher of Rastafari.

In 1933 Howell moved to St Thomas, a parish whose strong anti-colonialist attitudes resonated with his preaching and personal convictions. His radical and revolutionary opinions soon attracted the displeasure of the authorities and he was arrested following an open-air meeting in the village of Trinity Ville, St Thomas, on 16 December 1933. At that time Howell was promoting six propositions:

1.  The Black men are reincarnations of the ancient Israelites and were exiled to the West Indies because of their transgressions.
2.  Haile Selassie is the living God and the Emperor of the World.
3.  Ethiopia is Heaven. The Jamaican situation is hopeless Hell.
4.  The Black men are superior to White men, they will soon rule the world.
5.  Soon Black men will avenge themselves on the White man.
6.  That their God and Emperor will soon arrange for their homeland, Ethiopia.[14]

Howell, who was announced as being the representative of Ras Tafari, King of the Ethiopians, was charged with sedition against both the British and the island governments. He was eventually released from gaol in 1940 and shortly afterwards formed 'The Ethiopian Salvation Society' which purchased an abandoned estate in the hills of St Catherine's, north-west of Kingston. Here he established a commune which was called the 'Pinnacle'. At its height, membership reached about 1,500 members. Howell took thirteen common-law wives and lived in the main house.[15] The members of the community received teaching and instruction in

---

[14] R. Dix, *The Rastafarians*, 13.
[15] Ibid. 14.

Rasta and worked the land to cultivate yams, cow peas, red peas and sweet potato for food, and ganja (marijuana) for the community's use and as a cash crop. In addition they had fowls, goats and cows. An ex-member of the Pinnacle recalled that most households of the community in fact provided for their own needs working small private plots granted by the 'Prince Regent' as Howell was known to the residents.[16] It was Howell's Pinnacle community which brought the Rastafari communities to value and practise smoking ganja.

Howell's organisation was dominated by his charismatic leadership. He alone made the decisions and meted out punishments on those who did not comply with his regulations. On some occasions his retributions could be harsh. A former member of the Pinnacle recalled:

> There were certain restrictions that not even the Government was pleased about, such as punishment. Suppose you disobey him, him order you fi get lash, and if it is in your hand, you have fi take it. If is twenty, take the twenty in you hand. If you violate what him say, you get flogging, and if you refuse, you was sent out of the compound.[17]

Perhaps not surprisingly Howell was arrested in 1941 on charges of assault and spent a further two years in prison.

In 1953 after a further spell in gaol Howell went back once more to the Pinnacle. This time he determined to heighten security and set up a strong guard who adopted a fierce appearance with beards and dreadlocks in an attempt to ward off unwelcome intruders. They also used ferocious dogs to deter interference. The guard were known as 'Ethiopian warriors'. Despite these stronger measures the Pinnacle was raided in 1954, 163 members being arrested and the community finally broken up. The police turned the remaining members off the reservation and they were forced to relocate in the slums of Kingston. By this time Howell was advancing in age and possibly as a result of the onset of senility began to proclaim himself to be divine. He was committed to Kingston Mental Hospital in 1960 where he died.

---

[16] Chevannes, *Rastafari Roots and Ideology*, 122.
[17] Ibid. 124.

The Pinnacle was an important stage in the development of Rastafarianism. It was there that a number of important rituals and practices began to emerge. These included the smoking of ganja at meetings, men adopting dreadlocks and the women plaiting the hair. Ivor Morrish observed that by the close of 1954 there were at least twelve different Rastafarian groups in West Kingston alone with memberships of anything from 20 to about 150.

Joseph Hibbert (1894–1985) was another Garvey follower. Hibbert began his mission in St Andrew in a district known as Benoah. Unlike Howell and Dunkley he built his organisation on occultism. Like Dunkley he also appears to have been in possession of a copy of the book of Maccabees which impressed many of his followers. But it was his reputation as a magic practitioner which drew people to him. In this he was assisted by his common-law wife whose power as a medium was impressive.

After being released from prison with Leonard Howell, Robert Hinds (d. 1950) decided to set up on his own. Instead of continuing his association with Howell, Hinds organised his own group. His headquarters were known as the King of Kings Mission. Much of Hinds' group was captivated by his dominant shepherding. Members looked to him as a prophet. Below him in a well-defined hierarchy were secretaries, two chaplains, an armour bearer, twelve male officers and another dozen water-mothers. The secretaries kept records of the proceedings and read the Scriptures at meetings. The chaplains and water-mothers fulfilled an important function at the baptismal ceremonies.

Hinds was adamant in his belief that Haile Selassie was 'King of Kings' and that he was destined to overthrow the power of England together with that of all other colonising nations. He found biblical support for this conviction in the book of Revelation 17:10–14. Hinds' following had a number of clashes with the police, particularly on account of their expressed opposition to the governments in the form of protest marches.

The King of Kings Mission was in decline by the mid-1940s. There seem to have been several reasons for this: Hinds ran into moral problems with other men's wives,[18] his political activism brought opposition and his sudden unexplained anti-Garvey stance

---

[18] Chevannes, *Rastafari Roots and Ideology*, 140.

turned others away. A large section of his members defected and started a new group led by an individual named Morris. Hinds died in Kingston Hospital on 12 May 1950 without a single follower and was given a pauper's funeral. Morris' group survived until 1960 under the title of Ethiopian United Body.

## Further Developments

By the close of 1954 there were at least twelve Rastafarian groups in Kingston alone. These ranged in membership size from around 20 to 150. In March 1958 representatives of these different factions held a Rastafarian 'Universal Convention' at the 'Back-O-Wall' headquarters in Kingston. There were nightly rituals of singing and dancing and some clashes with the police took place. Two of the major topics discussed at the conference were the issues of unity among the groups and repatriation. There were a number of police raids and arrests under the Jamaican Dangerous Drugs Law for using ganja. The Jamaican evening paper gave the following coverage to the convention:

> For the first time in local history members of the Rastafari Cult are having what they call a 'Universal Convention' at their headquarters known as the Coptic Theocratic Temple in Kingston Pen. Some 300 cultists of both sexes from all over the island have assembled at Back-O-Wall headquarters since Saturday, March 1. The convention is scheduled to last until April 1. The convention was said to be 'the first and the last' in that they were expected to migrate to Africa their homeland.[19]

## The Claudius Henry Repatriation Scheme

The repatriation issue had been the primary focus of the Back-O-Wall convention and there were calls for the Jamaican government to take matters in hand. Unfortunately their response was not sufficiently early to prevent the national emergency caused

---

[19] *The Star*, 6 March 1958, cited Barrett, *The Rastafarians*, 92.

by the Rev Claudius Henry. This gentleman had been invited to return to his native Jamaica to participate in the convention and duly arrived back from New York City in 1958. The following year he established an organisation in West Kingston which he named The African Reformed Church. His powerful ability as a leader and communicator quickly enabled him to gain control over a wide section of Jamaica's Rastafarian population.

Matters reached fever pitch when Henry, who styled himself the 'Repairer of the Breach', began to issue a large number of cards on tickets to the island's inhabitants. Each one contained the following statement of a promise of return to Africa.

> Pioneering Israel's scattered children of African Origin 'back home to Africa'. This year 1959, deadline date Oct. 5th; this new government in God's Righteous Kingdom of Everlasting Peace on Earth. 'Creation's Second Birth.' Holder of this Certificate is requested to visit the Headquarters at 18 Rosalie Avenue . . . August 1st, 1959, for our Emancipation Jubilee, commencing 9 a.m. sharp. Please reserve this Certificate for removal. No passport will be necessary for those returning to Africa, etc. We sincerely, 'The Seventh Emmanuel's Brethren' gathering Israel's scattered and anointed prophet, Rev. C.V. Henry, R.B. Given this 2nd day of March 1959, in the year of the reign of His Imperial Majesty, 1st Emperor of Ethiopia, 'God's Elect' Haile Selassie, King of Kings and Lord of Lords, Israel's Returned Messiah.[20]

These tickets which were sold at a shilling each were purchased in their thousands by those who were convinced that Haile Selassie was their returned Messiah and that Claudius Henry had been raised up to lead them back to their promised land. By the time the 5 October deadline had arrived people from all over Jamaica had gathered at the African Reformed Church's headquarters in Rosalie Avenue hoping to leave the island by boat. It was soon apparent that their hopes had been dashed to the ground since no planes had come for them, nor was there any sign of a ship. Additionally, no passports had been arranged and no passages booked.

---

[20]  Text given in Morrish, *Obeah, Christ and Rastaman*, 74.

Claudius Henry now found himself in an impossible situation of his own making. According to the *Daily Gleaner* of 7 October 1959, hundreds had nowhere to go.[21] Many had left their homes and were ashamed to return while others from the countryside had sold their possessions and had no place to which they could return. A distraught Henry tried unsuccessfully to explain that he had never anticipated the 5 October deadline as the departure day to Africa. Rather this was simply the day on which he had anticipated that the government would respond to the demands of Jamaica's African population. Henry was arrested but eventually he was discharged since the court came to the view that he was a religious fanatic rather than a political agitator. He was fined £100 and bound over to keep the peace for a year.

Claudius Henry did not make a positive response to the lenient treatment he had received and became increasingly antagonistic towards the authorities. This eventually culminated in his arrest together with nine of his followers on 7 April 1960. The police raided the church's premises and seized a large cache of weapons which included over 2,500 electrical detonators, a shotgun, a 32 calibre revolver, a large quantity of machetes and several sticks of dynamite. People referred to the incident as 'the Henry fiasco' and its instigator as 'seditious Henry'. Henry was convicted and on this occasion given a lengthy sentence. Even this did not bring matters to an end because Henry's son, Ronald, and several others, came to the island and resumed the fight. This ended in disaster when two soldiers of the Royal Hampshire Regiment were killed in a clash. In the trial it became apparent that seven of the eight were members of the First African Corps, a New York based black terrorist group. Ronald Henry was hanged for murder in March 1961.

After his eventual release Claudius Henry's ordination certificate and passport were taken away by the Jamaican government. Henry himself founded the International Peacemaker's Association which had several branches in Jamaica with the primary aim 'to establish peace in the earth'. He predicted peace would come to the world through Jamaica after 1 April 1972. Despite his failings in the prophetic area Claudius Henry used his practical skills to set up a large bakery business which sold bread and cakes to shops across the

---

[21] *Daily Gleaner*, 7 October 1959, cited Barrett, *The Rastafarians*, 97.

island. The profits from this venture were ploughed back into the Association. Henry's endeavours had a distinctively millenarian aspect to them. He firmly believed that by repairing waste places and creating prosperity he was bringing in the Kingdom. While Ethiopia might still be the promised land the focus of Henry's activities were Jamaica as the new Zion.

## The Jamaican Government Report on Rastafarianism

The Claudius Henry catastrophe prompted the government of Jamaica to set up a full enquiry into the problems which then faced the Rastafarian communities. In particular they sought to examine the grievances of the poor of which Rasta communities were a major expression. Dr Arthur Lewis, head of the University of the West Indies, authorised three top scholars to produce a report which contained recommendations to the Jamaican Premier. The report which was published in 1960 made a number of unanimous recommendations:

1. The Government of Jamaica should send a Mission to African countries to arrange for immigration of Jamaicans.
2. Preparations should be discussed immediately with representatives of the Ras Tafari brethren.
3. The general public should realise that the great majority of Ras Tafari brethren are peaceful citizens, willing to do an honest day's work.
4. The police should complete their security enquiries rapidly and cease to persecute peaceful Rastafari brethren.
5. The building of low-rent housing should be accelerated, and provision made for self-help co-operative building.
6. The Government should acquire the principal areas where squatting is now taking place, and arrange for water, light, sewage disposal and collection of rubbish.
7. Civic centres should be built with facilities for technical classes, youth clubs, child clinics etc. The churches and the University College of the West Indies should cooperate.

8. The Ethiopian Orthodox Coptic Church should be invited to establish a branch in the West Indies.
9. Ras Tafari brethren should be assisted to establish cooperative workshops.
10. Press and radio facilities should be accorded to leading members of the movement.[22]

As a direct result of these recommendations the government sent a mission to Africa in April 1961. It spent time in Ethiopia, Nigeria, Ghana and Liberia. A second mission followed in 1962. The most significant result was to secure agreements with these African countries which were willing to receive Jamaicans. In the main they were only prepared to take in those with specific technical and professional skills. The arrangement held out little hope of repatriation for the mass of Jamaicans.

## The Visit of Haile Selassie to Jamaica

One other major event in the development of Rastafarianism in Jamaica was the visit of His Imperial Majesty, Haile Selassie, to the island in April 1966. The initial planning of the Emperor's coming was not in any way connected with the Rastafarians. He was on a scheduled trip to Trinidad and Tobago at the request of Dr Eric Williams, the region's Prime Minister. Various Jamaican organisations then sent a telegram requesting him to include Jamaica in his itinerary. When news of his acceptance of their invitation appeared in the press the various Rastafarian groups once more raised their hopes of an immediate return to the African continent. Crowds estimated to be 100,000 were at the airport to greet him. The Rastas who were estimated to be at least 10,000 roared with joy the moment the Emperor's plane touched down on the runway. They swarmed in round the aircraft so that it was more than thirty minutes before the Emperor was able to leave for the King's House. Some of the Rastafari Back-to-Africa brethren were invited to meet the Ethiopian ruler. The rank and file were deeply impressed that the 'King of Kings and Lord of Lords' had been prepared to

---

[22] Dix, *The Rastafarians*, 47.

leave his throne in Ethiopia and sit on a chair among ordinary people in the West Indies. The Emperor for his part was totally bemused that people who had never before seen him should have come to follow him in such large numbers.

The visit of Haile Selassie had two important results for the Rastafarian community in Jamaica. In a private communication the Emperor urged the members not to seek entry into Ethiopia until they had first liberated their own land. So a new principle was established of 'liberation before migration'. In consequence of the visit 21 April became a major celebration day for the island's Rasta population. As sociologists of religion would understand it the notion of 'liberation before migration' represented a slowing down or 'routinization' of the sect.

The death of Haile Selassie in 1975 in the Marxist *coup d'état* led by Colonel Mengistu might well have been expected to bring the hopes of Rastafarians to an end. History reveals, however, that millenarian aspirants are not always easily discouraged and many of them develop fail-safe coping mechanisms. Thus, despite the fact that his mortal remains are currently resting in Addis Ababa's Orthodox Cathedral, there are those who believe that Negus' spirit lives on and that he will ultimately return to lead his followers out of 'Babylon' to their promised rest in Africa. On this understanding Rastafarians have been able to absorb into their theological system what might appear to have been the death knell of their movement. Just as mainstream Christians believe that the tomb was not the end for Jesus but that he would come again to rule in majesty, so the Rastafarians are still eagerly looking forward to the dawning of a new day when all the oppressions suffered by the black peoples will be brought to an end.

## Rastafarianism in Jamaica and the UK since 1960

There can be no doubting that Rastafarianism represents a very important religious sectarian movement in Jamaica. Its numbers were estimated at between 70,000 and 100,000 in 1970.[23] Of these, the majority were between seventeen and thirty-five years of age.

---

[23] Morrish, *Obeah, Christ and Rastaman*, 89.

A decade later there was little to indicate any significant decrease. As with most sectarian groups, the membership, at least in the beginning phase, was predominantly from the lower-class elements of society. As long as conditions of oppression and poverty persist in the island it is likely that membership will remain at relatively high levels. Should social conditions improve, however, one of the cornerstones from which Rastafari exists, namely freedom from poverty and exploitation by the white peoples, will be removed. Membership would then be likely to decline.

In the period after the Second World War, significant numbers of West Indians began to arrive in Britain to take up some of the many job opportunities which had become available as a result of post-war reconstruction and renewed economic growth. Inevitably many brought with them their Rastafarian hopes and aspirations. The 'United Afro-West Indian Brotherhood' which was a Rastafarian organisation was first observed in London in 1955. Another group emerged in Brixton in 1958.[24]

In 1968 a branch of The Ethiopian World Federation was established in London along with the Ethiopian Orthodox Church. Four years later, Claudius Haughton, a Jamaican living in Birmingham, established a second branch in Birmingham. In the 1970s the Rastafarian image underwent something of a change. Whereas in the 1960s Rastas were what Patterson termed 'cultural outcasts' in the 1970s they became more of a positive cultural force in art and music, particularly reggae. Most prominent was Robert (Bob) Marley (1945–81) whose music so well expressed Rastafarian aspirations. His lyrics were not only inspired by his personal faith, they were both singable and memorable. He wrote and sang about the inequalities of the white capitalist system and of the hope of a return to Africa. He was brought into the movement by his wife, Rita, and became a member of The Twelve Tribes of Israel, one of the larger Rastafarian groups.

Starting in 1976, when he released his most influential album 'Rastaman Vibration', Marley proclaimed the Rastafarian gospel in the US, Canada, parts of Europe, Africa and Australasia. Some of his songs were an incisive critique of the white-dominated world, others criticised the futuristic heaven preached from many church

---

[24] See O. Patterson, 'Ras Tafari: The Cult of Outcasts'.

pulpits. In another song, 'Exodus', Marley forthrightly sang about the assurance of the Rastafarians' heritage and their pilgrimage from Babylon to the land of their Father.[25] Marley died of cancer in 1981 and was immediately hailed as a second Garvey by his black followers. He clearly had a major impact on the growth of the movement in the 1970s and 1980s.

In these two decades numerous Afro-Caribbean youths suffered deprivation and a lack of educational opportunity. They felt angered by a white-structured society which consistently left them at the bottom of the pile. In this context Rastafari became a vehicle through which they could express their sense of anger and frustration. Many Blacks therefore came to adopt Rasta dress, customs and ideals without necessarily being committed to the core beliefs about salvation through a black Messiah.

## Rastafarian Beliefs

As we have already noted Rastafarianism is an extremely diverse movement, it will be no surprise that as many as twenty-one different groups were known in the cities of Kingston, Spanish Town, May Pen and Montego Bay in the 1960s, each having special names and separate leaderships. In the British Isles there were four main groups by the 1970s. The Universal Black Improvement Organisation, The Twelve Tribes of Israel, The Ethiopian World Federation and The Nyabingis. Each of these had their origins in the West Indies. The Ethiopian World Federation is the oldest of these denominations and dates from the time when Haile Selassie covenanted Ethiopian land in the 1930s to those Africans in the West who offered to help in the struggle against the Italian invasion. Each of these established structures and networks and sought to draw in members of the black communities. More recently two other groups, The Prince Emmanuel and The Boboshantis, have taken root in parts of England. All of these six strands share a number of doctrines and practices but The Twelve Tribes of Israel developed by Dr Vernon Carrington, has some distinctively Christian aspects

---

[25] Cited E.E. Cashmore, *The Rastafarians*, 6.

which the others do not share. The core ideals which are common to most Rastafarians were set out by Ras Sam Brown.

Ras Sam Brown, born in Frelawney in 1925, proved himself an able pupil at his primary school. He worked in a variety of job situations including the print trade. In 1961 he created something of a public stir by running as an independent candidate for West Kingston elections under the title of 'The Black Man's Party'. His manifesto was set out in twenty-one points. These have since come to be regarded as 'The Charter of Rastafarianism':

1. Members of the Rastafarian Movement are an inseparable part of the Black people of Jamaica.
2. As such we cannot and do not proclaim any higher aims than the legitimate aims and aspirations of the Black people of Jamaica.
3. The Rastafarian Movement consists of the most advanced, determined and uncompromising fighters against discrimination, ostracism and oppression of Black people in Jamaica.
4. The Rastafarian Movement stands for freedom in its fullest sense and for the recovery of the dignity, self-respect and Sovereignty of the Black people of Jamaica.
5. Many deplore and accuse the Black people of raising the colour question in this island. But white supremacy was the official policy of this island for hundreds of years and white supremacists never regarded Black men as good as the dogs in their yards.
6. To white supremacy has been added brown-man supremacy and the mongrel children of the Black woman came to think and behave contemptuously of Black people.
7. Time has removed some of the grosser aspects of white and brown-man supremacy; but discrimination, disrespect and abuse of the Black people are still here in many forms.
8. For instance, in their employment policies, the big guns get generous salaries, house allowance, travelling expenses and bonuses. The poor Black man working in the same industry or enterprise cannot get adequate food, money, and has to accept poor treatment and insults as part of the price of holding the job.
9. In their housing policy, they have houses for the rich, housing for the middle-class and housing for the under-privileged.

'Underprivileged' is only another name in Jamaica for poor Black people.

10. God did not say 'come let us make underprivileged man, middle-class man, and rich man'. He said 'come let us make man'. The existence of underprivileged man in Jamaica is a product of white and brown-man supremacy.

11. The Rastafarian Movement has as its chief aim the complete destruction of all vestiges of white supremacy in Jamaica, thereby putting an end to economic exploitation and the social degradation of the Black people.

12. The Rastafarian Movement stands for Repatriation and power and for the fullest co-operation and intercourse between the Governments and people of Africa and a free and independent people of Jamaica.

13. The Rastafarian Movement, for the furtherance of these ends, must have the backing of its support to, or lead, a political movement of its own.

14. The Rastafarian Movement has the backing of no party. We are subject to persecution and discrimination.

15. The Rastafarian Movement has lent its support to the two big Parties, this support has been in vain because no improvement has taken place in our condition. Neither are we offered nor do we see any hope.

16. The Rastafarian Movement therefore has decided to actively join the political struggle and create a political movement with the aim of taking power and implement measures for the uplift of the poor and oppressed.

17. Because we have no other aims than the legitimate aims of all Black people in this island as stated in clause 2, this movement is open to all Black people, irrespective of class, religion or financial standing.

18. We are not declaring against the political leadership of white men and brown men because of their colour, but because of the wickedness that they represent and invite them to repentance.

19. Consequently, if a man be as Black as night, his colour is in our estimation of no avail if he is an oppressor and destroyer of his people.

20. All men therefore are free irrespective of colour to join this
    political crusade. The only condition is that he must abandon
    evil.
21. Suffering Black people of Jamaica, let us unite and set up a
    righteous Government, under the slogan of Repatriation and
    Power.[26]

Laurence Breiner found that Jamaican attitudes to the Bible
were 'complex'.[27] Many believed that the Bible was originally
written in Amharic by and about the Ethiopians, the 'Israelites'.
The majority of Rastafarians regard the Bible as the product of the
white slave masters, with the result that it now exists only in a
corrupt form appropriately named the King James Version! The
result of this is that most Rastafarians try to see through what they
take to be distortions so that they can 'restore the original sense of
the true Bible'.[28] In contrast to most sects the Rastafarian
hermeneutic is a complex mixture of fundamentalism and
symbology. Where the Bible appears to support Rastafari practice
such as the use of ganja or the subservient role of women, it is
taken with great literalism. Where it appears to conflict with their
ideology, such as in the matter of 'slaves obey your masters' it is
seen as a subverted text which must be reconciled with the major
themes of the Exodus and the deliverance from Babylonian
captivity. In summary, some Rastafarians see the Bible as a source
book for their practices such as abstention from pork, long hair
and the use of marijuana. Others regard it as containing wisdom
which predated Rastafarian ideology.

The Emperor Haile Selassie was a regular reader of the Bible and
encouraged others to do so. For this reason many Rastafarian
groups and individuals read several chapters of the Bible at their
meetings or on their own without commenting or reflecting on its
meaning.

---

[26] Dix, *The Rastafarians*, 44–6.
[27] L.A. Breiner, 'The English Bible in Jamaican Rastafarianism', 31.
[28] Ibid. 32.

## The Divinity of Haile Selassie

All Rastafarian groups venerate Haile Selassie, Emperor of Ethiopia. To each, except the Twelve Tribes, Haile Selassie is 'the true and living God', the black Messiah, who arose in Africa and will lead black peoples back to the African continent, which is the real Zion. The Twelve Tribes assert that Jesus is essential to salvation. Further, that it is only after you have received his forgiveness that you can see in Haile Selassie a reflection of Christ. The other Rastafarian groups are of the view that Haile Selassie alone, apart from Christ, is the Messiah and deliverer. For the Rasta, God is black. For most of their number the authorised version of Jeremiah 8:21 is sufficient proof:

> For the hurt of the daughter of my people am I hurt; I am black; astonishment hath taken hold on me.

The book of Revelation speaks of the coming Messiah as 'King of Kings and Lord of Lords', and as the 'conquering Lion of the tribe of Judah', while Psalm 87:3–4 declares:

> Glorious things are spoken of thee, O city of God. Selah. I will make mention of Rahab and Babylon to them that know me: behold Philistia, and Tyre, with Ethiopia; this man was born there.

To the Rastafarians the fact that Haile Selassie was black, that he was from Ethiopia and that he took the titles 'Lion of the Tribe of Judah' and 'King of Kings and Lord of Lords' can only mean that he is the promised Messiah. Rastafarians are in the habit of calling out 'Jah! Ras Tafari' meaning Haile Selassie is Jehovah. Rastafarians saw Haile Selassie as a real Messiah in the flesh until August 1975, but consider him to be in a spiritual body since the time of his death. 'Jah Rastafari' cannot die. He is God and has the power over death. All Rastafarians who believe and trust in him will live eternally and never see death. He is in all things their God. They pray to him, sing hymns to him and believe his presence is with them in all that they do. Members regard themselves as having been spiritually born again and therefore sons of 'Jah Rastafari'.

## Black Peoples Are the True 'Israel'

Just as God is black so for the Rastafarian the true Israelites are also black. For them the terms 'Israelite' and 'Ethiopian' are one and the same. Most are of the view that they have been punished for their sin through slavery to the Whites. As true members of the House of Israel they observe the strict dietary and hygiene laws of the Old Testament. Members of the 'Twelve Tribes of Israel' branch of Rastafari believe themselves to be the ten lost tribes of Israel. Each individual is able to identify the tribe to which he or she belongs by the month in which they were born. So, for example, if you were born in the month of April you are regarded as belonging to the tribe of Reuben. In fact the months are taken from new moon to new moon so that it might happen that a person is born on 26 March but is still of the tribe of Reuben. 'The Twelve Tribes of Israel' Rastafarians see themselves as the dry bones of Ezekiel 37 coming together in the last days.

The concomitant of this view of the black peoples is that the white races are inferior. This idea emanated primarily from the teachings of Garvey who taught that the white man was the oppressor and therefore evil. Despite this rhetoric many Rastafarians do not automatically assume that white people are evil and in fact numbers of Whites have themselves become Rastafarians. The Twelve Tribes of Israel treat white races on equal terms.

Most Rastafarians are of the opinion that Blacks will ultimately emerge as rulers of the world. They derive this view from their particular understanding of Daniel 2:31–42. The stone which became a great mountain is believed to be the rising African nations which destroyed the 'great image', interpreted as the nations which had formerly colonised Africa.

## Eschatology

From the very beginnings of Rastafarianism, there has been a core belief that salvation would come out of Africa. Marcus Garvey himself was reputed to have said just before his departure to the US, 'Look to Africa for the crowning of a Black King; he shall be the redeemer.' Early leaders taught that Africa was the world's most ancient and cultured civilisation. Ethiopia in particular came to be the focus of this ideology because it was the one nation which had been able to escape white colonisation during the so-called scramble for Africa in the nineteenth and early twentieth centuries.

For many Rastafarians Jamaica is a symbol for hell. It represents a place of oppression where Africans in exile first had to suffer under the whip of the slave driver and then endure a marginalised lifestyle of poverty and economic deprivation. For this reason some Rasta groups understandably are unwilling to enter into any close relationship with Whites. As Sam Brown put it: 'We are the people in Jamaica who are definitely opposed to any form of integration or assimilation with the White oppressor, or any non-African races and ourselves.' He continued, 'We are those who do not accept the name Jamaican, knowing we are Africans in exile.'[29]

In the 1960s Jamaican-based Rastafarians organised classes on Ethiopian history and culture but in more recent times there has been less stress on a future heaven in a black promised land and more emphasis on present justice. Nevertheless repatriation still figures in the thinking of most Rastafarians. They look forward to being established in Ethiopia before the cataclysmic end-time conflict takes place at Armageddon. According to their scheme the Antichrist will appear and this final and decisive battle involving major world powers, including the Chinese, will take place. After this a third of the earth will pass away and Satan will be bound. It is at this point that the Messianic Kingdom will finally be established.[30]

## Rastafarian Meetings

Most Rastafarians see worship primarily as an individual and personal affair rather than a corporate experience. Very few Rastafarians attend the worship of other denominations. Members of the Twelve Tribes are required to read a chapter of the Bible a day and are encouraged to pray individually and with their family.

---

[29] Barrett, *The Rastafarians*, 117.
[30] Interview in Manchester, 18 March 1999, with a member of the 'Twelve Tribes' who wishes to remain anonymous.

Rastafarian groups hold various meetings for differing purposes. These may be weekly, monthly or quarterly. The frequency is varied according to what is felt necessary at the time. In 1999 the 'Twelve Tribes' were meeting every three months. On these occasions the assembly is in the hands of twelve leaders one from each of the Twelve Tribes. Each will read one chapter from the Bible. In addition twelve women, one from each of the twelve tribes will read a chapter, making a total of twenty-four chapters in one meeting. Each of the twenty-four readers will also give a brief testimony. Usually three hymns are sung, one after the Bible readings, one after the testimonies and one at the end. Notices and other communications come before the end and the gathering concludes with the singing of the Ethiopian national anthem.

The content of these meetings differs from one Rastafarian group to another. Only the Twelve Tribes allow women a public role and the privilege of reading and bringing a testimony. The Twelve Tribes believe it is important that people are filled with the Holy Spirit. This is seen as a gradual process as members go on believing in Jesus. Prayers are said at the gatherings, including for the sick and needy. Some are set in form. For example, the following intercession is often repeated:

> May the hungry be fed,
> The sick nourished,
> The aged protected,
> And the infant cared for.

Another common ascription at meetings is

> For the preaching of the cross is unto them that perish foolishness but unto us it is the power of God. For that reason we now say in the name of the Father, the Son and the Holy One of creation as it was in the beginning, so let it be done in the end.

The Ethiopian prayer 'Princes and princesses shall come out of Ephraim, Ethiopians shall stretch forth their hands unto God' and the Lord's Prayer are regular aspects in the meetings of The Twelve Tribes.

Baptism is regarded by the Twelve Tribes as a baptism of fire or purification which takes place within a person as a result of God's presence working in their lives. There is a ritual involving the reading of Scripture and prayers of blessing.

A controversial aspect of Rastafarian denominations is the smoking of ganja or marijuana which is spoken of as the 'wisdom weed'. This has both a religious and a social function. Various biblical texts are cited in justification of the practice, notably Genesis 1:12: 'And the earth brought forth grass, and herb yielding seed after his kind, and the tree yielding fruit, whose seed was in itself, after his kind: and God saw that it was good.' The smoke which rises from the chillum pipes is believed to be a sending up of incense to Jah as described in the biblical books of Deuteronomy and Revelation. In some Rastafari gatherings just before the lighting of ganja the following prayer is said: 'Glory be to the Father and to the maker of creation. As it was in the beginning is now, and ever shall be, World without end: Jah Rastafari: Eternal God Selassie!'[31]

Rastafarians also have an emphasis on festivals although they do not recognise Christmas or Easter. The Twelve Tribes celebrate four major days in the year: the founding of the Organisation of African Unity on 25 May, Haile Selassie's birthday on 23 July, Haile Selassie's state visit to England on 14 October and his coronation on 2 November. The OAU celebration lasts for about an hour and a half with hymns and prayers and testimonies from six men and six women, the testimonies highlighting what the day stands for. After a closing prayer there is a stage show with tap and African dancing and celebration food. Most branches of Rastafarianism celebrate Haile Selassie's birthday and coronation but not all keep the founding of the OAU and Haile Selassie's state visit to England.

## Rastafarian Practices

Many Rastafarians refer to themselves not as 'I' but as 'InI' which is shorthand for 'I and I'. In this way they constantly remind themselves and test their awareness that they have both a physical and a

---

[31] Barrett, *The Rastafarians*, 131.

spiritual being or nature. One of the ways by which Rastafarians are most easily recognised is their long hair. There are various reasons for this practice. Some see it as an imitation of the tribal warriors of Ethiopia. Others have justified it from texts such as Leviticus 21:5 and 1 Corinthians 11:6. Rastafarians regard long hair as a symbol of submission to God in the same way that the Old Testament Nazarite took a vow 'to let the locks of hair of his head grow long' in Numbers 6:5. The Bible, as Rastafarians see it, teaches that a person must let their hair grow long as a means of cleansing themselves. As one adherent put it, 'it is important to have locks in your heart'. The dreadlock has other connotations. 'Dread' means rebellion and so for many Rastas it is a sign of their rejection of white oppression and materialistic values of which they disapprove. Long hair is thus a way of announcing their rejection of an alien culture.

Rastafarians turn away from the use of chemically processed goods. They do not use shampoo or soap. Hair is often washed in water using herbs. Rastas also keep to the Mosaic injunctions not to tattoo the skin or cut the flesh. As true Israelites they observe the Old Testament dietary laws. They do not eat pork or shellfish and they do not drink any kind of liquor, milk or coffee, although they will imbibe herbal tea. Some abstain from sugar and salt which are felt to hinder spiritual purity. They avoid all genetically modified foods and in general keep a natural wholesome diet. 'Ital' is the word Rastafarians use of permitted food.

Women in most Rastafarian groups were treated as subservient to the men. This has been changing somewhat in recent years and within the Twelve Tribes group there is an almost complete equality. Here women can take an active role in the meetings. In many Rastafarian groups in the 1970s the woman's role was to serve the man and attend to his needs. Her prime responsibility, except during her menstrual flow, was to bring up the children and to cook. With the women's rights movement of the 1980s and 1990s many Rasta women now go out to work and are increasingly treated much more as equals.[32] It is still the case that in The Ethiopian Association, the Boboshantis, Prince Emmanuel and Nyabingi sections women are not allowed to take a public role in the meetings.

---

[32] Interview, 18 March 1999.

## Rastafarian Symbols

As with other religious communities Rastafarians have certain key symbols. The most important is that of the 'Lion' which represents Haile Selassie, the 'Conquering Lion of Judah' and the 'Messiah.' The Lion also symbolises the dominant role of men within the movement. Rastafarian men strive to cultivate the spirit and the strength of the Lion. Colours are important, particularly red, gold and green, the colours of Ethiopia. Red symbolises the blood of the martyrs which was shed, gold stands for wealth and green for land.

## Rastafarians and the Historic Christian Churches

With the exception of The Twelve Tribes who are much closer to orthodox Christian creedal beliefs, Rastafarians differ in their Christology from the historic Christian denominations. They do not see Jesus as the unique and complete revelation of the God of the Old Testament.

For some Rastafarians, Jesus is the white man's God and Selassie is for the black man. For others Jesus is the Son of Jah and Haile Selassie is a manifestation of him. Mainstream Christianity acknowledges that Jesus has been and is reflected in the lives of great saints but see this as altogether different from asserting that Haile Selassie is a manifestation or incarnation of Jesus. The mainline Catholic and Protestant churches do not worship or ascribe divine status to any other than the Trinitarian God – Father, Son and Holy Spirit. In most Rastafarian teaching there is no doctrine of the Trinity and Haile Selassie is regarded as the incarnation of Jehovah. There is no baptism or Lord's Supper in Rastafarian worship. For the movement's members, smoking ganja is their sacrament. The wisdom weed or herb is regarded as being a source of spiritual food and a source of enlightenment. Rastafarians also have a detailed and developed eschatology in which they feature prominently in a repatriated Ethiopia. In these matters there are clear points of difference from mainstream Christianity. Rastafarianism represents a reaction to the colonial white-dominated Christianity proclaimed by missionaries who operated out of an imperialistic culture in the eighteenth, nineteenth and twentieth centuries. Its desire for a relationship with God which is direct, immediate and relevant to the circumstances of living is a challenge to both Protestants and Catholics alike. Rastafarians have drawn deeply from the great Old Testament themes of liberation and redemption. They see themselves as living in Babylon which could be a political regime or simply spiritual oppression. Like the ancient Jews they look forward to the hope of a promised land which they believe is Africa and more particularly Ethiopia.

# Chapter 12

# The Appeal of Sectarian Religion

Sectarian religion has an appeal and a holding power not matched by the historic Christian denominations. Taken as a whole the sectarian movements considered in this volume have in the region of 300,000 adherents. Most sects are growing steadily or holding on to their existing members – while at the same time membership of mainstream religion is declining steadily. There are a variety of reasons for this attracting power of sectarian movements.

## Certainty

The postmodern era of the third millennium is a world of uncertainty. There is no metanarrative about God, world origins, meaning, purpose or destiny. Richard Roberts suggested that postmodernity is characterised by the collapse of grand narrative, a crisis of legitimation, fluidity and individualism.[1] Furthermore there are no longer any generally accepted norms as to relationships or social and personal morality. It was in this context that Alisdair MacIntyre asserted that the established Christian churches stand between what he termed the 'defeated tradition' and 'an increasingly alien human and social reality'.[2] Growing numbers of people are reaching a point where they find it hard to distribute the load of uncertainties which press in on them in the course of their daily existence. Inevitably, therefore, they will be attracted to any

[1] R.H. Roberts, 'A Postmodern Church? Some Preliminary Reflections on Ecclesiology and Social Theory', in D. Ford and D.L. Stamps, *The Essentials of Christian Community*, 179–95.
[2] Cited Roberts, 'A Postmodern Church?' 183.

movements that offer definite answers to ultimate questions or even clear solutions to social and political issues which the authorities try to keep on hold. All of the sectarian movements examined in the previous chapters put forward clear black-and-white answers to the question of salvation. They have straightforward schemes about God's plans and purposes for the human race and the future destiny of the present world order. Many of those who join sectarian groups testify that these seemed like the one sure thing in a world where everything else is in a state of chaos and flux.

There is that in everyone which seeks to get things taped and buttoned up, especially so when it comes to the issues of life and death. Speaking in general terms, most of the historic or older Christian churches and denominations tend not to deal in certainties. Their theologies are open-ended and allow for a fairly wide divergence of views. A universal branch of Christendom like the Anglican Communion offers a 'Broad Church' with a range of opinion on issues such as the atonement, the sacraments, the role of women, future judgement and final destiny. The general impression created by the public persona of the Church of England, for example, is one of confusion and uncertainty on many key doctrinal issues. Therefore people who are looking for answers to their own and the world's problems are not going to be drawn by those religious organisations that lack the ability to set out a clear, straightforward scheme rooted in the biblical text.

Many sectarian movements not only have a strong conviction that they alone have the truth about salvation, they also market their message with enthusiastic missionary strategies. Frequently this is done with major input from the young enthusiastic members of their group, supported, where possible, by celebrities such as the Osmans, in the case of the Latter-day Saints, or Bob Marley of the Rastafarians. Large numbers of people have been captivated by the warm enthusiasm of young Mormon missionaries who came knocking on their doors. Numbers are impressed by the courage of the student members of the Church of Christ witnessing on buses, tubes and university campuses, or the boldness of the Jesus Army on the streets of the inner-city areas. Yet others have been convinced by steady persistence of the 'publishers' from their local Jehovah's Witness Kingdom Hall who come to offer them the *Watchtower* magazine.

## Morality

Another aspect of the appeal of sectarian religious movements is their strong adherence to definite moral codes. When Ernst Troeltsch first analysed 'church' and 'sect' types, he observed that churches were essentially 'compromising institutions'. They were ready to adapt and change their doctrines and moral codes in response to the surrounding culture in which they were operating. In contrast, Troeltsch noted that sectarian membership was composed of 'strict and definite believers'. They were not those who explained away eternal verities or watered down what they took to be biblical standards of social behaviour. There is a growing disillusionment on the part of many with contemporary Western society. Rising crime rates, racism, a seemingly ineffectual justice system, juvenile delinquency and teenage pregnancies are the tip of the iceberg of decaying family life. Ever-increasing mobility and short-term contracts have also dispersed what was the extended family. Increasing numbers of young couples no longer live close to either parents who in earlier times could have provided additional support and stability. It is no surprise, therefore, that people are drawn to religious movements which have family and strong behavioural values at their core. Such frameworks for living, which most sectarian movements operate, are what Juan Luis Segundo categorised as the 'easy' morality which readily 'distinguishes the realm of the permitted from the realm of the prohibited'.[3]

From an early age all who belong to the Latter-day Saints are taught to respect one another and not to be judgemental, to be honest, kind and generous, loyal and truthful. The Latter-day Saints maintain that over 70 per cent of their teenage members are actively involved in the life and worship of their church, which, as already mentioned, prohibits alcohol, tobacco and premarital sex.[4] Groups such as the Jesus Fellowship maintain high standards of personal behaviour among those who live in its community houses. Male and female members are strictly segregated and, as has been noted, dating procedures are carefully monitored by the movement's leaders. Each fellowship house is seen as a family unit with elders

---

[3] J.L. Segundo, *The Community Called Church*, 112.
[4] Le G. Richards, *A Marvellous Work and a Wonder*, 391.

keeping a careful eye on discipline and behaviour. This has a particular attraction for those who come from dysfunctional home backgrounds or situations of brokenness and pain. Christadelphians and Jehovah's Witnesses are also among those religious movements which preserve a strict morality and encourage family values. Young people from the Witnesses are chaperoned on dates with the opposite sex and receive guidance and advice about marriage commitment from the local leaders. These high standards of morality are further reinforced by a variety of disciplinary and expulsion procedures. Although some of these measures might strike the outsider as harsh and unreasonable, for the adherents they provide further guarantees of stability and are seen as appropriate means of upholding core values and standards. Bryan Wilson pointed out that in this stand for traditional religious codes of conduct sects are conservative and yet have an appealing radical element. Sects are conservative in that they often seek to reassert moral and religious precepts which have been neglected by the traditional churches. At the same time, they are radical in that they often denounce synods, bishops and clergy for failing to maintain original religious values.[5]

In upholding strict and definite values and standards of behaviour sectarian leaders adopt straightforward, face-value and sometimes literal interpretations of the biblical literature. This for many would-be members has a further appeal because they are seen to be those who take the Bible seriously. They are regarded as people of real faith who do not compromise the meaning of the text. Here are men and women who are seriously committed and take God at His word. Many young people, particularly those who have become disenchanted with middle-class materialism, find the challenge to radical discipleship put forward by movements such as the Jesus Army and the London Church of Christ one to which they can readily respond. Mary Grey in her critique of contemporary society aptly summarised the mood of the younger generation. Writing as a parent, she commented: 'We have seen them grow from bored but obedient teenagers, who found that their concerns for peace, ecology, justice and meaningful participation were better met outside the church.'[6]

---

[5] B. Wilson, *Religion in a Sociological Perspective*, 105–10.

[6] M. Grey, *Beyond the Dark Night: A Way Forward for the Church*, vii.

## Identity

When Ernst Troeltsch first analysed the distinction between church and sect types of religious community he noted that sects were essentially smaller, more vibrant and intensive in their approach. In their corporate life members were 'bound together' in a tight-knit bond by virtue of the fact that all had experienced 'new birth'. Here they could find a sense of belonging among people of their own class and background. For many, their religious community became also a refuge from the hostility and the rejection of the wider world.

With the passage of time membership of many established sects has a tendency to prosper and adopt middle-class values. However, in the initial phase of their development, membership was frequently drawn from the disinherited and those on the margins of society. Such, for example, was the case with the Christadelphians, the Jehovah's Witnesses and the Latter-day Saints. Within the Ecclesia, the Kingdom Hall or the local ward church, members were able to create their own subculture based on their particular values and standards. Here they could accept and affirm one another and find an identity which for most was not possible in the depersonalised and harsh environments of the nineteenth-century mine and factory. In many instances the sect became their total way of life. It was almost their sole source of identity. For many, the small sectarian community continues to function in this way for, as Anthony Thistleton observed, 'all persons . . . enhance their identity in relationality with others and with the other'.[7]

This provision of identity which sects offer is perhaps best observed in immigrant communities. To attend the worship and activities of a religious group which reflects the ethnicity, traditions and heritage of the homeland can serve as a cushion against excessive 'culture shock' brought about by the environment of the new country. The Amish, for example, who were organised by Jacob Ammann in 1693, emigrated to America and Canada. Here they sought to retain their identity by keeping aspects of their European peasant culture and traditions. Even to this day they live in communal reservations mostly in the US and Canada, wear

---

[7] A.C. Thistleton, *Interpreting God and the Postmodern Self: On Meaning, Manipulation and Promise*, 162.

sixteenth-century-style clothes, drive horse and buggies instead of motorised transport, reject the use of radios, televisions and telephones, and live without electricity in their homes.

In the 1960s and 1970s many Afro-Caribbean people residing in the UK found their identity by joining one of the predominantly West Indian sects such as the Rastafarians or the Church of God of Prophecy or the New Testament Church of God. Here the music, colour dress codes, rhythmic swaying, clapping, dancing and general intensity all combined to produce an environment with which they could identify and in which they could be themselves. In summary, identity is achieved by belonging to a group and being accepted and valued by its membership.

## Community

Closely related to the concept of identity is that of the community within which individuals begin to express themselves and to experience a process of self-discovery. There are a number of reasons why people look for community. For some it is the case, as Dietrich Bonhoeffer observed, that they are afraid to be alone.[8] For others a stable community is the missing ingredient in their life for which they have long been searching. In the Western world, and in Britain in particular, there is a very high divorce rate. A large number of young people come from broken and dysfunctional families in which they have lacked any sort of encouragement or affirmation. Many sectarian groups have a strong appeal for teenagers and university students who crave the loving care and support they lacked in their home environment. David Yakqub Mohammed typifies many thousands who have found a solid base within a sectarian community. Born of mixed race in Birmingham in 1964 his father died when he was two years old. While still at junior school he began stealing designer clothes from washing lines and selling them. At the same time he learned the art of manipulating pinball machines to make jackpots. By the time he reached the age of nine he was taken into care and all semblance of family life was over. As a result of Jesus Army members visiting the café which had

---

[8]  D. Bonhoeffer, *Life Together*, 57.

become his home, he began to attend their meetings. He felt God drawing him as if he were being pulled by a rope. Now fully committed to the Jesus Army he says: 'I have found a true family. One which brings security and healing. Once I had no mum and dad, now I have lots of mums and dads . . . It's brilliant the way God has become a father to me, and how He has brought me into His family. I just long for others to find what I have found.'[9]

The distinctive aspects of the Jesus Fellowship communities are also reflected in the London Church of Christ in that they too operate household communities. As Keith Newell observed, 'the household restores family to those who have lost it, and is intended to bring emotional healing and personal growth'.[10] Mary Grey also noted that 'what people want is a form of community where they experience meaningful participation'.[11] However, the fact remains that not all who live in sectarian community have survived the experience. For some life under such conditions is too confining and too structured. Nevertheless many do stay and go on to make long-term commitments to group living. This clearly resonates with Andrew Walker's contention that 'There will be no future for the broad church in a postmodern world. We will have to return to structures . . . akin to the monastery, the religious community and the sect.'[12]

Movements such as the Latter-day Saints and the Jehovah's Witnesses offer secure environments for their members. Although these are not in community households they might be termed extended domestic households in which welcome, hospitality and support are freely given. Some sectarian groups are well known for the way in which they provide not only Sunday meals but activities and structured meetings almost every night of the week. Some individuals locate their entire lives in this context. Members develop a strong bond with each other. They share a common core of beliefs and subscribe to a corporate vision. They worship, pray, study the Bible and socialise together. They have gone from door to door

---

[9] *Jesus Life* 46 (Fourth Quarter, 1998), 5.
[10] K. Newell, *Charismatic Christianity: Sociological Perspectives*, 127.
[11] Grey, *Beyond the Dark Night*, 25.
[12] A. Walker, *Telling the Story: Gospel Mission and Culture* (SPCK, 1996), 190.

with their message, stood in the rain and snow witnessing or invit-ing people to neighbours nights, guest services or friendship banquets. United in a tight-knit body of believers they are often so involved with their movement's activities that they have few other friends or contacts. The people they are closest to and the ones they trust are those within their group. Community for most sectarian members, even if it is largely closed to the outside world, is their security. It is this aspect which retains their commitment. They provide warmth, stability, care and friendship in what is for many a hostile and confusing world.

## Immediacy

Members of sects frequently speak of coldness and indifference in the worship of the mainstream denominations. They perceive church services as sedate, predictable and unemotional. Salvation in the historic churches is for the most part a matter of reason and operating one's life on the basis of trust in certain doctrinal propositions. It is essentially a lifelong process to be worked at and persevered with to the end. Much of this emphasis manifestly fails to resonate with the prevailing culture of the new millennium which stresses immediacy and markets instant products. Establishment religion is bottom of the confidence ratings among the under thirty-fives and only slightly higher among those over fifty. In fact, like their religious counterparts, many traditional secular institutions are also struggling for survival.

The contemporary scene is a world characterised by instant credit, fast foods, short-term contracts, divorce on demand and immediate access to information from the Internet. It is reckoned that a quarter of the population of the British Isles are addicted to something. The root of that addiction in many cases is pain. Many are therefore looking for that same instant overwhelming experi-ence which will dull their sufferings and lift them above the hurts, stresses and complexities of their daily living. The youth culture seeks for such a remedy in drugs, sexual experimentation and possi-bly the occult. Older generations look for short-term relief and escape routes in shopping, travel, entertainment, the Internet, eating out and house comforts. Most are unlikely to be attracted by the prospect of what appears to be a long-term commitment to a God which involves steady discipline, faith and perseverance. Against this background the element of experience and immediacy present in many sectarian movements has an appeal not matched by the older traditional churches. As Bryan Wilson observed, 'new religious movements offer reassurance to men in more immediate ways'.[13] The sociologist Peter Berger regarded this element of immediacy as the defining characteristic of sectarian religion. 'The Sect', he argued, 'may be defined as a religious grouping based on the belief that the spirit is immediately present. And the church, on the other hand, may be defined as a religious grouping based on the belief that the spirit is remote.'[14]

A number of sectarian movements appeal because they are able to offer a package which is not only immediate, but is also emotionally satisfying. For example, many are drawn to the Spiritualists because in the messages received for them by the clairvoyant, or the improvement they feel from attending a healing service, they encounter a new and satisfying level of experience. Glen Hoddle, the former England football coach, was captivated by Eileen Drewery's practice of absent healing, which enabled her to repair overnight what had been diagnosed as a long-term injury and likely to keep him out of football for six weeks. This same element of immediacy through healing is also an attracting aspect of Christian Science. Numbers testify to having joined the Church as a result of hearing testimonies of healing or having themselves received healing through the prayers of a Christian Science practitioner.

Similarly Rastafarianism's dancing, reggae music and communal smoking of ganja offers a deep and intense emotional experience which brings relief and escape from an alien culture. For this reason in the 1970s and 1980s, large numbers of young unemployed Afro-Caribbean immigrants embraced the life and worship of groups such as The Ethiopian World Federation and The Twelve Tribes. It is a different, yet immediate, experience of an altogether different kind which is offered by the Jesus Fellowship and the Jesus Army which has had such drawing power for young white people and particularly those coming from backgrounds of crime and

---

[13] Wilson, *Religion in a Sociological Perspective*, 131.
[14] P. Berger, *Invitation to Sociology*, 474.

broken families. Wilf Copping, for example, attended a meeting of the Jesus Fellowship at Bugbrooke and found the atmosphere 'electric'. As he put it in his own words, 'It felt like a little LSD trip! I enjoyed it! It lasted too long! It was too much!'[15]

This element of immediacy is also present in the reception of new converts into warm and supportive communities. Walter Martin observed of the Latter-day Saints that they concentrated on programmes which 'make its church organisation a home away from home for Mormon children and young people, and the absence of juvenile delinquency is in a marked proportion among Mormons'.[16]


## Authority

In one way the postmodern world is fertile ground for the growth of sectarian groups because absolute truth is dead. There is no one version of the Christian message to which everyone or even a substantial majority adheres. Individuals are therefore increasingly thrown back on their own views and what they feel is right. From the clamour of voices which compete for people's allegiance in the religious marketplace it is often the sectarian groups with 'charismatic' leaders who prove most successful in the recruitment stakes.

Sectarian movements, as we have seen, are usually founded by men and women who have 'charisma' or natural gifts of personality and authority. Max Weber emphasised that this charisma is a quality of spiritual endowment rather than any ability to administrate.[17] It is also frequently the case that at the local level sects often continue to be led by similar charismatic individuals who are possessed with energy and enthusiasm. Many people are attracted by groups which have this kind of strong dynamic leadership which is confident and self-assured. They find security in a clearly expressed doctrinal basis and straightforward programmes of action which are carried forward with efficient firmness. The Latter-day Saints, as we have

---

[15] *Jesus Life* 46 (Fourth Quarter, 1988), 22.

[16] W. Martin, *The Kingdom of the Cults*, 147.

[17] M. Hill, *A Sociology of Religion*, 148.

seen, have a developed hierarchy under the authority of the chief prophet and President of the Church. This Council of the Seventy are responsible for overseeing the worldwide organisation including building, missionary activity and the distribution of literature. The Church with its bright, modern buildings and its clear teachings has inevitably expanded both its UK and worldwide membership rapidly during the past two decades.

Other sectarian groups also attract new members for the same reason. For example, many young people have joined the Jesus Army because they are impressed by the strong uncompromising leadership set by its director Noel Stanton. Members of the London Church of Christ with whom I spoke had a high regard for their local elders and spoke of them warmly in first-name terms. Although significant numbers of those who have left the Church professed to find the system of disciplining oppressive, others with whom I spoke professed to feel secure within it.

## Mission

The majority of sectarian movements, although not all, have a strong missionary impetus with a strategy to plant new congregations.[18] For many, particularly the young, this has a strong appeal. It gives a heightened sense of purpose and a feeling of being actively involved in extending the Kingdom and purposes of God. People in general are not attracted to static or declining institutions, rather they look for energetic groups which have clear goals and objectives and are on the move. This contention is demonstrated by the fact that there has been considerable transference of membership from decaying institutions such as the Church of England into the so-called New Churches such as Pioneer, and more particularly the Vineyard denomination.

Sectarian missionary activism is well illustrated by the upbeat words of Noel Stanton, the Senior Pastor of the Jesus Fellowship. Writing a comment in *Jesus Life*, he declared:

---

[18] This would not be true, for example, of Christian Scientists or Spiritualists.

JESUS EMPHATICALLY stated He would 'build His Church'. No power of demons or men would stop Him! He has been building now for upwards of 2000 years and will continue until his return. Jesus trained and commissioned Peter and His first disciples to be 'builders'. They would continue His building mission. We, in our turn, are now the builders, building the Church of Jesus Christ. 'We will build!' must be our cry.[19]

It is this kind of seriousness of purpose and commitment, not often present in the historic churches, which acts as a magnet for some people.

Taken as a whole, sectarian movements are a growing feature of the religious landscape in contemporary Britain. Some of those we have considered in this volume, such as the Exclusive Brethren, the Latter-day Saints, the Christadelphians and the Jehovah's Witnesses, have a history that extends back well into the nineteenth century. They are generally designated as 'established sects'. In contrast other movements such as the Jesus Fellowship and the Central London Church of Christ are comparatively recent. Taken together these groups are significant because they are an aggressive form of religious life and worship. As such they are likely to survive while establishment religion is probably set to decline yet more steeply. Dr George Carey, the Archbishop of Canterbury, in an address at Swanwick warned fellow bishops, missionaries and other members of the clergy that 'the Church is one generation away from extinction'.[20] While his statement was clearly hyperbolic the mainline churches would do well to learn from the wholehearted commitment and forthright evangelism of their sectarian counterparts.

---

[19] *Jesus Life* 46 (Fourth Quarter, 1998), 3.
[20] *Daily Telegraph*, 10 March 1999.

# Select Bibliography

*A Century of Christian Science Healing* (The Christian Science Publishing Society, 1966)

Adams, N., *Goodbye Beloved Brethren* (Impulse Publications, 1972)

Aebi-Mytton, J., '*An Exploratory Study of the Mental Health of Former Members of the Taylorite Branch of the Exclusive Brethren*' (unpublished MSc thesis, University of London, 1993)

*Alumni Dublinensis* (Alex Thom, 1935)

Anderson, R.I., 'Spiritualism Before the Fox Sisters', *Parapsychology Review* 18 (January–February 1987)

Arrington, L.J., and Bitton, D., *The Mormon Experience* (George Allen & Unwin, 1979)

Arthur, D., Jacoby, D., Lloyd, J., *Shining Like Stars* (Central London Church of Christ, 1987)

Barker, E., *New Religious Movements* (HMSO, 1992)

Barrett, D.V., *Sects, Cults and Alternative Religions* (Blandford Press, 1996)

Barrett, L.E., *The Rastafarians* (Heinemann, 1977)

Bassett, J., *100 Years of National Spiritualism* (The Spiritualist National Union, 1990)

Bauer, R., and Bauer, S., *The Boston Movement: Analysis, Commentary and Media Reports* (Freedom House, undated)

Berger, P., *Invitation to Sociology* (Penguin Books, 1966)

Bourne, F.W., *Billy Bray* (Epworth Press, 1937)

Breiner, L.A., 'The English Bible in Jamaican Rastafarianism', *Journal of Religious Thought* 42, Part 2 (1986)

Brodie, F.M., *No Man Knows My History* (no publisher, 1966)

Bushman, R.L., *Joseph Smith and the Beginnings of Mormonism* (University of Illinois Press, 1988)

Campbell, J., and Bird, J., *Christian Community in Central England* (New Creation Christian Community, Northampton, 1989)

Carter, J., *God's Way* (The Christadelphian, undated)

Cashmore, E.E., *The Rastafarians* (Pergamon Press, 1984)

Chevannes, B., *Rastafari Roots and Ideology* (Syracuse University Press, 1994)

*Church Alive* (Jesus Fellowship, 1996)

Clark, D., *Basic Communities: Towards an Alternative Society* (SPCK, 1977)

Clifton, A., *What is Christian Spiritualism?* (Greater World Spiritualist Association, 1998)

Close, F., *Table-turning not Diabolical: A Tract for the Times* (no publisher, 1853)

—, *The Testers Tested; or Table-moving, Turning, and Talking, not Diabolical: A Review of the Publications of the Rev Messrs Godfrey, Gillson, Vincent and Dibdin* (no publisher, 1853)

Collyer, I., *Robert Roberts* (The Christadelphian, 1977)

Cooke, G., *Who is White Eagle?* (White Eagle Publishing Trust, 1998)

Cooper, S., and Farrant, M., *Fire in Our Hearts* (Kingsway, 1991)

Darby, J.N., *Separation from Evil, God's Principle of Unity* (no publisher, undated)

*Dictionary of National Biography* (22 vols.; Oxford University Press, 1921–22)

Dix, R., *The Rastafarians* (Breda Centre, 1985)

Doyle, A. Conan, *History of Spiritualism* (Cassell, 1926)

Eddy, M.B., *Christian Healing: A Sermon Delivered at Boston* (First Church of Christ, Scientist, 1888)

—, *Church Manual* (The Christian Science Publishing Society, undated)

—, *Miscellaneous Writings* (The Christian Science Publishing Society, undated)

—, *No and Yes* (The First Church of Christ, Scientist, 1891)

—, *Retrospection and Introspection* (First Church of Christ, Scientist, 1953)

—, *Science and Health with Key to the Scriptures* (First Church of Christ, Scientist, undated)

*The Family: A Proclamation to the World* (Church of Jesus Christ of Latter-day Saints, 1995)

Farthing, G., *When We Die* (The Theosophical Publishing, 1968)

Fielding Smith, J., *Doctrine of Salvation* (Deseret Book Company, 1954)

—, *The Teachings of the Prophet Joseph Smith* (Deseret Book Company, 1977)

Fitzgerald, F., *Cities on a Hill* (Picador, 1987)

Franz, R., *Crisis of Conscience* (Commentary Press,1992)

Gardiner, A.J., *The Recovery of the Truth* (no publisher, undated)

Garmon, J., 'Reconstruction of the Brockton House Church', *Boston Bulletin* (9 October 1998)

*Gospel Principles* (Church of Jesus Christ of Latter-day Saints, 1988)

*The Greater World Christian Spiritualist Association Information Leaflet* (Greater World Association Trust, 1998)

Grey, M., *Beyond the Dark Night: A Way Forward for the Church* (Cassell, 1997)

Ha, B., *Rapture in October 1992* (no publisher, 1992)

Harper, M., *A New Way of Living* (Hodder & Stoughton, 1973)

Hill, M., *A Sociology of Religion* (Heinemann, 1976)

History and Information about the UK Churches of Christ (Web site www.icoc.org.uk/London, 26 November 1998)

Hoekema, A.A., *Christian Science* (Paternoster Press, 1973)

Holl, K., 'Der Szientismus', *Gesammelte Aufsätze Zur Kirchen-geschichte* (J.C.B. Mohr, 1921–28)

Homer, M., 'Sir Arthur Conan Doyle: Spiritualism and "New Religions" ', *Dialogue* 23 (1990)

Howe, E.D., *Mormonism Unveiled* (no publisher, 1834)

Hunckley, G.B., *Truth Restored* (Church of Jesus Christ of Latter-day Saints, 1979)

*Information about the London Church of Christ* (INFORM, 1995)

*Introducing the Jesus Army* (Jesus Army pamphlet, undated)

Jacoby, D., *The Powerful Delusion: How to Study with Charismatics* (Central London Church of Christ, 1977)

*Jehovah's Witnesses in the Divine Purpose* (Watch Tower Bible and Tract Society, 1959)

*Jehovah's Witnesses in the Twentieth Century* (Watch Tower Bible and Tract Society, 1989)

*Jehovah's Witnesses: Proclaimers of God's Kingdom* (Watch Tower Bible and Tract Society, 1993)

Jensen, R.L., and Thorp, M.R., *Mormons in Early Victorian Britain* (University of Utah, 1989)

Jensen, J., and Armstrong, C., 'London Church of Christ Memorandum on The Roger Cook Report' (21 August 1990)

*Jesus Army Introduction* (Jesus Fellowship, 1987)

*Jesus: The Name Jesus: The Foundation* (Jesus Fellowship, 1992)

Jones, J., *What Does the Boston Movement Teach?* (Mid-America Books, 1991)

Juachon, S.J., 'This is My Open Letter to You about the ICOC' (lesid@fishnet.net)

Katz, I., 'The Theocrats', *Weekend Guardian* (6 July 1991)

*Knowledge That Leads to Everlasting Life* (Watch Tower Bible and Tract Society, 1995)

*The Leader's Resource Handbook* (Discipleship Publications, 1988)

*Let God Be True* (no publisher, 1946)

*The Lyceum Today: An Outline* (The Spiritualists' Lyceum Union, 1998)

MacDonald-Smith, F., 'The Jesus Army Wants You', *The Independent Magazine* (29 April 1995)

Martin, W., *Christian Science: Is This Religious Group Truly Christian or a Science?* (Bethany House Publishers, 1957)

—, *The Christian Science Myth* (Zondervan, 1955)

—, *The Kingdom of the Cults* (Marshall Morgan & Scott, 1968)

McKean, K., 'Revolution Through Resolution', *Upside Down* (April 1992)

Morrish, I., *Obeah, Christ and Rastaman* (James Clarke, 1982)

Moses, W.M., *More Spirit Teachings* (Spiritualist Press, 1974)

Nelson, G.K., 'Spiritualism in the Midlands: A Research Note', in A. Bryman (ed.), *Religion in the Birmingham Area: Essays in the Sociology of Religion* (University of Birmingham, 1979)

—, 'Ultimate Reality and Meaning', *Modern Spiritualist* 11 (1988)

Newell, K., *Charismatic Christianity: Sociological Perspectives* (Macmillan, 1997)

*Newness*, No. 2 (Jesus Fellowship, 1983)

Niebuhr, R., *Sources of Denominations* (New York, 1929)

Noel, N.L., *The History of the Brethren* (2 vols.; W.F. Knapp, 1936)

Norris, A., *The Things We Stand For* (Aletheia, 1974)

*On the March* (Jesus Fellowship, 1987)

Owen, A., 'Women and Nineteenth Century Spiritualism: Strategies in the Subversion of Femininity', in J. Obelkevich, L. Roper and R. Samuel, *Disciplines of Faith* (Routledge & Kegan Paul, 1987)

Paden, R., 'The Boston Church of Christ', in T. Miller (ed.), *America's Alternative Religions* (State University of New York Press, no date)

Patterson, O., 'Ras Tafari: The Cult of Outcasts', *New Society* 4 (1964)

Peel, R., 'The Christian Science Practitioner', *Journal of Pastoral Counselling* 4 (spring 1969)

—, *Mary Baker Eddy* (3 vols.; The Christian Science Publishing Society, 1966)

Penton, M.J., *Apocalypse Delayed* (Unversity of Toronto Press, 1985)

Pytches, D., *John Wimber: His Influence and Legacy* (Eagle, 1998)

*Qualified to Be Ministers* (Watch Tower Bible and Tract Society, 1955)

Ramsay, E.M., *Christian Science and Its Discoverer* (The Christian Science Publishing Society, 1963)

Raven, F.E., *Readings and Addresses 1898 and 1902* (Stowhill Bible and Tract Depot, undated)

Reay, B., *The Quakers and the English Revolution* (Temple Smith, 1985)

Richards, Le G., *A Marvellous Work and a Wonder* (Deseret Book Company, 1979)

Roberts, R., *Christendom Astray* (The Christadelphian, 1978)

—, *Dr Thomas: His Life and Work* (The Christadelphian, 1925)

Roberts, R.H., 'A Postmodern Church? Some Preliminary Reflections on Ecclesiology and Social Theory', in D. Ford and D.L. Stamps, *The Essentials of Christian Community* (T. & T. Clark, 1996)

Robertson, R., *The Sociological Interpretation of Religion* (Blackwell, 1985)

Russell, C.T., *The Time is at Hand* (Watch Tower Bible and Tract Society, 1916)

Rutherford, J., *The Finished Mystery* (Watch Tower Bible and Tract Society, 1917)

Ruthven, M., *The Divine Supermarket* (Chatto & Windus, 1989)

Saxby, T.J., *Pilgrims of a Common Life* (Herald Press, 1987)

Schnoebelen, W., *The Mormon Temple of Doom* (Triple J, 1987)

*Science and Health, its Pure and Complete Teaching* (The Christian Science Publishing Society, 1980)

Segundo, J.L., *The Community Called Church* (Gill & MacMillan, 1980)

Silberger, J., Jnr, *Mary Baker Eddy: An Interpretive Biography of the Founder of Christian Science* (Little Brown, 1980)

Smith, J., *History of the Church* (6 vols.; Deseret Book Company, 1980)

—, *Doctrine and Covenants* (Deseret Book Company, undated)

—, *Journal of Discourses* (no publisher, no date)

*Statement of Faith* (Leicester Ecclesia, 1902)

*The Story of White Eagle Lodge* (White Eagle Publishing Trust, 1986)

Stroup, H.H., *The Jehovah's Witnesses* (Columbia University Press, 1945)

Talmage, J., *The Lord's Tenth* (Church of Jesus Christ of Latter-day Saints, undated)

Taylor, J., Jnr, *Readings at Nostrand Avenue and Other Ministry* 4 (October 1970)

Tennant, H., *The Christadelphians: What They Believe and Preach* (The Christadelphian, 1988)

Thistleton, A.C., *Interpreting God and the Postmodern Self: On Meaning, Manipulation and Promise* (T. & T. Clark, 1995)

Thomas, M., and A., *Mormonism, A Gold-plated Religion* (Alpha, 1996)

Troeltsch, E., *The Social Teachings of the Christian Churches* (George Allen & Unwin, 1931)

Tucker, R., *Strange Gospels* (Marshall Pickering, 1991)

Twelves, H.A., *The Only Way of Salvation* (The Christadelphian, 1985)

Walker, A., *Restoring the Kingdom* (Eagle, 1998)

Wallis, R., *Rebirth of the Gods* (Queens University, 1978)

White, T., *A People for His Name* (Vantage Press, 1967)

*The White Eagle Lodge* (White Eagle Publishing Trust, 1990)

Widtsoe, J.A., *Discourses of Brigham Young* (Deseret Book Company, 1977)

Wilson, B., 'The Brethren: A Current Sociological Appraisal' (unpublished paper)

—, *Patterns of Sectarianism* (Heinemann, 1967)

—, *Religion in a Sociological Perspective* (Oxford University Press, 1982)

—, *Religion in Secular Society* (C.A. Watts, 1966)

—, *Religious Sects* (World University Library, 1970)

—, *Sects and Society: A Sociological Study of Three Religious Groups in Britain* (Heinemann, 1961)

Wimber, J., *Signs and Wonders and Church Growth* (Vineyard Ministries International, 1984)

*Women in the Church*, Flame Leaflet 10 (Jesus Fellowship, revised, April 1992)

*You Can Live For Ever in Paradise on Earth* (Watch Tower Bible and Tract Society, 1982)

Young, B., *Journal of Discourses* (26 vols.; Deseret Book Company, 1977)

*Your First Forty Days*, INFORM MS 1624 (London Church of Christ)

Zimmerman, D., *Controversy in the Boston Church of Christ* (INFORM MS, undated)

*Zion's Aims and Precepts* (Jesus Fellowship, 1994)

# Scripture Index

# Subject Index